SOCIO-RELIGIOUS MOVEMENT IN MODERN INDIA

Encyclopaedic History of India Series

SOCIO-RELIGIOUS MOVEMENT IN MODERN INDIA

Dr. Mahesh Vikram Singh
Professor, Deptt. of History
Mahatma Gandhi Kashi Vidyapeeth
Varanasi (UP)

Dr. Brij Bhushan Shrivastava
Head of Deptt., Ancient History, Archeology & Culture
SMMTPG College, Ballia (UP)

CENTRUM PRESS
NEW DELHI-110002 (INDIA)

CENTRUM PRESS
H.O.: 4360/4, Ansari Road, Daryaganj,
New Delhi-110002 (India)
Tel: 23278000, 23261597, 23255577, 23286875
B.O.: No. 1015, Ist Main Road, BSK IIIrd Stage,
IIIrd Phase, IIIrd Block, Bangalore-560085 (INDIA)
Tel: 080-41723429
Email: centrumpress@gmail.com
Visit us at: www.centrumpress.com

Socio-Religious Movement in Modern India

First Edition, 2011

ISBN 978-93-80836-83-6

PRINTED IN INDIA

Printed at Mehra Offset Press, Delhi

प्रो. विपिन चंद्रा
अध्यक्ष
Prof. Bipan Chandra
Chairman

नेशनल बुक ट्रस्ट, इंडिया
नेहरू भवन
5 इंस्टीट्यूशनल एरिया, फेज़-II, वसंत कुंज, नई दिल्ली-110 070
फोन/ Phone: 011-26121880 फैक्स/ Fax: 011-26121883

NATIONAL BOOK TRUST, INDIA
Nehru Bhawan
5 Institutional Area, Phase II, Vasant Kunj, New Delhi-110 070
ई-मेल / E-mail: chairman@nbtindia.org.in
वेबसाइट / Website: www.nbtindia.org.in

FOREWORD

The term 'history' is derived from the Greek word 'historia' that means knowledge acquired through investigation. Obviously, this knowledge can be correct if the method of investigation is objective and not vitiated by any kind of bias. In other words, if the study of human past is comprehensive and obtained through scientific inquiry, it can provide perspective on the present day problems and help one plan for the future.

A true historian has to identify the sources that can be most useful in a given context. Documents, coins, archaeology, anthropology, geography, travel accounts, oral traditions, mythology and so on can be useful but they can be used only after their veracity is tested and they are critically examined. They should be checked and counter-checked.

Over the centuries, one finds the study and writing of history vitiated by biases. There are numerous instances in which historical data have been distorted to support or oppose certain preconceived ideas and purposes. Strictly speaking such history is just like fiction to accord with preconceived notions and serve some ulterior purposes.

The study of the past has never been static. Conclusions go on changing because of the discovery of new materials and tools of investigation. To give a concrete example, the carbon 14 or radiocarbon dating test has revolutionized the study of civilizations and settlements, especially of prehistoric times, for which written documents, coins, etc. are seldom available. This method has enabled historians to determine more accurately than before the time period of a particular civilization or settlement. This method was discovered only 70 years ago by American scientists.

In our country, excavations brought to light the Indus Valley Civilization and its various features, hitherto unknown. Similarly, no complete text of Kautilya's Arthashastra was available before it was discovered by Shamasastry, the chief of the Mysore Government Oriental Library in the first decade of the last century. Likewise, people's knowledge of the history of the Buddhist period got extended after excavations at Sarnath and the ruins of the Asokan period at Patna. In the future, if the Harappan inscriptions are deciphered, our knowledge of the Indus Valley Civilization will increase enormously. All these instances underline the fact that our knowledge of history is never static and its frontiers go on extending.

In the light of what has been said above the encyclopedic history is going to be of great help to students interested in Indian history. It is comprehensive and as far as possible free from biases. It includes the latest materials, and objective conclusions.

Prof . Bipan Chandra

Professor Emeritus, JNU

Chairman, National Book Trust, India

Contents

	Preface	(*viii*)
1.	Arya Samaj Movement	1
2.	Brahmo Samaj	25
3.	Prarthana Samaj	95
4.	A History of Child Marriage in India	135
5.	Depressed Class Movement	157
	Bibliography	285
	Index	293

Preface

The people of India have had a continuous civilization since 2500 B.C., when the inhabitants of the Indus River valley developed an urban culture based on commerce and sustained by agricultural trade. This civilization declined around 1500 B.C., probably due to ecological changes. During the second millennium B.C., pastoral, Aryan-speaking tribes migrated from the northwest into the subcontinent. As they settled in the middle Ganges River valley, they adapted to antecedent cultures.

The political map of ancient and medieval India was made up of myriad kingdoms with fluctuating boundaries. In the 4th and 5th centuries A.D., northern India was unified under the Gupta Dynasty. During this period, known as India's Golden Age, Hindu culture and political administration reached new heights. Islam spread across the Indian subcontinent over a period of 500 years. In the 10th and 11th centuries, Turks and Afghans invaded India and established sultanates in Delhi. In the early 16th century, descendants of Genghis Khan swept across the Khyber Pass and established the Mughal (Mogul) Dynasty, which lasted for 200 years. From the 11th to the 15th centuries, southern India was dominated by Hindu Chola and Vijayanagar Dynasties. During this time, the two systems—the prevailing Hindu and Muslim—mingled, leaving lasting cultural influences on each other.

The first British outpost in South Asia was established in 1619 at Surat on the northwestern coast. Later in the century, the East India Company opened permanent trading stations at Madras, Bombay, and Calcutta, each under the protection of native rulers. The British expanded their influence from these footholds until, by the 1850s, they controlled most of present-day India, Pakistan, and Bangladesh. In 1857, a rebellion in north India led by mutinous Indian soldiers caused the British Parliament to transfer all political power from the East India Company to the Crown. Great Britain began administering most of India directly while controlling the rest through treaties with local rulers.

In the late 1800s, the first steps were taken toward self-government in British India with the appointment of Indian councillors to advise the British viceroy and the establishment of provincial councils with Indian members; the British subsequently widened participation in legislative councils. Beginning in 1920, Indian leader Mohandas K. Gandhi transformed the Indian National Congress political party into a mass movement to campaign against British colonial rule.

—Authors

1

Arya Samaj Movement

Swami Dayananda Saraswati

Maharishi Dayananda Saraswati February 12, 1824 – October 31, 1883) was an important Hindu religious scholar, reformer and the founder of the Arya Samaj, "Society of Nobles", a Hindu reform movement, founded in 1875. He was the first man who gave the call for *Swarajya*-"India for Indians" in 1876 which was later furthered by Lokmanya Tilak. Denouncing idolatry and ritualistic worship prevalent in Hinduism at the time, he worked towards reviving Vedic ideologies, subsequently philosopher and later President of India, S. Radhakrishnan, later called him one of "makers of Modern India" as did Sri Aurobindo.

One of his notable disciples was Shyamji Krishna Varma who founded *India House* in London and guided other revolutionaries like Madam Cama, Veer Sawarkar, Lala Hardyal, Madan Lal Dhingra, Bhagat Singh and others. His other disciples were Swami Shraddhanand, Lala Lajpat Rai and others who got their inspiration from his writings. His book *Satyarth Prakash* contributed to the Indian independence movementis one of his great contributions. He was a sanyasi (ascetic) from his boyhood, and a scholar, who believed in the infallible authority of the Vedas.

Dayananda advocated the doctrine of karma, skepticism in dogma, and emphasised the ideals of Brahmacharya (celibacy and devotion to God). The Theosophical Society and the Arya Samaj were united from 1878 to 1882, when the former adopted the name Theosophical Society of the Arya Samaj.

Among Maharishi Dayananda's contributions are his promoting of the equal rights of women-such as the right to education and reading of Indian scriptures-and his translation of the Vedas from Sanskrit to Hindi so that the common person may be able to read the Vedas.

Early Life

Dayananda was born on February 12 in 1824, in the village of Tankara near Morvi (Morbi) in the Kathiawar region (present Rajkot district), Gujarat, into a affluent and devout Brahmin family of Krishna Lal Tiwari and Yashodabai. Since he was born under Mul Nakshatra, he was named *Dayananda Mulshankar* and led a very comfortable early life, studying Sanskrit, the Vedas and other religious books so as to prepare himself for a future as a Hindu priest.

A number of incidents resulted in Dayananda's life questioning traditional beliefs of Hinduism and inquiring about God (Bhagwan) in early childhood. Still a young child on the night of Shivratri (literally: the night for God Shiva) when his family went to a temple for overnight worship, he stayed up waiting for God to appear to accept the offerings made to idol of God Shiva. While his family slept, Dayananda saw a mouse eating the offerings kept for the God. He was utterly surprised and wondered how a God, who cannot even protect his own "offerings," would protect humanity. He argued with his father that they should not be worshipping such a helpless God. The deaths of his younger sister and his uncle from cholera caused Dayananda to ponder the meaning of life and death and he started asking questions, which worried his parents. He was to be married in his early teens (common in 19th century India), but he decided marriage was not for him and ran away from home in 1846.

Search for Knowledge

He was disillusioned with classical Hinduism and became a wandering monk. He learned Panini's Grammar to understand Sanskrit texts, and learnt from them that GOD can be found. After wandering in search of GOD for over 2 decades, he found Swami Virjananda near Mathura who became his guru. Swami Virjananda told him to throw away all his books, as he wanted Dayananda to start from a clean slate and learn directly from the Vedas, the oldest and foundational books. Dayananda stayed under Swami Virjananda's tutelage for two and a half years. After finishing his education, Virjananda asked him to spread the knowledge of the Vedas in society as his *gurudakshina* (tuition-dues). It is during his mission, Dayananda Saraswati gave the call.

Dayananda's Mission

AUM or OM is considered by the Arya Samaj to be the highest and most proper name of God.

Dayananda set about the difficult task with dedication despite attempts on his life. He travelled the country challenging religious scholars and priests of the day to discussions and won repeatedly on the strength of his arguments. He believed that Hinduism has been corrupted by divergence from the founding principles of the Vedas and misled by the priesthood for the priests' self-aggrandisement. Hindu priests discouraged common folk from reading Vedic scriptures and encouraged rituals (such as bathing in the Ganges and feeding of priests on anniversaries) which Dayananda pronounced as superstitions or self-serving.

Far from borrowing concepts from other religions, as Raja Ram Mohan Roy had done, Swami Dayananda was quite critical of Islam and Christianity and also of the other Indian faiths like Jainism, Buddhism and Idol Worshipping in Hinduism-as may be seen in his book *Satyartha Prakash*. He was against what he considered to be the corruption of the pure faith in his own country. Unlike many other reform movements within Hinduism, the Arya Samaj's appeal was addressed not only to the educated few in India, but to the world as a whole as evidenced in the 6th principle of the Arya Samaj.

Arya Samaj allows and encourages converts to Hinduism.

Dayananda's concept of Dharma is succinctly set forth in his *Beliefs and Disbeliefs*. He said,

I accept as Dharma whatever is in full conformity with impartial justice, truthfulness and the like; that which is not opposed to the teachings of God as embodied in the Vedas. Whatever is not free from partiality and is unjust, partaking of untruth and the like, and opposed to the teachings of God as embodied in the Vedas-that I hold as adharma.

He had also said;

He, who after careful thinking, is ever ready to accept truth and reject falsehood; who counts the happiness of others as he does that of his own self, him I call just.

Dayananda's Vedic message was to emphasize respect and reverence for other human beings, supported by the Vedic notion of the divine nature of the individual-divine because the body was the temple where the human essence (soul or "Atma") could possibly interface with the creator ("Paramatma"). In the 10 principles of the Arya Samaj, he enshrined the idea that "All actions should be performed with the prime objective of benefitting mankind" as opposed to following dogmatic rituals or revering idols and symbols. In his own life, he interpreted Moksha to be a lower calling (due to its benefit to one individual) than the calling to emancipate others.

Dayananda's "back to the Vedas" message influenced many thinkers. Taking the cue from him, Sri Aurobindo decided to look for hidden psychological meanings in the Vedas. Sri Aurobindo Ashram, Pondicherry. 1972.

Arya Samaj

Swami Dayananda's creation, the Arya Samaj, is a unique contribution in Hinduism. The Arya Samaj unequivocally condemns idol-worship, animal sacrifices, ancestor worship, pilgrimages, priestcraft, offerings made in temples, the caste system, untouchability, child marriages and discrimination against women on the grounds that all these lacked Vedic sanction. The Arya Samaj discourages dogma and symbolism and encourages skepticism in beliefs that run contrary to common sense and logic. To many people, the Arya Samaj aims to be a "universal society" based on the authority of the Vedas..

Works

Dayananda Saraswati wrote more than 60 works in all, including a 14 volume explanation of the six Vedangas, an incomplete commentary on the Ashtadhyayi (Panini's grammar), several small tracts on ethics and morality, Vedic rituals and sacraments and on criticism of rival doctrines (such as Advaita Vedanta, Islam and Christianity). Some of his major works are Bhratnivaran, Sanskarvidhi, Ratnamala, Vedabhasya. The Paropakarini Sabha located in the Indian city of Ajmer was founded by the Swami himself to publish and preach his works and Vedic texts.

- *Satyarth Prakash* (1875) (Light of Truth-first English translation 1908
- Rigvedici-Bhasya-balmlike/An Introduction to the Commentary on the Vedas. ed. B. Ghasi Ram, Meerut (1925). reprints 1981, 1984
- *Glorious Thoughts of Swami Dayananda.* ed. New Book Society of India, 1966
- *An introduction to the commentary on the Vedas.* Jan Gyan-Prakashan, 1973.
- *Autobiography,* ed. Kripal Chandra Yadav, New Delhi : Manohar, 1978.
- Yajurveda bhasyam : Samskritabhasyam, Andhratikatatparyam, Anglabhavarthasahitanga.
- *The philosophy of religion in India,* Delhi : Bharatiya Kala Prakashan, 2005, ISBN 8180900797.

Death

According to Indian History, in 1883 Dayananda was invited by the Maharaja of Jodhpur, to stay at his palace. The Maharaja was eager to become his disciple and learn his teachings. Onc day Dayananda went to Maharaja's rest room and saw him with a dance girl. Maharaja loved this low-character dance girl. Dayananda boldly asked Maharaja to forsake that girl and all unethical acts and follow Darma of a true Aryan. Dayananda's suggestion went against to that dance girl and she decided to take revenge of this. Dance girl bribed Dayananda's cook to poison him. One evening when Dayananda was about to go to bed he brought him a glass of milk containing poison and ground glass. Dayananda took the glass of milk and went to sleep only to wake up later with a burning sensation. He realized immediately that he had been poisoned and attempted to purge his digestive system of the poisonous substance, but it was too late. The poison had already entered his blood stream. Dayananda was bedridden and suffered excruciating pain. Many doctors came to treat him but all was in vain. His body was covered all over with large bleeding sores. On seeing Dayananda's suffering the cook was overcome with unbearable guilt and remorse. He confessed his crime to Dayananda. On deathbed, Dayananda forgave him and gave him a bag of money and told him to flee the country lest he be found out and executed by the Maharaja's men.

Arya Samaj

Arya Samaj is a Hindu reform movement founded in Bombay (India) by Swami Dayananda in 1875. He was a sannyasi (renouncer) who believed in the infallible authority of the Vedas. Dayananda advocated the doctrine of karma and reincarnation, and emphasized the ideals of Brahmacharya (chastity) and sanyasa (renunciation). He founded Arya Samaj by meeting a guru named Vrajanand. There are approximately 3-4 million followers of Arya Samaj worldwide.

Founding of the Arya Samaj

Vedic Schools

Between 1869 and 1873, Swami Dayananda, a native of the Princely State of Gujarat, made his first earnest attempt at affecting a substantial and lasting reform in his native India. This attempt took the form of the establishment of several so-called "Vedic Schools" which, in contradistinction to other public schools at the time, put a marked emphasis on attempting to impart Vedic values, culture and religion to its students. The first was established at Farrukhabad in 1869 and reported 50 students as being enrolled in its first year. This initial success led to the founding of four additional schools in rapid succession at Mirzapur (1870), Kasganj (1870), Chhalesar (1870) and Varanasi (1873).

The Vedic Schools represented the first practical application of Swami Dayananda's vision of religious and social reform. They enjoyed a mixed reception. On the one hand, students were not allowed to perform traditional idol worship (*murtipuja* in Hindi) at the school, and were instead expected to perform *sandhya* (a form of meditative prayer using mantras from the Vedas) and participate in *agnihotra* twice daily. Also, disciplinary action was swift and not infrequently severe. On the other hand, all meals, lodging, clothing and books were given to the students free of charge, and the study of Sanskrit was opened to non-Brahmins. The most noteworthy feature of the Schools was that only those texts which accepted the authority of the Vedas were to be taught. This, in the opinion of Swami Dayananda, was critical for the spiritual and social regeneration of Vedic culture in India.

Due primarily to organizational problems, the Vedic Schools soon ran into many difficulties. Swami Dayananda had considerable trouble finding qualified teachers who agreed with his views on religious reform, and there existed a paucity of textbooks which he considered suitable for instruction in Vedic culture. Funding was sporadic, attendance fluctuated considerably, and tangible results in the way of noteworthy student achievement were not forthcoming. Consequentially, some of the schools were forced to close shortly after opening. As early as 1874, it had become clear to Swami Dayananda that, without a wide and solid base of support among the public, setting up schools with the goal of imparting a Vedic education would prove to be an impossible task. He therefore decided to invest the greater part of his resources in the clear formulation and widespread propagation of his ideology of reform. Deprived of the full attention of Swami Dayananda, the Vedic School system all but collapsed shortly thereafter, and the last of the remaining schools (Farrukhabad) was finally closed down in 1876 due to Muslim takeover.

Adi Brahmo Samaj

While travelling (1872 – 1873), Swami Dayananda came into close and extended contact with several of the leading Indian intellectuals of the age, including Navin Chandra Roy, Raj Narayan Bose, Debendranath Tagore and Hemendranath Tagore all of whom were actively involved in the Brahmo Samaj. This reform organization, founded in 1828, held many views similar to those of Swami Dayananda in matters both religious (e.g. a belief in monotheism and the eternality of the soul) and social (e.g. the need to abolish the hereditary caste system and uplift the masses through education). Debendranath Tagore had written a book entitled *Brahmo Dharma*, which serves as a comprehensive manual of religion and ethics to the members of that society, and Swami Dayananda had studied it thoroughly while in Calcutta.

Although Swami Dayananda was persuaded on more than one occasion to join the Brahmo Samaj, there existed several points of contention which the Swami simply could not overlook, the most important being the position of the Vedas. Swami Dayananda held the Vedas to be divine revelation, and refused to accept any suggestions to the contrary. Despite this difference of opinion, however, it seems that the members of the Brahmo Samaj and Swami Dayananda parted on good terms, the former having publicly praised the latter's visit to Calcutta in several journals and the latter having taken inspiration from the former's activity in the social sphere.

The Light of Truth

Swami Dayananda made several changes in his approach to the work of reforming Hindu society after having visited Calcutta. The most significant of these changes was that he began lecturing in Hindi. Prior to his tour of Bengal, the Swami had always held his discourses and debates in Sanskrit. While this gained him a certain degree of respect among both the learned and the common people alike, it prevented him from spreading his message to the broader masses. The change to Hindi allowed him to attract increasingly larger crowds, and as a result his ideas of reform began to circulate among the lower classes of society as well.

After hearing some of Swami Dayananda's speeches delivered in Hindi at Varanasi, Raj Jaikishen Das, a native government official there, suggested that the Swami publish his ideas in a book so that they might be distributed among the public. Witnessing the slow collapse of the Vedic Schools due to a lack of a clear statement of purpose and the resultant flagging public support, Swami Dayananda recognized the potential contained in Das' suggestion and took immediate action.

From June to September 1874, Swami Dayananda dictated a comprehensive series of lectures to his scribe, Pundit Bhimsen Sharma, which dealt with his views and beliefs regarding a wide range of subjects including God, the Vedas, Dharma, the soul, science, philosophy, childrearing, education, government and the possible future of both India and the world. The resulting manuscript was edited by Sharma and others, and was eventually published under the title Satyarth Prakash or The Light of Truth in 1875 at Varanasi. This voluminous work would prove to play a central role in the establishment and later growth of the organization which would come to be known as the Arya Samaj.

First Attempt at a 'New Samaj'

While the manuscript of the Satyarth Prakash was being edited at Varanasi, Swami Dayananda received an invitation to travel to Bombay in order to conduct a debate with some representatives of the Vallabhacharya sect. The Swami arrived in Bombay on the 20th of October, 1874. The debate, though greatly publicised, never materialized. Despite this, however, two members of the Prarthana Samaj approached Swami Dayananda and invited him to deliver a few lectures at one of their gatherings, which were received with appreciation by all those present. The members of the Prarthana Samaj of Bombay recognized in Swami Dayananda an individual in possession of the knowledge and skills necessary for promoting their aims, the greatest and most comprehensive of which being the general uplift of Hindu society at large and its protection from what they perceived to be the advancing threat of Christian and Muslim efforts to convert Hindus.

After his having spent over a month at Bombay, 60 new-found admirers of Swami Dayananda – among them, prominent members of the Prarthana Samaj – proposed the notion of founding a 'New Samaj' with the Swami's ideas serving as its spiritual and intellectual basis. A committee was formed to draw up a constitution, and a high court lawyer was employed to finalize the draft. However, pressure was exerted upon the still-forming group by high-profile orthodox caste members in the area – so much, in fact, that the effort to establish a Samaj was aborted quickly.

Second Attempt at Ahmedabad

After having received a personal invitation from Judge Gopalrao Hari Deshmukh, Swami Dayananda left Bombay and travelled to Ahmedabad, Gujarat, arriving on the 11th of December, 1874. Once there, he conducted a debate with local pundits on the issue of idol worship, and emerged victorious. It is reported that the formation of a Samaj and the founding of a Vedic School at Ahmedabad was proposed following the widely acknowledged and publicized success of the debate, but it was found that not enough support for such a venture could be mustered.

Initial Success at Rajkot

On an invitation from Hargovind Das Dvarkadas, the secretary of the local Prarthana Samaj, Swami Dayananda decided to travel to Rajkot, Gujarat and arrived on the 31st of December, 1874. However, instead of delivering his standard program of lectures, he allowed members of the audience to choose the topics they would like to have him discourse upon. A total of eight topics were chosen, and Swami Dayananda delivered impromptu lectures on all of them to the overwhelming satisfaction of all present. Gifts were bestowed upon the Swami as tokens of gratitude for his masterly orations, and it was announced that the Rajkot Prarthana Samaj was henceforth dissolved and was ready to be reorganized as a new Samaj under the auspices of Swami Dayananda. The Swami, after much deliberation, chose the name 'Arya Samaj' or 'Society of Nobles'. Swami Dayananda himself drafted a list of 28 rules and regulations for the Rajkot Arya Samaj, which he later had printed for distribution.

Setback at Ahmedabad

On his way back to Bombay, Swami Dayananda stopped off in Ahmedabad and related the news of Rajkot, Gujarat, distributing copies of the rules and regulations to those present. A meeting was held on the 27th of January, 1875 to discuss the proposal of forming an Arya Samaj there, yet no conclusive decision was reached. Unwilling to wait for the deliberations to come to an end, Swami Dayananda continued on his way to Bombay.

While travelling, the Swami received word that the still fragile Rajkot Arya Samaj had involved itself in some political dispute and managed to have a government warning issued against it and its members. Thus, the collapse of the just established society was already looming large.

Lasting Success at Bombay

Swami Dayananda reached Bombay on 29 January 1875, and immediately the appeal to establish an Arya Samaj there was renewed. However, the Swami did not want a protracted debate to ensue as had occurred at Ahmedabad, bringing with it the possibility of endless deliberations. Thus, a membership drive was initiated which would circumvent the need for discussions. Within a short time, 100 individuals enrolled themselves as prospective members.

While the membership drive was underway, Swami Dayananda held a now famous discourse with the congregation at Bombay. Someone in the audience asked the Swami: "Should we set up a new Samaj?" Dayananda responded:

"If you are able to achieve something for the good of mankind by a Samaj, then establish a Samaj; I will not stand in your way. But if you do not organize it properly, there will be a lot of trouble in the future. As for me, I will only instruct you in the same way as I teach others, and this much you should keep clearly in mind: my beliefs are not unique, and I am not omniscient. Therefore, if in the future any error of mine should be discovered after rational examination, then set it right. If you do not act in this way, then this Samaj too will later in become just a sect. That is the way by which so many sectarian divisions have become prevalent in India: by making the guru's word the touchstone of truth and thus fostering deep-seated prejudices which make the people religion-blind, cause quarrels and destroy all right knowledge. That is the way India arrived at her sorry contemporary state, and that is the way this Samaj too would grow to be just another sect. This is my firm opinion: even if there be many different sectarian beliefs prevalent in India, if only they all acknowledge the Vedas, then all those small rivers will reunite in the ocean of Vedic Wisdom, and the unity of *dharma* will come about. From that unity of *dharma* there will result social and economic reform, arts and crafts and other human endeavours will improve as desired, and man's life will find fulfilment: because, by the power of that dharma all values will become accessible to him, economic values as well as psychological ones, and also the supreme value of moksha."

On the 10th of April, 1875, the Bombay Arya Samaj was officially established. The original membership amounted to exactly 100 persons, including Swami Dayananda. The members appealed to the Swami that he should serve as either the President or the Guru of the Samaj, but he kindly refused, and instead requested that he be listed as a regular member. In the list of members, which was organized alphabetically, Swami Dayananda's name appears as No. 13.

Principles of Arya Samaj

On the 24th of June, 1877, the second major Arya Samaj was established at Lahore. However, the original list of 28 rules and regulations drafted by Dayananda for the Rajkot Arya Samaj and used for the Bombay Arya Samaj were deemed by the Lahore community to be too unwieldy. Therefore, it was proposed that the principles should be reduced and simplified, while the bylaws should be removed to a separate document. Everyone present, including Swami Dayananda, agreed, and the 10 Principles of the Arya Samaj as they are known around the world today came into existence.

All subsequently established branches of the Arya Samaj have been founded upon the Lahore principles. However, each new branch of the Society has a degree of freedom in determining the exact bylaws under which it shall operate. Everyone who wishes to become a member of the Society must agree to uphold these principles in their entirety. However, nothing beyond these 10 Principles has any binding force on any member of the Arya Samaj. For this reason, the early Samaj proved to be attractive to individuals belonging to various religious communities, and enjoyed a notable degree of support from segments of the Hindu, Sikh and Muslim populations of Indian society.

Drawing what are seen to be the logical conclusions from these principles, the Arya Samaj also unequivocally condemns practices such as polytheism, idolatry, iconolatry, animal sacrifice, ancestor worship, pilgrimage, priestcraft, the belief in avatars or incarnations of God, the hereditary caste system, untouchability and child marriage on the grounds that all these lack Vedic sanction.

The Arya Samaj and the Theosophical Society

There continues to this day a considerable controversy regarding the exact nature of the relationship which existed between the Arya Samaj and the Theosophical Society from 1877 to 1882. What follows is a report of the chain of events as understood by members of the Arya Samaj today.

Initial Relationship

In 1877, a meeting occurred in America between some leading members of the Theosophical Society, founded in 1875, and Mulji Thakarshi, an individual who had played an instrumental role in the establishment of the Bombay Arya Samaj that same year. During the course of the exchange, it became clear that the two societies held many views in common, and efforts were undertaken to bring their respective leaders into closer contact. As a result, correspondence began between Henry Steel Olcott, one of the co-founders of the New York Theosophical Society, and Harish Chandra Chintamani, the acting president of the Bombay Arya Samaj.

At the suggestion of Chintamani, Olcott composed a letter addressed to Swami Dayananda dated the 18th of February, 1878 which is reported to have contained, among other things, the following notable passage: "There exist a number of Americans and others who earnestly seek spiritual knowledge. They place themselves at your feet and pray you [sic] to enlighten them. They are united in the object of gaining wisdom and becoming better. For this purpose they organized themselves into a body called the Theosophical Society three years ago. Finding in Christianity nothing that should satisfy their reason or intention they (...) have turned to the East for light and openly proclaimed themselves foes of Christianity. We come to your feet as children to a parent and say: 'Look at us, our teacher. Tell us what we ought to do. We place ourselves under your instructions."

Unwilling to wait for what they were led to believe would be a positive response, the heads of the Theosophical Society decided to go ahead with their plans to recast their organization as a branch of the Arya Samaj. On the 22nd of May, 1878, the Theosophical Society was renamed 'The Theosophical Society of the Arya Samaj of Aryavarta' and Swami Dayananda was announced as its director in chief.

Reconsideration and Reorganization

This unilateral move on the part of the Theosophists, however, eventually proved to be grossly miscalculated. While Olcott's open profession of faith in the Vedas was positively received and publicly praised by Swami Dayananda on more than one occasion, when he came to learn of the details of the tenets held by the Theosophists, including their belief in ghosts, mediumistic abilities, miracles and other occult matters, the Swami, taking up the role of teacher, was quick to admonish Olcott for what he termed 'humbuggery' and 'superstition' unbefitting of a seeker of truth. The Theosophists, however, were unwilling to give up their faith in these matters, and the gulf which had always existed between the two societies suddenly became apparent to all involved. Therefore, in September 1878, the Theosophical Society was reverted to its former status as an independent organization. However, a second organization was simultaneously formed and given the now familiar name 'The Theosophical Society of the Arya Samaj of Aryavarta'. It was agreed that membership of the new society, which itself was to remain a common branch of both the Theosophical Society and the Arya Samaj, would be open to any persons who wished to remain associated with both societies.

Irreconcilable Differences

This tentative solution, however, proved incapable of bridging the growing divide. Between 1879 and 1881, the founders of the Theosophical Society, Henry Olcott and Helena Blavatsky, paid Swami Dayananda several visits while touring India. Through the course of their discussions and correspondence, it became clear that the differences between the two societies were not, as previously assumed, limited to relatively minor issues, but in fact extended to what the Swami viewed as central tenets of the Vedic Religion. The main point of contention was in regards to the nature of God. While the Theosophists asserted that the highest Divinity is an impersonal Principle, Swami Dayananda maintained that the Vedas and their allied literature clearly teach that God is a personal Being – in his words, "the Personification of Being, Knowledge and Bliss". Thus, the line dividing the two organizations was clearly identified and neither party saw themselves in need of reconsidering their views. Therefore, on the 28th of March, 1882, Swami Dayananda announced that the Arya Samaj had officially cut off all ties with the Theosophical Society.

It has been stated that many of the difficulties and subsequent hostilities which arose between the Theosophical Society and the Arya Samaj were due to an unfortunate combination of personal intrigue and poor translations. Both parties have claimed to have been misrepresented on several occasions and members of each have accused the other of being responsible for the failure of the undertaking. Regardless, the theological and ideological differences between the Theosophical Society and the Arya Samaj persist to this day.

Relations with Sikhs

In 1875, the Arya Samaj established itself in Punjab, and some of its members began stating publicly that Sikhism should be considered a branch of Hinduism using what was seen as derogatory language in reference to Sikh Gurus and their writings. Leaders in the Sikh community, however, showed resolve in maintaining the status of their religion as independent and unique, and the statements of the Arya Samaj activists were summarily denounced as acts of aggression with the intent of destroying Sikh religious identity. It was also alleged that the Arya Samaj, which had taken an increasingly active role in certain Sikh Gurdwaras, was introducing practices that were contrary to Sikh principles and behaving in ways which would prove detrimental to the Sikh faith. In response, organizational efforts such as Singh Sabha and Gurdwara Sudhar Movement were launched for countering Arya Samaj influence and peacefully reclaiming control of Sikh Gurdwaras.

Mahatma Hansraj

Lala Hansraj (1864-1938) also known as Mahatama Hansraj, was an Indian educationist and a follower of Arya Samaj movement founder, Swami Dayananda, and who founded Dayananda Anglo-Vedic Schools System (DAV) in Lahore in 1886, along with Guru Dutt Vidhyarthi, where the first DAV school was set up, in the memory of Swami Dayananda who had died three years earlier.

He was also a compatriot of freedom fighter Lala Lajpat Rai. He served as the principal of Dav College for 25 years, and committed the rest of his life in Social service. Today DAV runs over 669 colleges, schools, professional and technical institutions

Early Life and Education

Born in a small town, Bajwara, in Hoshiarpur district, Punjab in 19 April, 1864, Hans Raj lost his father before he was 12 and thereafter he was looked after and educated by his elder brother. Subsequently his family moved to Lahore where he joined a missionary school. Meanwhile he heard Swami Dayananda's lecture and this was chanage his life course forever. He went on to complete his B.A. degree with excellent marks.

Career

Upon completing his B.A., instead of taking up a job, he decided to start a school, the first DAV school along with a fellow Arya Samaji, Guru Dutt Vidyarthi. Later he became the Principal of the Dayananda Anglo-Vedic College, Lahore, and president of the provincial Arya Pradeshik Pratinidhi Sabha, the DAV section of Arya Samaj in Punjab. In 1893, the Arya Samaj split into two in Punjab, one section lead by Lala Hans Raj and Lala Lajpat Rai retained the control over DAV College Lahore, while the radical section was under the leadership of Pandit Lekh Ram and Lala Munshi Ram, who was later known as Swami Shraddhanand, formed Punjab Arya Samaj and led Arya Pratinidhi Sabha. He served as the principal of DAV College, Lahore for the next 25 years, and after his retirement committed the rest of his life in Social service.

He died on November 14, 1938 in Lahore.

Legacy

Today, many educational institutions are named after him, including Hans Raj College Delhi University, where Mahatma Hans Raj College Road, is situated at the heart of University's North campus.

Swami Shraddhanand

Swami Shraddhanand (1856-1926) was an Indian educationist and a Arya Samaj missionary who propagated the teachings of Swami Dayananda which included the establishment of educational institutions, like the Gurukul Kangri University, and played a key role on the *Sangathan* (consolidation) and the *Shuddhi* (re-conversion) a Hindu reform movement in 1920s.

His death at the hands of a Muslim fanatic caused religious strife in India.

Early Life and Education

He was born on 22 February 1856 in the village of Talwan in the Jalandhar District of the Punjab Province of India, and was the youngest in the family of Lala Nanak Chand, was a policeman in the East India Company administered United Provinces (now Uttar Pradesh). His given name was Brihaspati, but later he was called Munshi Ram by his father, a name that stayed with him till he took Sanyas in 1917, variously as Lala Munshi Ram and Mahatma Munshi Ram.

His school education began at Varanasi and ended at Lahore. His father, His early education was interrupted because of his father's frequent transfer to different locations.

Career

Despite this handicap he started his career as a 'Naib-Tehsildar' and later had a successful career as a lawyer from 1885 to 1892, meanwhile his meeting with Swami Dayananda in 1882 gave a new direction to his life, and he immediately took to the cause of Arya Samaj. In 1892, when Arya Samaj split into two factions over making Vedic education the main stay of the curriculum at the DAV College Lahore, he left the organization and formed Punjab Arya Samaj, and in 1902 established a Gurukul in Kangri near Haridwar which is now a recognized University known as Gurukul Kangri University. Previously in 1897, after the assassination of Lala Lekh Ram, he became his successor, and headed the 'Punjab Arya Pratinidhi Sabha', and started its monthly journal, *Arya Musafir*.

In 1915, upon his return from South Africa, M. K. Gandhi stayed at the university campus and met Swami Shraddhanand, it was during this visit that Swami Shraddhanand gave Gandhi, the title of *Mahatma* (great soul), after that he was best known around the world as Mahatama Gandhi to this day..

In 1917, Swami Shraddhanand, till now know as Mahatma Munshiram took sanyas, left Gurukul to jump full-fledged into Hindu reform movements and the Indian Independence movement, working with Congress, which he invited to hold its session at Amritsar in 1919 when due to Jalianwala tragedy no one in the Congress Committe agreed to have a session at Amritsar. Swami shraddhanand presided that session at Amritsar. He joined the nationwide protest against the Rowlatt Act, in the same year, defiantly protested in front of a posse of Gurkha soldiers, at the Clock Tower in Chandni Chowk, after which he was allowed to proceed. In early 1920s he emerged as important force in the Hindu Sangathan (consolidation) movement which was a by product of the now revitalized Hindu Maha Sabha

Swami Shraddhanand was the only Hindu Sanyasi who addressed a huge Muslim gathering from the minarates of the main Jama Mosque, New Delhi, for national solidarity and Vedic Dharma starting his speech with the recitation of Ved Mantras.

He wrote on religious issues in both Hindi and Urdu. He published newspapers in the two languages as well. He promoted Hindi in the Devanagri script, helped the poor and promoted the education of women. By 1923, he left the social arena and plunged whole-heartedly into his earlier work of the shuddhi movement (re-conversion to Hinduism), which he turned into an important force within Hinduism In late 1923, he became the president of *Bhartiya Hindu Shuddhi Sabha,* created with an aim to reconvert Muslims specially 'Malkana Rajputs' in western United Province, this antagonized the Muslims against him irrevocably and brought him in direct confrontation with Muslim clerics and leaders of the time, and on 23 December 1926 he was assassinated by a Muslim fanatic named Abdul Rashid, who entered his home at Naya Bazar, Delhi, posing as a visitor.. Upon his death, Gandhiji moved a condolence motion at the Guwahati session of the Congress on December 25, 1926

Today, the 'Swami Shraddhanand Kaksha' at the Archeological Museum, Gurukul Kangri University, Haridwar houses a photographic journey of his life

Personal Life

He married Shiwa Devi, but when he was only 35 years old she died and he was left with two sons and two daughters.

Dayananda Anglo-Vedic Schools System

General

The Dayananda Anglo-Vedic Schools System, also familiarly known as the D.A.V. Public Schools System is the single largest non-governmental education society in India. It is based on the ideals of the religious and social reformer, Swami Dayananda Saraswati.

The DAV system also comprises colleges offering graduate and post-graduate degrees in various areas of study all over India.

Founded in 1886, in Lahore by the efforts of Lala Hansraj, it manages 667 institutions today, 461 of which are high school level institutions, with an annual budget of more than 2 billion rupees.

These schools are run by the Dayananda Anglo-Vedic College Trust and Management Society, also commonly known as the Dayananda Anglo-Vedic Education Society..

It holds the record for producing the largest number of CBSE (class Xth and XIIth) toppers as a single institution in the last 10 years.

English is the primary language of instruction, with students also receiving compulsory education in Hindi and Sanskrit or a regional language.

Anglo Vedic, the name itself implies a perfect blend of modern education and the essence of traditional Indian culture.

Satyarth Prakash

The *Satyarth Prakash* (English title: The Light of Truth) is a 1875 book written by Swami Dayananda, the founder of Arya Samaj, and is considered its central text.

Overview

During the Middle Ages of Indian history, many faiths and sects sprang up in religious and social spheres of Hindu Society. They drifted away from the teachings of the Vedas and attached greater significance to their founders and their preachings. From then onwards polytheism commenced. Great differences developed among the different sects and divided and weakened Hindu society. The caste system based on birth became strong and gave rise to further fragmentation. Superstition, ignorance and blind faith spread and caused the degradation of the Hindu religion and society.

It was at this time that Swami Dayananda wrote the Satyarth Prakash in order to spread the knowledge of the Vedas and to educate people on the true qualities of God. The Satyarth Prakash contains exposition and clarifications of Vedic principles. Some of the important topics in the Satyarth Prakash are worship one God, explanation of the main principles of the Vedas, the relationship between Religion and Science and between devotion and intellect, elimination of the caste system and of different religious beliefs for the strengthening of society, eradication of superstitions, false notions and meaningless customs, shunning narrow-mindedness and promoting brotherhood of man.

Contents of Satyarth Prakash

The book, written in 1875, contains fourteen chapters, the contents of which are detailed below:

Chapter Content:

1 The first chapter is an exposition of "Om" and other names of God.

2 The second chapter provides guidance on the upbringing of children.

3 The third chapter explains the life of *Brahmacharya* (bachelor), the duties and qualifications of scholars and teachers, good and bad books and the scheme of studies.

4 Chapter 4 is about marriage and married life.
5 Chapter 5 is about giving up materialism and starting to carry out community service.
6 Chapter 6 is about Science of Government
7 Chapter 7 is about Veda and God.
8 Chapter 8 deals with Creation, Sustenance and Dissolution of the Universe.
9 Chapter 9 deals with knowledge and ignorance, and emancipation and bondage.
10 Chapter 10 deals with desirable and undesirable conduct and permissible and forbidden diet.
11 Chapter 11 contains criticism of the various religions and sects prevailing in India.
12 Chapter 12 deals with the Charvaka, Buddha (Buddhist) and Jain religions.
13 Chapter 13 has his views on Christianity (the Bible).
14 Chapter 14 has his views on Muhammadism (Quran).

Shuddhi Movement

The socio-political movement, derived from ancient rite of *shuddhikaran*, or purification was started Arya Samaj, and its founder Swami Dayananda Saraswati and his followers like Swami Shraddhanand, who also worked on the *Sangathan* consolidation aspect of Hinduism, in North India, especially Punjab in early 1900s, though it gradually spread across India.

Shuddhi had a social reform agenda behind its belligerent rationale and was aimed at abolishing the practise of untouchability by converting outcasts from other religions to Hinduism and integrating them into the mainstream community by elevating their position, and instilling self-confidence and self-determination in them. The movement strove to reduce the conversions of Hindus to Islam and Christianity, which were underway at the time.

In 1923, Swami Shraddhanand founded the 'Bhartiya Hindu Shuddhi Mahasabha' (Indian Hindu Purification Council) and pushed the agenda of reconversion peacefully, but ultimately created a flashpoint between Hindus and Muslims as it offended Muslim exceptionalists, who argued that Hindus, being dhimmis, do not have any rights to convert others to their faith unlike the

Muslims, who are munim. The main point of contention was the reconversion Malkana Rajputs in western United Province Subsequently the movement became controversial and antagonized the Muslims populace to no end and also led to the martyrdom of the leader of the movement, Swami Shraddhanand in 1926. Gradually the movement faded away especially with the rise of nationalistic fervour during the Civil Disobedience movement of Mahatma Gandhi in the 1930s.

The aggressive Hinduism preached by the Arya Samaj was not political in its conception. That it has been strengthened by political considerations cannot, however, be denied.

This is an appropriate place for examining the origin and bearings of the *Shuddhi* movement of which we have heard so much of late. The movement is as old as the Arya Samaj or even the Sikh religion.

The Arya Samaj claims that the religion preached by it is universal religion, and aims at bringing the whole world under its banner. In this respect its claims are as ambitious and wide as those of Christianity and Islam. There was a time when the more orthodox section of the Arya Samaj used to proclaim from the housetops that they were non-Hindus; and that they were free to eat and drink and marry with non-Hindus; and that even Hindus should undergo a certain amount of *Shuddhi* before they could be admitted into the Arya Samaj.

The other section, which was believed to be more political-minded, was opposed to all these claims of the Mahatma party of which Swami Shraddhanand (then Lala Munshi Ram) was the head. *Shuddhi* with the latter was purely the ritual of conversion, i.e., admission into their Church. It had no political significance whatsoever.

For a time, Lala Munshi Ram's party maintained this attitude, and some of them attempted to put into practice what they believed in theory. It was then that the now-famous Dharmpal was made a hero. Soon after, however, they found that by insisting on this idea and putting it into practice they were bound to lose the practical sympathy of the Hindu community. This they could not afford to do, as it was the general Hindu community that greased the various mills they were running. So better counsels prevailed, and they changed their attitude.

I know it as a fact, however (as I was an active member of the Arya Samaj then), that serious efforts were made even then to bring the Malkana and other Rajputs of the United Provinces and Rajputana into the fold of the Arya Samaj. Some were actually so brought at Aligarh and in the neighbouring districts. The Malkanas, however, did not want to be "Aryas"; what they desired was to be re-admitted into their own caste, and brotherhood on equal terms. To this the orthodox Rajputs would not agree. So the matter remained in suspense for a number of years, until the orthodox Rajputs consented to take them in. What was at the back of the latter's mind in this change of attitude, is also clear. It was the communal demands of the Muslim community, the policy of Mian Fazl-i-Husain and the Multan riots, which created the necessary atmosphere.

The principle of *Shuddhi* has now been accepted by the Hindu Mahasabha, and I am free to confess that the idea at the back of this decision is partly political, pardy communal, and partly humanitarian, the latter element being more in evidence in the *Shuddhi* of the untouchables.

It was, it must be confessed, only natural that the Muslims should be exasperated at this change in the attitude of the orthodox Hindus, because the change opens out an entirely new chapter in Indian history. The question raised by the movement is a fundamental one, and although one can understand and appreciate the Muslim point of view, one can see no way of stopping the movement as long as non-Hindu agencies are free to carryon their proselytizing work. The movement has come to stay, and this fact should be philosophically accepted. That it has direct political bearings cannot be denied, and the only way to minimise its importance is to do away with communal representation. For the present, the decisions arrived at by the Delhi Unity Conference may be accepted as the final word in the matter.

At this stage we might discuss the *Sangathan* and the *Tanzim* movements too. The *Sangathan* movement also (or to call it by its proper name, the Hindu Sabha movement) represents an old idea. The object was present to the mind of the founder of the Arya Samaj. But the Samaj signally failed to realise it, as it went on developing its sectarian proclivities. I remember that when I was a student of the Lahore Government College in the early eighties, a Hindu Sabha was formed at the house of Raja Harbans Singh of Sheikhupura in Lahore. That Sabha died in its infancy. Then the movement was revived towards the end of the last century at the house of the late Lala Balmokand, Reis, Lahore. Even this organization, however, remained almost lifeless until the late R. B. Lal Chand put life into it.

But somehow or other, the movement never took root. It has benefited individual members, but it has done no good to the Hindu community as a whole. It had two formidable rivals: on the political side the Indian National Congress, on the socio-religious side the Arya Samaj. Fixed between these two mill-stones, it was never able to lift its head sufficiently high to be a success. The present movement is a reaction of the Hindu-Muslim situation. There is nothing in its aims and objects or its constitution that need make it anti-Muslim, but to be frank, the fact that it is anti-Muslim is the only thing that keeps it alive.

The Khilafat Committees which were originally established to support the Khilafat agitation have regularly and systematically carried on a religious propaganda to which is directly traceable a part, at least, of the present bitterness between Hindus and Muslims. At Cocanada, it was given out that the Khilafat Committee would be used to organise the Indian Muslims. *Tanzim* is its other name. It is obviously anti-Hindu.

Personally, I would welcome both the movements, i.e., the *Sanghathan* and the *Tanzim*, if they could unite the different sections of the Hindus into one organization, in one case, and all the different sections of the Muslims, in the other; for then it would be a comparatively easy thing for the two main organizations to come to terms with each other. But the task is hopeless. In my judgment the only purpose which the two movements are likely to serve is to increase the already existing estrangement between the two communities. The Muslim movement is also intended to keep the Pan-Islamic movement going. One cannot help noticing, and noticing with regret, that while the Muslims do not open their purses for the relief of Indian sufferers from famine, floods, earthquakes, etc., and that while very little Muslim money is spent to improve the educational and economic condition of Indian Muslims, thousands and lakhs [=hundreds of thousands] are sent abroad under one name or other. The phenomenon is confined to India. One finds no evidence of it in other Muslim nations like Egypt, Turkey, Morocco, Sudan, Syria, etc.

As far as internal organization is concerned, both movements are bound to fail. The canker of sectarianism is as fatal in one case as in the other.

In the case of *Sanghathan*, the Arya Samaj and the Sanatan Dharam Sabha will not allow it to flourish and succeed. They do not seem prepared to transfer any of their functions or influence to the Hindu Sabha. In the case of *Tanzim*, the different Muslim sects will not unite to let it be a success. Both the movements will, however, be much advertised though, to keep alive anti-Muslim feeling in one case, and the anti-Hindu feeling in the other.

2

Brahmo Samaj

Brahmo Samaj is the societal component of Brahmoism. According to J.N Farquahar, "It is without doubt the most influential socio-religious movement in the evolution of Modern (Greater) India." It was conceived as reformation of the prevailing Bengal of the time and began the Bengal Renaissance of the 19th century pioneering all religious, social and educational advance of the Hindu community in the 19th century. From the Brahmo Samaj springs Brahmoism, the most recent of legally recognised religions in India and Bangladesh, reflecting its non-syncretic "foundation of Ram Mohan Roy's reformed spiritual Hinduism (contained in the 1830 Banian deed) and scientifically invigorated by inclusion of root Hebraic-Islamic creed and practice."

Meaning of Names

For Modern usage reflecting subsequent Legislation, Constitution and Legal rulings see Brahmo.

The Brahmo Samaj is a community of people assembled for orderly public meeting, discussion or worship of the Eternal, Immutable Supreme Being, Author and Preserver of the Universe, "but not under or by any other name designation or title peculiarly used for and applied, to any particular being or beings by any man or set of men whatsoever".

Brahmo literally means "one who worships Brahman", and Samaj mean "community of men".

History and Timeline

Brahmo Sabha: On 20 August 1828 the first assembly of the Brahmo Sabha (progenitor of the Brahmo Samaj) was held at the

North Calcutta house of Feringhee Kamal Bose. This day is celebrated by Brahmos as Bhadrotsab. This Sabha was convened at Calcutta by religious reformer Raja Ram Mohan Roy for his family and friends settled there. The Sabha regularly gathered on Saturday between seven o'clock to nine o'clock. These were essentially informal meetings of Bengali Brahmins (the "twice born"), accompanied by Upanishadic recitations in Sanskrit followed by Bengali translations of the Sanskrit recitation and singing of Brahmo hymns composed by Ram Mohan. These meetings were open to all Brahmins and there was no formal organisation or theology as such.

On 8 January 1830 influential progressive members of the closely related Kulin Brahmin clan (scurrilously described as Pirali Brahmin *i.e.* ostracised for service in the Mughal Nizaamat of Bengal) of Tagore (Thakur) and Roy (Vandopadhyaya) zumeendar family mutually executed the Trust deed of Brahmo Sabha for the first Adi Brahmo Samaj (place of worship) on Chitpore Road (now Rabindra Sarani), Kolkata, India with Ram Chandra Vidyabagish as first resident superintendent.

On 23 January 1830 or 11th Magh, the Adi Brahmo premises were publicly inaugurated (with about 500 Brahmins and 1 Englishman present). This day is celebrated by Brahmos as Maghotsab.

In November 1830 Ram Mohan Roy left for England.

Decline of Brahmo Sabha

With Ram Mohan's departure for England in 1830, the affairs of Sabha were effectively managed by Trustees Dwarkanath Tagore and Pandit Ram Chandra Vidyabagish, with Dwarkanath instructing his diwan to manage affairs. Weekly service were held consonant with the Trust directive, consisting of three successive parts: recitation of the Vedas by Telegu Brahmins in the closed apartment exclusively before the Brahmin members of the congregation, reading and exposition of the Upanishads for the general audience, and singing of religious hymns.

The reading of the Vedas was done exclusively before the Brahmin participants as the orthodox Telegu Brahmin community and its members could not be persuaded to recite the Vedas before Brahmins and non-Brahmins alike. By the time of Ram Mohan's death in 1833 near Bristol (UK), attendance at the Sabha dwindled and the Telugu Brahmins surreptitiously revived idolatry. The zumeendars, being preoccupied in business, had little time for affairs of Sabha, and flame of Sabha was almost extinguished.

Tattwabodhini Period

In 1839 Debendranath Tagore, son of (Prince) Dwarkanath Tagore, founded the Tattwabodhini (Truth-seekers) Sabha.

Foundation of Samaj

On 7th Pous 1765 Shaka (1843) Debendranath Tagore and twenty other Tattwabodhini stalwarts were formally invited by Pt. Vidyabagish into the Trust of Brahmo Sabha. The Pous Mela at Shantiniketan starts on this day which is considered as foundation of the 'Adi' (First) Brahmo Samaj which was named the Calcutta Brahmo Samaj.

First Schism

The admittance of Keshub Chandra Sen (a non-Brahmin) into the Calcutta Brahmo Samaj in 1857 while Debendranath was away in Simla caused considerable stress in the movement, with many old Tattvabodhini Brahmin members leaving the Samaj and institutions due to his high-handed ways. These events took place intermittently from 1859, coming to a head publicly between the period of 1 August 1865 till November 1866 with many tiny splinter groups styling themselves as Brahmo. The most notable of these groups styled itself "Brahmo Samaj of India". This period is referred to in the histories of these secessionists as the "First Schism".

Spread of Influence

Although the Brahmo Samaj movement was born in Kolkata, the idea soon spread to the rest of India. That happened to be the period when the railways were expanding and communication was becoming easier. Outside Bengal presidency some of the prominent centres of Brahmo activity were: Punjab, Sind, and Bombay and Madras presidencies. Even to this day, there are several active branches outside West Bengal. Bangladesh Brahmo Samaj at Dhaka keeps the lamp burning.

Social & Religious Reform

In all fields of social reform, including abolition of the caste system and of the dowry system, emancipation of women, and improving the educational system, the Brahmo Samaj reflected the ideologies of the Bengal Renaissance. Brahmoism, as a means of discussing the dowry system, was a central theme of Sarat Chandra Chattopadhyay's noted 1914 Bengali language novella, Parineeta.

Focus of Modern Brahmo Reform:

- Denunciation of polytheism,
- Rejection of the caste system and its abolition,
- Rejection of the dowry system and its abolition,
- Emancipation of women,
- Widow remarriage,
- Reform of educational system,
- Opposition to sati (the practice of burning widows alive),
- Spread of knowledge by universal access to information,
- Legal reform especially in fields of personal and secular law,
- Simplicity and purity in public and private affairs
- Opposing corrupting influences like intoxicants, television, devadasi system, politicians etc.

After controversies, including the controversy over Keshub Chunder Sen's daughter's child marriage rituals wherein the validity of Brahmo marriages were questioned, the Brahmo Samaj Marriage Bill of 1871 was enacted as the Special Marriages Act of 1872 and set the age at which girls could be married at 14. All Brahmo marriages were thereafter solemnised under this law which required the affirmation "I am not Hindu, nor a Mussalman, nor a Christian". The Special Marriages Act 1872 was repealed by the new Special Marriages Act in 1954 which became the secular Marriage law for India. The old Special Marriages Act of 1872 was allowed to live on as the Hindu Marriage Act 1955 for Hindus-Brahmo Religionists are excluded from this Act; which is applicable, however, to Hindus who follow the Brahmo Samaj. On May 5, 2004 the Supreme Court of India, by order of the Chief Justice, dismissed the Government of West Bengal's 30 year litigation to get Brahmos classified as Hindus. The matter had previously been heard by an 11 Judge Constitution Bench of the Court (the second largest bench in the Court's history). As of 2007 the statutory minimum age for Brahmos to marry is 25(M)/21(F) versus 21(M)/18(or 15F) for Hindus.

It also supported social reform movements of people not directly attached to the Samaj, such as Pandit Iswar Chandra Vidyasagar's movement which promoted widow remarriage.

Doctrine

The following doctrines, as noted in Renaissance of Hinduism, are common to all varieties and offshoots of the Brahmo Samaj:

Brahmo Samajists have no faith in any scripture as an authority.

Brahmo Samajists have no faith in Avatars.

Brahmo Samajists denounce polytheism and idol-worship.

Brahmo Samajists are against caste restrictions.

Brahmo Samajists make faith in the doctrines of Karma and Rebirth optional.

Ram Mohan Roy

The renaissance in modern Indian literature begins with Raja Ram Mohan Roy. Roy was born in Radhanagar village in west Bengal's Hooghly district on May 22, 1772, to conservative Bengali Brahmin parents. His father Ramakanta Roy's family belonged to the Vaisnava (who worship Lord Vishnu-the Preserver; followers of Sri Caitanya Maha Prabhu) a liberal sect that flourished in Bengal and South India. His mother Tarini Devi's orthodox priestly family (Bhattacharyas of Chatra) on the other hand belonged to the Shakta sect (worshippers of Goddess Kali-the Shakti-the Mother Energy of the universe). Roy did his elementary education in the village school in Bengali, his mother tongue. At the age of 12, Roy went to a seat of Muslim studies in Patna where he mastered Persian and Arabic. His knowledge of Arabic enabled him to read the Koran in the original, as well as the works of Sufi saints. He also devoured Arabic translations of the works of Aristotle and Plato. When he was 16, Royclashed with his orthodox father on the issue of idol worship and left home. Toacquaint himself with the Buddhist religion, he travelled across northern India and Tibet for the next three years. Hisquestioning mind objected to the deification of the Buddha and this did not godown well with some of the lamas. He then visited Varanasi where he learnt Sanskrit and studied ancient Hindu scriptures.

In 1803, he secured a job with the East India Company and in 1809, he was posted to Rangpur. In Rangpur, he learnt about

Jainism and studied the Jaintexts. Roy was drawn to certain aspects of Christianity that led some of the followers of the religion to suggest that he convert; but he politely declined.

Roy's understanding of the different religions of the world helped him to compare them with Vedantic philosophy and garner the best from each religion. Sufi mysticism had a great influence on Roy. He loved to repeat three of their maxims: "Man is the slave of benefits"; "The enjoyment of the worlds rests on these two points-kindness to friends and civility to enemies"; and "The way of serving God is to do good to man".

To pursue his interests, Roy resigned from the East India Company a few years later and came to Calcutta in 1814. Dissatisfied with the system of education and the rote method of teaching English, he formed an association of English and Hindu scholars. He also invested his own money in the starting of a school where he introduced subjects like science, mathematics, political science and English. Roy felt that an understanding of these" modern" subjects would give Indians a better standing in the world of the day.

Though initially antagonistic towards British rule in India, Roy later began to feel that the country would benefit in terms of education and by exposure to the good points of Christianity. For this he was called a stooge of the British.

Along with a group of like-minded people, Roy founded the Atmiya Sabha in 1814. The group held weekly meetings at his house; texts from the Vedas were recited and theistic hymns were sung. Roy was drawn to the Unitarian form of Christianity that resulted in him supporting a Unitarian Mission to be set up in Calcutta in 1824.

Historical Significance

In the early 1800s, the General Assembly of the Church of Scotland sent Reverend Alexander Duff, a young and dedicated missionary, to Kolkata to set up an English-medium institution. Though Bengalis had shown some interest in the spread of Western education from the beginning of the 19th century, both the local church and government officers were skeptical about the high-caste Bengali's response to the idea of an English-medium institution. Raja Ram Mohan Roy helped by organizing the venue and bringing in the first batch of students. He also assured the guardians that reading the Bible did not necessarily imply religious conversion. Although his ultimate aim was the spread of English education, Duff was aware that without a good command on one's native language, it was impossible to master a foreign language. Hence in his General Assembly's Institution (as later in his Free Church Institution), the teaching and learning of the Bengali language and literature was given high priority. Duff was keen on sports and had accumulated different kinds of sports-related equipment for use in his institution. When he introduced political economy as a subject in the curricula, the Church strongly criticized him.

In 1840, Duff returned to India. At the Disruption of 1843, Duff sided with the Free Church. He gave up the college buildings, with all their effects and with unabated courage, set to establish a new institution, which came to be known as the Free Church Institution. He had the support of Sir James Outram and Sir Henry Lawrence, and the encouragement of seeing a new band of converts, including several young men born of high caste. In 1844, governor-general Viscount Hardinge opened government appointments to all who had studied in institutions similar to Duff's institution. In the same year, Duff co-founded the Calcutta Review, of which he served as editor from 1845 to 1849. These two institutions founded by Duff, *i.e.*, the General Assembly's Institution and the Free Church Institution would be merged later to form the Scottish Churches College. After the unification of the Church of Scotland in 1929, the institution would be known as Scottish Church College.

Along with Raja Ram Mohan Roy, the father of modern India, Dr. Duff played a significant role in supporting Lord Macaulay in drafting his famous Minute for the introduction of English education in India. Successive eminent missionary scholars from Scotland, *viz.* Dr. Ogilvie, Dr. Hastie, Dr. Macdonald, Dr. Stephen, Dr. Watt, Dr. Urquhart and others contributed to the spread of the liberal Western education.

Along with other educational institutions like Serampore College, Hindu College, the Scottish Churches College played a pivotal role in ushering the spirit of intellectual enquiry and a general acceptance of the ideals of the European Enlightenment, among Bengalis, in what came to be regarded as the Young Bengal Movement and later, the Bengal Renaissance. Duff's contemporaries included such luminaries as Reverend Mackay, Reverend Ewart and Reverend Thomas Smith. Till the early 20th century the norm was to bring teachers from Scotland (like William Spence Urquhart, Leslie Stephen, H.M. Percival, Ian Fairweather etc.) but eminent Indian scholars were also engaged as teachers by the college authorities. Scholars like Surendranath Banerjea, Kalicharan Bandyopadhyay, Jnan Chandra Ghosh, Gouri Shankar Dey, Adhar Chandra Mukhopadhyay Sushil Chandra Dutta, Mohimohan Basu, Sudhir Kumar Dasgupta, Nirmal Chandra Bhattacharya, Bholanath Mukhopadhyay and Kalidas Nag had all contributed hugely to enhance the academic standards of the college.

Dr. Duff played a leading part in founding the University of Calcutta in 1857, he was associated with the Agro-horticultural Society and the establishment of a medical college, the first in India. He also aimed at breaking down caste-barriers by founding several girls schools. The Scottish Church College played a pioneering role in women's education as well as co-education in the country. Female students comprise half the present roll strength of the college. With the added interest of the missionaries in educational work and social welfare, the college stands as a monument to Indo-Scottish co-operation. The aims and principles of the College are essentially those of its founder namely, the formation of character through education based on Christian teaching.

Raja Ram Mohan Roy (1772-1833) was born into a Brahmin family in Bengal and experienced the orthodox practices of Hinduism in his youth. He studied the Quran, Buddhism and the New Testament. He disliked Idol worship and hated the practice of Sati, after seeing his brother's widow burnt alive on her husband's funeral fire. He fought to abolish polytheism, idol worship, the caste system, child marriage, animal sacrifice and Sati which is the practice of a widow being burnt alive on the funeral pyre.

In 1828, Raja Ram Mohan Roy founded the Brahmo Samaj (Society of Brahma) in an attempt to reform Hindu religious beliefs and practices. Brahmo Samaj's hall of worship has no images, statues or pictures. Only prayers and Hymns are sung, selecting one God for concentrating their prayers. Members offered prayers as a group. This community worship was a new aspect to Hinduism. The form of worship under Brahmo Samaj system was based on the Christian school of thought as the founder was inspired by the Western ideas. The Samaj inspired progressive development in

Hindu Society, religion and politics. The indirect result of the reform movement of Ram Mohan Roy was the abolition of Sati, child marriage, untouchability, caste distinction, and established women's right to property and widow remarriage.

Science in the Vedas

Vedic Physics by the 33-year old Dr. Raja Ram Mohan Roy is an ambitious work by a physical scientist who-thanks to his upbringing in a traditional household-also had the benefit of a Vedic schooling from childhood. His goal is to show that the Vedas, in keeping with their name meaning 'knowledge', contain a good deal of scientific knowledge that was lost over millennia, which he seeks to recover by suitably interpreting them. In particular, he regards the Rigveda as a book on particle physics and cosmology that has much in common with modern physics, but sometimes more subtle, especially when it comes to explaining the origin and evolution of the universe.

Such a claim is of course not new; there is no shortage of books claiming that the Vedic seers had seen everything and modern science is only a rediscovery. The author makes no such claim. His position is that by following a path of discovery quite different from that followed by modern science, the Vedic sages had arrived at a model of the universe, supported by a theory of atomic and subatomic particles that bears some similarity to modern physics; but Vedic cosmology is quite different from modern theories of the universe. What lends credence to the author's claim is his comprehensive grasp of modern physics. This allows him to construct-possibly reconstruct-a Vedic model of the universe that avoids some of the difficulties of modern theories like the Big Bang.

This may sound similar to some other books on the subject like Fritj of Capra's Tao of Physics, but there are important differences. For one, the author's grasp of the Vedic texts is surer, based on primary readings and often, original interpretations. Next, he offers some remarkable insights that go beyond contemporary knowledge of cosmology and even physics. Most significantly, he reconstructs a theory of the universe that may be a serious competitor to modern theories like the Big Bang. In other words, he is not satisfied with a comparison between Vedic knowledge and modern science; his goal is it to shed new light on important problems of nature. His approach is based on a careful reading of Vedic texts combined with a firm grasp of science. And therein lies the book's strength.

Before going into the details of Mr. Roy's book, it is useful to have an idea of different approaches to the study of the Rigveda. The most widely known is the nineteenth century reading favoured mostly-but not exclusively-by Western Indologists, which holds the Rigveda to be the record of 'Aryan invaders' from Eurasia and their conquest of India then populated by dark skinned natives. This has justly fallen into disrepute though some Western academics and their Indian followers continue to cling to some variant of it if only because they have nothing better. It is not hard to see that two dominant nineteenth century European ideas-colonial conquests and racism-went into this interpretation though political and Christian missionary interests also had major influence. The values underlying this version have fallen into disrepute, but their creation called 'Indology' continues to hold sway in academia, though it is rapidly crumbling.

When we turn to Indian interpretations, we run into problems of a different kind-break in tradition. Although we look at the four Vedas as from a single genre, there is considerable difference between the Rigveda and the other three. To take an example, the same verses from the Rigveda that appear in the Yajurveda are sometimes read and even interpreted differently.

Where the Yajurveda is generally treated as 'Karma-kanda'-or what may loosely (and incorrectly) be called 'ritualistic', the real meaning and purpose of the Rigveda remains something of a mystery. This is by no means a recent phenomenon. The ancient commentator Yaska (c. 3100 BC) tells us that even in his time scholars no longer had the intuitive grasp of the Vedic hymns that the ancients possessed. For whatever reason, even before the third millennium, the true meanings of the Rigveda had been greatly diluted if not lost, and various artificial interpretations like Karma-kanda came to be imposed on them.

Another point to be kept in mind is the extreme sophistication of structure and language of the Rigveda. Even superficially seen, its metrical forms and linguistic structures are the most sophisticated the world has even known. To go with this, its language, far from being elaborate, is concise yet flexible-at times bafflingly so. As Sri Aurobindo observed, the Vedic language is "just and precise and sins rather by economy of phrase than by excess, by over-pregnancy rather than by poverty of sense." From this it is possible to see that the Rigveda records not the beginning of a civilization but a culmination, containing knowledge-or 'Veda'-coded in the form of what we call Rigvedic hymns. In other words, the language of the Rigveda could well be technical in nature, like what we find in a modern book on physics or mathematics. A convincing key to unlocking this body of knowledge remains to be found. This is what the author in his book has set out to do.

In his words: "Most of the verses in the Vedas are mysterious. This is so because we don't know the actual scientific meaning of these verses. My aim in furnishing complete hymns is to give my learned readers as much information as possible, so that they can help in finding the lost Vedic science." His book is an admirable step in that direction, and, as this review seeks to explain, a great deal more.

The message of the book under review may be summarized as follows: one of the keys to unlocking the secrets of the Rigveda consists in reading many of the words like 'gau' and 'ashva' as well as names of gods like 'Marut' and 'Indra' as technical terms used in the natural sciences, and the hymns themselves as descriptions of laws of nature. In other words, the Rigveda contains a description of the forces of nature and the laws that govern them, written in cryptic even coded language. The author's goal is to extract their meaning by making sense of important hymns that appear enigmatic or even incoherent when interpreted in a conventional way. Though his effort cannot be considered complete, it nonetheless sheds new light on important Vedic passages.

For example, in the Vedic literature we have frequent statements like 'agni was pashu' and 'pashus are agneya' that make no sense when read literally. The author, however, identifies 'pashu' with particle and 'agni' with energy. Then a whole series of Vedic passages including the ones just cited become comprehensible and even coherent. Similarly, he identifies Vayu with field-one of the most important concepts in physics. Surya of course stands for light, and the seven horses yoked to Surya's chariot are the seven colours of the light spectrum. The word 'gau' (cow), which Yaska tells us also means light, actually refers to the particle state of light or the photon. Based on his approach, the author suggests that the great Rigvedic hymn 1. 123 by Dirghatamas, actually describes the creation and annihilation of particles, which some liken to Shiva's Dance of Creation. It should be emphasized that this brief description-necessarily simplified-does not do full justice to the author's interpretations.

This approach offers some interesting possibilities. The author observes: "Our universe is matter dominated. If matter and antimatter are created together in same amount, then we should find equal amount of antimatter. Whyis it we don't find much evidence of antimatter as far as we can observe? Are remote parts of the universe antimatter dominated? Did matter and antimatter somehow get segregated in different corners of the universe? Scientists don't think so. Scientists believe that when universe was very young, for some reason a small excess of matter over antimatter was generated. As matter and antimatter annihilated each other, this small excess remained, and this small excess is our universe. The Vedas take a different view. According to the Vedas, matter and energy are constantly being created at the surface of the universe, and there is an imbalance in their creation. Matter and antimatter continually annihilate each other and the small excess of matter has accumulated over the age of the universe."

This is a profoundly different cosmic view, which the author supports with the help of Rigvedic passages including 2.20.7 and 6.47.21. The latter may be read as: "Everyday Indra removes half of the people, similar to the other half but black in colour, born in his house." (The author uses the past tense, which I have rendered into the present following Panini's rule for the Vedic usage: chandasi lung lat litah.) The author goes on to observe: "Indra is considered responsible for killing the black people in the Rigveda. As matter and antimatter are attracted towards each other due to the opposite nature of electric charge resulting in annihilation, electric force is indeed responsible for this phenomenon."

So black refers to antimatter! In addition to the author's remarkably original reading of an obscure passage, it highlights the utter superficiality of European Indologists and their Indian followers in giving such passages a racial meaning. If the author's insights can be supported, this is the kind of knowledge that was lost over the millennia. There is evidence however, that some fragments of it survived as late as the time of Sayana (1315-87). In his Rigveda Bhashya he gives a value for the velocity of light that in modern units works out to 186,000 miles per second. So it is not easy to dismiss the author's interpretations as speculation, obtained by 'retrofitting' modern scientific findings on to the Vedas. In any event, the Vedic cosmology worked out by the author has important differences with modern theories of the universe.

After presenting his interpretation of Vedic passages in the light of modern physics, the author gives a lucid summary of modern theories (Big Bang and Steady State) followed by a discussion of the Vedic model. He points out some of the basic problems of the Big Bang theory, highlighting the following: singularity, horizon, flatness, age, monopole, entropy and antimatter. He discusses the same problems in the Vedic context and shows how they may be elegantly accounted for. This can be illustrated with the help of the singularity problem. In the author's words:

> *"Universe started with an explosion according to the Big Bang model. At time equal to zero, all the mass-energy was concentrated in a point. This is certainly an unimaginable feat, as the universe is immense.*
>
> *According to Pauli's exclusion principle, not even two electrons can occupy the same state, and here the whole universe is considered to be inside a point....*
>
> *The situation is a direct result of the conservation of mass and energy [or mass-energy], the most sacred principle of physics. Considering that the universe is expanding, extrapolating backward in time, the universe was as small as a point. As mass-energy of the universe must be conserved, all the mass-energy must have been there at time zero as well. We should note that conservation of mass-energy is violated in this case as well. This is equivalent to saying that all the mass-energy was created at time zero. Mass-energy density of the universe was infinity at time equal to zero, which is called a point of singularity."*

To get around this obvious difficulty, scientists have introduced an entity called 'inflation', which has mysteriously disappeared from the present universe. The singularity problem does not arise in the Vedic approach to creation. As the author observes: "Inflation has not solved the singularity problem, as inflation only produces part of the mass-energy of the universe, and as long as even a tiny amount of matter-energy was present at time zero, singularity problem will be there. The Vedas tell us that at time zero there was no mass-energy in the universe. It was a complete void. Space, mass and energy are continuously being created. As universe had zero mass-energy at time zero, the universe did not start with singularity."

This obviously violates the conservation principle. But Vedic cosmology has a conservation principle of its own that includes space along with mass and energy. It is a very subtle principle and yet stunning in its simplicity. The author describes it as follows:

> *"... the Vedas have returned to tell an even greater truth [than mass-energy equivalence]: equivalence of space, mass and energy. Space is no different from matter and energy. In the beginning there was no mass-energy in the universe because there was no space. Mass-energy is created due to expansion of the universe. The universe cannot expand without creating mass-energy and universe cannot contract without annihilating mass-energy. Thus the universe started with zero mass energy and will end up with zero mass-energy as well. Thus there was no singularity in the beginning and there will be no singularity at the end."*

The author recognizes that since the universe is now in an expanding mode, we must be witnessing the creation of mass-energy in the universe. As evidence he points to gamma-ray bursts that scientists have observed but have no clue as to its source. In 1973 it was discovered that about three times a day, the sky flashes with a powerful burst of gamma-rays. The author observes: "The gamma-ray bursts are intense, bulk of their radiation is in the range of 100,000 to 1,000,000 electron volts, implying a very hot source and its sources release more energy within minutes than sun will release in its entire lifetime."

Astronomers believe that these bursts are coming from distances that range from three to ten billion light years. Various explanations have been offered-from black holes to collapsing neutron stars-but none is satisfactory. It is possible to account for it using Vedic cosmology. According to Vedic science, mass-energy is continuously being created at the surface of the universe. This is related to the expansion of the universe. In the author's words: "As the universe is huge now, its expansion will create immense radiation."

What is extraordinary is that these gamma-ray bursts-corresponding to the creation of mass-energy according to Vedic science-takes place three times a day. This is exactly the frequency given in the Rigveda in at least three passages. (3.56.6, 7.11.3, 9.86.18). The second of these tells us: "O Agni! We know you have wealth to give three times a day to mortals."

Another fundamental difference between the Big Bang model and the Vedic model is that the latter postulates rotation of the universe around an axis. This means it has a preferred direction, or, in the parlance of physics, the Vedic universe is non-isotropic. Here too the author invokes an unexplained scientific phenomenon in support-violation of parity observed in weak interactions. As the author observes:

> *"It is obvious that model of the universe should not contradict the nature of these interactions. Weak interaction has complete disregard for many conservation laws including parity... What is so special about weak interaction? Why is it that it does not obey conservation laws like other interactions?... It has been more than forty years since the discovery of parity violation, but cosmologists have not taken into account what particle physicists have proved."*

The author shows that this can be seen as an indirect proof of the rotating universe implied in the Vedic model. He then cites possible direct evidence also. He notes that observations by Borge Norland and John P. Ralston on the polarization of light from distant galaxies indicate that the universe is rotating. (This is on top of the well-known Faraday Effect. Since the rate of rotation is slow, one has to look very far to find physical evidence of it.) Their results are disputed by other scientists for the reason that it violates the idea of an isotropic universe, but that is only to be expected. As the author notes: "Rotation of universe and continuous creation of matter and energy are two salient features of the Vedic cosmology."

This brings us to the author's reconstruction of the Vedic universe, which he summarizes as follows: "Like the Big Bang model, the Vedic model assumes that the universe started from a point and is expanding. However, unlike the Big Bang model, universe starts cold with zero mass-energy, and is rotating as well as expanding. There is a similarity with the Steady State model that mass-energy is constantly being created. The difference is that [in the Vedic] the universe is not considered infinitely old, and the creation of mass-energy is only during the expansion phase of the universe. During the contraction phase, the mass-energy is annihilated, so that the universe ends without a singularity."

Clearly, the author's study of the Vedas combined with his knowledge of modern physics has allowed him to present an impressive synthesis of the two. There are some minor difficulties. His reading of the Vedas leads him to postulate the existence of particles not known to modern physics. His interpretations of the symbolism of the Harappan seals are speculative, and sometimes wrong. We are of course on much firmer ground today-thanks to Jha's decipherment of the Harappan script, and the subsequent work of Jha and this reviewer.

Also, it is a little puzzling that he should read the famous description of the Sarasvati River-giribhya a samudrat-to mean 'from the ocean', when the causative case (pancami vibhakti) suggests the opposite. The book also has passages on the Puranas and the development of Hinduism that add nothing to it but interrupts the flow of reasoning that is central to its theme. But these are minor quibbles that do not seriously detract from what is beyond doubt a significant achievement.

We are now in the midst of a Renaissance of sorts in the study of ancient India, including the Vedas. More are less coinciding with the collapse of the colonial-missionary creation known as the Aryan invasion model of India, a new school of research-inaccurately called the Indo-American school-has been pursuing a path of study that combines ancient learning and modern science. Freeing itself from the racial, political and religious biases that influenced Indology for more than a century, this new school has made significant contributions to the history of the ancient world. Among notable members of this school one may cite K.D. Sethna, David Frawley, Shrikanth Talageri, Natwar Jha and several others. Dr. Roy, the author of the book under discussion, is a major new entrant to the field. He has opened an important way of looking at ancient texts-and possibly also the universe.

All told Vedic Physics is an impressive tour de force by a young scholar, offering fresh insights into the Vedas without compromising on the science. At the very least, it has opened new avenues for research, which one hopes will be pursued by scientists working closely with traditionally schooled Vedic scholars. This alone holds promise of a sane approach to problems if we hope to avoid the inanities-and the insanities-that have plagued Indology for over a century.

Nineteenth century Bengal witnessed a few reform movements among Muslims as well as Hindus. The Islamic Reform movements, such as Faraizi, Tariqah-i-Muhammadiyah, Taaiyuni and AHL-I-HADITH, occupied a conspicuous position among them. These were revivalist in character and stirred deep religious sentiments among Muslims throughout east, west and north Bengal, and succeeded considerably in rousing the Muslim masses to action. The Tabligh Jamaat and Seerat Conference movements, which recently stirred similar mass enthusiasm in Bangladesh, are reminiscent, and to a great extent also the spiritual progeny, of these movements of the preceding century.

Universal Perspective Religious movements being social phenomena have to be studied in the wider context. Islamic revivalist movements had taken such hold of Bengal in the 19th century that historians rated them as the persistent sign of life in a subjugated and decadent Muslim community. Religious revivalism in itself was not, however, peculiar to the Muslims of Bengal, but had become widespread throughout the Muslim world, affecting the Muslim Ummah as a whole. There is a suggestion that it had cropped up in different parts of the world under the impact of imperialism.

Thus considered, the Wahhabism of Arabia appears to have arisen under the impact of Ottoman imperialism. Mughal and British imperialism produced the movement of Shah Waliullahi and the Teriqah-i-Muhammadiyah. The Fariazi, Taaiyuni and Ahl-i-Hadith movements arose under British imperialism. The Fulani and Sannusiyah of North Africa arose under French and British imperialism, and the Paduri and Muhammadiyah movements of Indonesia under the impact of Dutch imperialism.

In popular parlance these religious reform movements came to be associatively known as Wahhabism and Islamic revivalism, tajdeed al-Islam, as against a somewhat Western Renaissance-oriented Muslim modernism and Pan-Islamism, ittihad al-Islam. The movements, in general, were universal; both aimed at re-awakening Muslims all over the world; and both carried the slogan: 'Islam in danger'. Therefore, there existed considerable mutual sympathy and a good deal of unity of purpose and identity of sentiments between them. Yet, they pursued different goals and occasionally expressed disapproval of each other's programmes and scrupulously maintained exclusiveness and independence of each other's stance.

Local perspective Although Bengal was occupied by the Muslims in the beginning of the 13th century AD and ruled by them till 1757, it was not fully Islamised. It comprised a cosmopolitan society consisting of Muslims, Hindus and Buddhists, who lived side by side in adjacent but separate villages and hamlets under a tolerant regime that ensured universal justice and security. In this local cosmopolitan historical perspective, the social scene in Bengal in the 19th century, as far as reform was concerned, sharply contrasted with the slothful situation obtaining in the 18th century. Intellectual life in Bengal during the 19th century became especially quickened and enlivened by the impulse of socio-religious reform which took hold of both Muslim and Hindu communities. In the second decade of the century, it made an intelligent section of both the communities question the compatibility of the current patterns of their life with their respective religious inspirational sources, and also with the immediate and future prospects of their communities. The immediate cause of such a reawakening was the impact of British rule on Bengal.

The rule of the *East India Company* in Bengal had completely shattered the social frame of the country, firstly, by sapping the authority and status of the Mughal Ruling class which comprised Muslims and Hindus in equal numbers; secondly, by destroying the traditional lifestyle of the rural well-to-do class; and thirdly, by setting up the Hindu Banyans of Calcutta, who were mainly marwari businessmen and moneylenders and worked as Gomastahs (commercial agents of the English in India), often styled as 'black Gomastahs of white men'. The zamindars, feudal lords newly created by the *Permanent Settlement* of 1793, perpetrated atrocities on the masses.

The gomastas and the zamindars were joined by a third group of ambitious fortune hunters, Englishmen looking for opportunities for capital investment in rural Bengal. Many of them probably brought money and skills from the lost colonies of America, and as indigo planters gave a 'royal colour' to the scourging of the peasantry.

The combined impact of these developments upon the social structure of a subjugated people can be well imagined. Such a pattern of a 'protected scourging' thus formed a corresponding 'take-over process' of the East India Company's rule over Bengal (1757-1857) as against the systematic destruction of the Mughal administration, which has been designated by Lathrop Stoddard as the policy of 'pacific penetration' by Western imperialism. This policy had created many social and economic anomalies especially in the rural life of Bengal.

Little wonder, therefore, that it aroused a deep sense of pity in the minds of Christian missionaries, and a sense of remorse in some good souls from the ranks of English administrators, and also considerable sympathy amongst humanist groups in England. With their blessings, encouragement, help and participation, Raja Ram Mohan Roy laid the foundation of a 'Renaissance' type of modernist/Western social reform movement in Calcutta around 1814, which spurred numerous other social reform movements in Bengal and India for remodelling the Hindu social system.

However, if the British challenge had produced a somewhat positive response among the Hindu elite of Bengal, during the corresponding period it produced a negative response among the Muslims and spurred a number of 'revivalist' religious reform movements, beginning with the Faraizi movement of HAJI SHARIATULLAH in Bengal and the Tariqah-i-Muhammadiyah movement of Sayyid Ahmad Shahid of Rai Bareilly in Delhi, both of which came into existence about the year 1818 AD.

In contrast to the Muslim revivalist movements, Raja Ram Mohan Roy's reform movement is generally regarded as a Renaissance movement. It should, nevertheless, be observed that it differed from the European 'Renaissance model', especially as it was deeply infused with a revivalist desire to restore a pristine Hindu or Aryan religious spirit. The European Renaissance aimed at integrating the classical, secular, Graeco-Roman spirit of the 'rationalism' of the 'past' with the merciful Christian 'morality' of the 'present', to create a 'humanism' that could be the foundation of a happy and civilized 'future' world. In comparison, however, Raja Ram Mohan Roy's Renaissance aimed at resuscitating a pristine Aryan 'Unitarianism of God' with the help of the modern Western rationalist spirit. In the heart of hearts, it was not secular but deeply religious. Consequently some other important Hindu reform movements, such as the Arya Samaj, were antagonistically spurred by Ram Mohan's reformist activities and inspiration.

Islamic revivalism and the Hindu Renaissance thrived within the same space and about the same time. They affected each other, unfortunately more by their mutually antagonistic revivalist impulse, than by the actual or imagined 'rational' impulse of the Renaissance. Thereby they tended to break asunder the time-honoured Islamic or Mughal peace of 'religious tolerance' and began fostering a new form of Hindu-Muslim communalism.

Local Islamic perspective Bengal, from the Muslim conquest (1205) till the Battle of Palashi (1757), continued to be a well-secured stronghold of the world Muslim community. Politically also, it remained a bastion of Muslim power in the Indian subcontinent. But the Battle of PALASHI brought in the English, and as a consequence, Muslim society decayed and shrank under constant stress. The period of subjugation under the British can be subdivided into two periods: first-pure slavery of 100 years under the East India Company's rule and second-protected subjecthood for 90 years under the British Crown, the Great Revolt of 1857 drawing the dividing line between the two.

In the first period, Muslim society moved from light to darkness, from hope to despair, from Darul Islam to Darul Harb, that is, from the abode of peace to the abode of war. Muslims waged a relentless and unlimited war against the enemies of Islam to defeat their conspiracy against Muslim society and the religion of Islam. It was a war unto death-Jihad or Hijrat, which eventually gave birth to the Faraizi movement of Haji Shariatullah and DUDU MIYAN, the Tariqah-i-Muhammadyah movement or so-called Indian Wahhabism of Sayyid Ahmad Shahid, TITU MIR, Maulana Wilayat Ali and Maulana Inayat Ali, the Ahl-i-Hadith movement of Shah Ismail Shahid, and Maulana Nazir Husain and also the Taaiyuni movement of Maulana KARAMAT ALI of Jaunpur.

In the second period, following the great shake-up of 1857, the Muslims-not as a community, but individually-endeavoured to adjust themselves to the alien political power, to tame their nature before adjusting to the modern civilization of the West, to compete along with other subject peoples of the British empire in order to grab the amenities of a happy and cultured life under Pax Britannica, to exchange jihad for the protection of the British law,

Aman. In a word, they tried for a transition from the abode of war (Darul Harb) to an abode of protection (Darul Aman) by means of giving up political ambition and accepting wholeheartedly the administrative peace, the rule of law, as the be-all and end-all of a happy modern life. These ideals and the accompanying sentiments and emotions became crystallised in one word-loyalism.

The Islamic revivalist movements thrived in Bengal with high emotional fervour from about 1820 to 1870, most of the time at a frantic sentimental level until they were systematically destroyed or tamed as non-political, religious movements by the British government. Thus considered, they may be said to form a 'transitional bridge' from the state of slavery to the state of protectorate. Until the struggle fizzled out, the slogan of 'Darul Aman' and the idea of protectorate could not take hold of Muslim society. After the revivalist movements fizzled out the Renaissance type of Muslim modernism, overtly or covertly pronouncing the slogan of 'loyalism', took charge of leading the Muslim community nearer to the English rulers along the road of constitutional progress.

Functions Coming into being as a puritan reaction to the impact of imperialism, as an international jihad movement and as a move to re-organise and reintegrate local Muslim society in the local socio-political perspective discussed above, the first and foremost task before the Islamic revivalist movements of Bengal was to revive the original doctrines of religion. This was also the main task set before Hindu reform movements such as the Brahma Samaj and Arya Samaj. In their reformist endeavour, both the groups called for purging their respective societies, but offered grounds for the fresh community-wide contact between them and their like-minded co-religionists across provincial barriers.

One of the functions of Islamic revivalism was thus the 'breaking of isolation' of the Muslims of different parts of the Indian sub-continent which had been caused by the shrinking of the Mughal power during the preceding century.

Secondly, it may be noted that, in all, there were four Islamic revivalist movements that gained popularity in Bengal. Out of them, the Faraizi, Tariqah-i-Muhammadiyah and Ahl-i-Hadith aimed at reviving the pristine teachings of Islam and purging Muslim society of un-Islamic local accretions. The fourth, the

Taaiyuni movement led by Maulana Karamat Ali Jaunpuri, had split off from the Tariqah-i-Muhammadiyah and wanted to retain some traditional institutions of Muslim society such as Fatiha, Milad and Urs, which were rejected by the other three. Moreover, following the revolt of 1857 the Ta'aiyuni movement joined hands with the Muslim modernists and declared India under the British Crown as an 'abode of protection' or protectorate (Darul Aman), which according to Maulana Karamat Ali absolved the Muslims from the religious obligation of jihad, that is, fighting unto death for the liberation of the Muslim community, and from Hijrat, that is, migration to an abode of Islam. Moreover, the reformist trend of Shah Waliullah of Delhi had influenced the Ahl-i-Hadith movement.

The Faraizi movement arose under the direct influence of the Wahhabism of Arabia and had no direct link with the movement of Shah Waliullah or the Tariqah-i-Muhammadiyah of Delhi. On the other hand, the movement of Titu Mir was a direct extension of the Tariqah-i-Muhammadiyah of Delhi.

Being manifestations of a universal type of Islamic revivalism, these reform movements emphasized the social egalitarianism of Islam, equality of mankind as the creation of one Allah, brotherhood of Muslims, the unity of the Muslim world and the need for waging jihad for the liberation of Muslim lands from the hands of the infidels. For this purpose, the upholders of these movements also sought to resuscitate the Islamic Ummah, which became in course of time a central part of their reform programme. For this reason, the Islamic revivalist movements everywhere in the world, overtly or covertly, aimed at establishing an Islamic social order and political State, and as a matter of policy, turned directly to the masses.

A second important function of Islamic revivalism was, thus, reinfusing a deep sense of organic unity of the Ummah and of the value of Islamic egalitarianism and brotherhood in the consciousness of the Muslims.

Moreover, their strategy of mass contact and fiery speeches delivered with equal fervour from the pulpit and the political platform, for rousing religious sentiments against internal corruption of Muslim society as well as against the conspiracy of the foreign rulers, succeeded considerably in waking up mass consciousness to the deplorable political and economic situation of the Muslims all over the world.

A third important function of Islamic revivalism in Bengal was thus the widening of general awareness, psychological re-invigoration, and reform and re-organisation of society. In the early 1820s when Sayyid Ahmad Shahid visited the city of Calcutta, he apparently received no opposition from any quarters of the Muslims, Hindus or the government administration. But in the first flush of its mass popularity in rural Bengal, in parts of 24 Parganas and Nadia under Mir Nisar Ali alias Titu Mir from about 1827 to 1831, it came upon the quicksands of a conspiracy of the new class of Hindu zamindars and gomastahs with whom the European indigo planters also joined hands.

However, Haji Shariatullah had lived at Mecca from 1799 to 1818. While he was a student he had closely observed the conflict of the Wahhabis of Arabia with Ottoman imperial power and watched how they were destroyed by Khedive Mohammad Ali at the behest of the Ottoman sultan. The Haji took shelter in patience and sobriety, and saved his movement by retreating completely from politics into the arena of social and religious reform. [Muin-ud-Din Ahmad Khan]

Peace on Earth

Peace on Earth: Time to Rekindle Passion for Unity

In India, many civilisations have come together over the years, creating new patterns of universal oneness. Raja Ram Mohan Roy ushered in the age of new thought in 1828. He wrote: "All mankind is one great family of which numerous nations and tribes existing are only various branches".

In Bengal, Rabindranath Tagore's father passed on these thoughts to the poet who wrote: "I love India not because I have had the chance to be born on her soil, but because she has saved through tumultuous ages the living words that were issued from the illuminated consciousness of her sons".

All religions tell us that the divine is within us. The Gospel according to St. Thomas says: "He who has heard and assimilated my word is as I". In Sanatana Dharma it is Tat Tvam Asi. To find divinity within oneself it is important to act with compassion towards all beings.

Mexican poet Octavia Paz wrote: "In India there is a passion for unity". Maulana Azad once asked: "If religion expresses the universal truth, why should conflicts arise amongst different beliefs, each claiming to be the sole repository of truth, and condemning others as false?"

One reaches the infinite through love, not through violence. "Ahimsa hi param dharma, Sarva dharma samabhava". The trishul of Shiva represents the three dimensions of space, earth and sky and the three gunas that each of us must strive to overcome in our own lives.

Guru Vyasa spoke of the folly of men who choose the way to destruction through discord when all legitimate material satisfaction could be had through the way of fellowship and harmony. Ours is a multifarious heritage. On the Sindhu-Gangetic plains the tribes were known as Sindhus and Hindus. Hindu became Indus to the Greeks and the country on the bank of the Indus became India. There was no caste, no temple, only prayers in the oral tradition of the Rig Veda.

Caste became an ugly name much later. Yet, Rishi Parasar (the law giver) was the son of a Chandala, Rishi Vashishta's mother was a fisherwoman, Viswamitra was a Kshatriya, Valmiki a hunter. All became great gurus. In the oral verse of the Rig Veda, men and women were equal.

Sanatana Dharma was meant to be India's gift to the world, a way to realise peace and harmony. Increasingly, however, ancient customs are being taken out of context for political purposes. Cattle were extremely important for the Vedic people and so became symbols of spiritual experience. Go, the name for cow and bull, also connotes the earth and the speech of rishis. Gokula means temple; it also means Krishna's dwelling place.

Today, politicians fight over cow protection. Why protect only the cow? What about the beautiful birds of the sky? And the donkeys and the street dogs that are constantly being ill-treated? The environment, too, needs protection. Majestic trees are regularly being chopped down. This decreases forest cover and causes more pollution. So the iist is long and painful.

Ecological awareness is the intuitive awareness of the oneness of all life. Our ancient heritage advocates protection not only for human beings and animals but for the elements, too.

Listen to the words of the Atharva Veda, written 4,000 years ago: "We are birds of the same nest,/We may wear different skins,/ We may speak different languages,/We may believe in different religions,/We may belong to different cultures,/Yet we share the same home-Our Earth./For man can live individually,/But can survive only collectively/Born on the same planet/Covered by the same skies/Gazing at the same stars/Breathing the same air/We must learn to happily progress together/Or miserably perish together".

Brahmo Samaj ("Assembly of Brahman")

Doctrines

Brahman is worshipped as the sole creator and supporter of the universe. This monotheism is based on the interpretation of the early Vedanta, the Upanishads, and the Brahma Sutra. Ram Mohan Roy, founder of Brahmo Samaj, identified the monotheism of Christianity and Islam as of universal validity. Codification of the doctrines came with the main principles of the Nava Samhita, New Dispensation, of Keshub Chandra Sen, the third leader of the movement, in 1881. These are: 1) Harmony of all scriptures, saints, and sects. 2) Harmony of reason and faith, of devotion and duty, of yoga and bhakti. 3) The church of the Samaj stands for One Supreme God, to be worshipped without form. No idolatry in any form may enter the precincts of the church. 4) The church stands for universal brotherhood without distinction of caste or creed or sect. One might add to this the principle of Roy that religious authority should be based on reason and ability, not on priestly caste. Texts from all world religions are used for prayer and worship.

History

Ram Mohan Roy was born in 1774 to a Brahmin family in the Bengal village of Radhanagar. He was influenced in his youth by studies in Advaita and the monotheism of Islam, and later by the Unitarian movement. The superior kulina castes stood aloof from the British. Roy however was the son of a non-kulina Brahmin and the non-kulina Hindus reaped the benefit of working with the British. By 1815 Roy was a financial success and went to live in Calcutta to devote himself to social, moral, and religious reform. The non-kulina Hindus were being urged by Christian missionaries to convert. To keep their Hindu identity and to acquire Western culture as well as to improve their religious status-for their religious leadership came from the kulinas-a new form of Hinduism was needed. Ram Mohan Roy provided this by the creation of the Brahmo Samaj in 1828 and he became the religious leader. He was followed by other non-kulinas and this new type of religious leader also led other new religious movements in the nineteenth century. Thus started the first modern Hindu reform movement. Roy sought to reform Hinduism from within, to restore Hinduism to its primitive purity. He started the restoration of the Vedas to public awareness for both study and religious inspiration, and he regenerated the Vedantic tradition, still of importance to educated Hindus today. Roy worked tirelessly to better social, moral, and religious conditions, one of his great successes being his contribution to the abolition of suttee in 1829.

Under the successors of Roy, Debendranath Tagore (1817-1905) and Keshub Chandra Sen (1838-1884), the work of Roy continued and the Samaj developed into a vital movement for social and religious reform. Swami Vivekananda as a young man was involved in the most westernising, reformist faction of the Brahmo Samaj. Gandhi too was a beneficiary of the vision of Roy.

The Samaj contributed to the process of making the Vedas "the active basis of numerous ideologies for socio-religious change. In this way they played an important part in the creation of modern India..." (Lipner 1994, 66).

Symbols

Keshub gave concreteness to the otherwise abstract monotheism of the Samaj by introducing into the church the Pilgrimage to saints, the Homa ceremony, the Baptismal ceremony, the Lord's supper, the Flag ceremony, the Arati, the vow of Poverty, the Savitri Vrata, the Nightingale Vrata, and other innovations. He also introduced extempore prayers and speeches from the pulpit rather than fixed stereotyped liturgy. However, Keshub himself became a symbol as a master and avatar.

Adherents

The Brahmo Samaj survives as a relatively small but progressive sect mainly in West Bengal. The Tagore family supported the Samaj for three generations.

Hinduism

The Religion of Divine Immanence and An Hereditary Graded Social Structure

Hinduism, dating from around 1500 B. C., is the oldest living religion having a membership (1982) of 477,991,300 confined largely to India. It is the most complex, diverse, and tolerant of the world's religions. One can find within Hinduism almost any form of religion--from simple animism to elaborate philosophical systems--which has ever been conceived or practiced by mankind. Hinduism has met the challenge of other religions, primarily, by absorbing them and their practices and beliefs into the mainstream of Hindu religious expression.

The Aryans (noble ones) invaded the Indus valley from Persia in the second millennium B.C. They were basically wandering nomads who spoke an Indo-European language which became the basis for Sanskrit. This early Aryan society developed into three basic socio-economic classes. The priests or Brahmins became the ruling class. The tribal chieftains and their warriors or Kshatriyas were next in line, with the commoners and merchants or Vaishyas rounding out the Aryan society. A fourth group, the conquered pre-Aryan people or Shudras, were at the bottom of society. Eventually these divisions developed into a religiously supported caste system.

The Vedas are the sacred scriptures of Hinduism. The four basic Vedic books are the Rig-Veda, the Yajur-Veda, the Sama-Veda, and the Atharva-Veda. Each of the Vedic books is divided into four parts. Each contains a section of hymns to the gods (Mantras), a section of ritual materials (Brahmanas), a section of guidance for hermits (Aranyakas), and a fourth section of philosophical treatises (Upanishads). The Mantra and Brahmana sections are the oldest materials with the Aranyakas and Upanishads added later. This Vedic literature evolved during the classical period of Hinduism.

The fourteen principal Upanishads form the basis of Hindu philosophy. They assume there is one reality, the impersonal god-being called Brahman. All things and beings are an expression of Brahman. Everything in the world and experience which is not Brahman is illusion (maya). All phenomenal existence (pleasure, worldly success, wealth) is illusion arising from ignorance of the true nature of reality. Those who continue in this ignorance are bound to life by the law of karma which keeps them endlessly in the cycle of birth, life, death, and rebirth. When man discovers the Path of Desire is not fulfilling he is ready to start on the Path of Renunciation. Here he recognizes his duty to others, family and community, and dedicates himself to a life of service. This is rewarding but he still yearns for infinite being, infinite awareness, and infinite joy.

To achieve these ultimates of experience we must realize the basic purpose of life is to pass beyond imperfection. That which is beyond the limitations and imperfections of life can be found within. Underlying our physical existence and personality is an infinite reservoir of reality. This infinite centre of every life, this hidden authentic self or Atman is no less than Brahman, the Godhead. By detachment from the finite, illusory self and commitment to Atman-Brahman, we achieve infinite being, infinite awareness, and infinite joy.

This philosophy of the Upanishads is a reaction to the sacrificial, priestly form of worship in Hinduism. It emphasizes meditation as a means of worship and teaches that ignorance is man's basic plight. Historically, the priestly sections of the Vedas have directed the religion of the masses in India while the Upanishads have attracted a relatively small number of Indian intellectuals. Contemporary Western people who are attracted to Eastern thought tend to identify Hinduism with the philosophy of the Upanishads.

Classical Hinduism also produced the ethical Code of Manu which teaches that the caste system is divinely ordained. The first three castes (Brahmins, Kshatriyas, and Vaishyas) are "twice born" people while the Shudras are "once born" manual labourers. The only upward mobility through this caste system is by means of repeated incarnations. Although the caste system is outlawed in contemporary India, its social influence is still strong.

The Code of Manu also teaches the various stages through which a man is expected to pass in a successful life: student, householder, hermit, and wandering beggar. These stages are only for twice born men. Women should stay in the home under the protection and control of the chief male in the household. The code requires the cultivation of pleasantness, patience, control of mind, non-stealing, purity, control of senses., intelligence, knowledge, truthfulness, and non irritability. The killing of cows is listed among the greatest of sins.

The composition of the great epic poem, the Bhagavad-Gita, sometime between the second century B.C. and the third century A.D. marks the end of the period of classical Hinduism. The Bhagavad-Gita is found within the text of a much longer poem and is probably the most highly esteemed scripture of Hinduism. In the poem Arjuna, a Hindu knight, for the first time in the recorded history of Hinduism, raises the question of the propriety of killing people. He is answered by his charioteer, Krishna, who turns out to be an incarnation of the god Vishnu. Arjuna is told he must be loyal to his duty as a warrior and kill. The Gita also teaches a variety of means of personal salvation. One may achieve release from life (Nirvana) through asceticism, through meditation, through devotion to and worship of the gods, or through obedience to the rules of his caste,

After the close of the classical period subtle changes gradually appear in Hinduism. Out of the millions of major and minor gods, worship tended to centre around the Trimurti: Brahma, the creator; Shiva, the destroyer; and Vishnu, the preserver. Among this trinity, Brahma receives the least attention. Shiva is the most popular probably because he is the god of sex and reproduction and appeals to the deprivation experienced by the masses. His various goddess consorts such as Kali are equally revered. According to mythology, Vishnu has appeared on earth in nine forms and will come a tenth time to bring the world to an end. Among his appearances are Krishna; Gautama, the Buddha; Matsya, the fish who saved Manu from the great flood; and Christ.

The majority of the people of India seek salvation through devotion to the gods while many of the wealthy and educated seek salvation through the way of knowledge. This intellectual Hinduism centres around six systems of philosophy: Samkhya, Yoga, Mimamsa, Vedanta, Vaiseshika, and Nyana. All claim to be based on the Vedas and revolve about common themes. The only basic difference among them is their view of ultimate reality. The Vedanta system is monistic and asserts that the only essence in the universe is Brahman; all else is illusion. The Samkhya, Yoga, Vaiseshika, and Nyana systems are dualistic and assert that the universe is composed of two forces, matter and spirit. The Mimamsa system is basically atheistic and teaches that salvation comes through the correct observance of Vedic rituals. Jainism and Buddhism began as reform movements in Hinduism and it has absorbed much of their thinking. During the Middle Ages Hinduism and Islam competed for followers in India. The two religions are in many ways opposites and there has been much bloodshed in their struggles. Sikhism arose in an attempt to bring reconciliation between the two. Tradition credits the disciple Thomas for bringing Christianity to India. During the three centuries of British rule Christianity had considerable influence on the growing edge of Hinduism.

The nineteenth and twentieth centuries brought three main reform movements in Hinduism. Ram Mohan Roy, called the Father of Modern India, was a monotheist who tended to agree with Christian missionaries in their attempt to suppress the suttee, child marriage, polytheism, and idolatry in Hinduism. The greatest reformer was Sri Ramakrishna, a follower of non dualistic Vedanta, who believed there was one single reality, God, behind all religions and that truth is essentially one. His disciple, Dutt, later known as Vivekananda, became the first Hindu missionary to the modern world. He described Vedanta Hinduism as the mother of all other religions. The best known Indian reformer is Mohandas K. Gandhi who was influenced by the teachings of Jesus and the Jain doctrine of non injury (ahimsa) espoused civil disobedience and nonviolence which were largely responsible for bringing India freedom from British rule. Gandhi, in turn, became a major influence in the political thinking of Martin Luther King, Jr. and many of the leaders of the "peace movement" in Western Civilization.

The Hindu Reformation

"...Thus it may be said that as early as 1820 India had come into the direct current of European thought and had begun to participate in the fruits of Europe's intellectual quest. The Brahmo Samaj lived up to this ideal. Its social message was Westernization, to purge Hinduism of the customs and superstitions with which it was overlaid, to raise the status of women, to bridge the yawning gulf between popular and higher Hinduism, to fight relentlessly against caste, social taboo, polygamy and other well entrenched abuses. To the educated Hindu, who felt unsettled in mind by the attack of the missionaries, the Brahmo Samaj provided the way out.

The Brahmo tradition has become so much a part of the Indian way of life now, that one is inclined to overlook its distinctive contribution. It does not lie primarily in the fact that it enabled Hinduism to withstand the onslaught of the missionaries, but in that it introduced the modern approach to Indian problems..."

Introduction...

The Hindu Reformation of the nineteenth century is one of the great movements of the age which by its massiveness and far-reaching significance takes its place with the most vital developments of modern history.

As it was a slow process and took place under the cover of British authority and was not always obvious to the outsider, it has so far escaped attention. A further reason why, in spite of its tremendous import, it passed unnoticed is that, by its very nature, it was an internal movement which did not touch or influence outside events. But India's independence and emergence into the modern world would hardly have been possible without the slow but radical adjustments that had taken place within the fold of Hinduism for a period of over 100 years.

In order to appreciate this movement fully it is necessary to understand what the position of Hinduism was in the beginning of the nineteenth century. 700 years of Islamic authority over the Indo-Gangetic Plains from Delhi to Calcutta had left Hinduism in a state of depression. It was the religion of a subject race, looked down on with contempt by the Muslims as idolatry. It enjoyed no prestige and for many centuries its practice had been tolerated only under considerable disadvantage in various areas. It had no central direction, no organization and hardly any leadership. When the British took over the rulership of Northern India, Hinduism for the first time in 700 years stood on a plane of equality with Islam. But a new and even more dangerous portent appeared on the stage.

The missionaries, feeling that there was almost a virgin field here in a society which appeared to be on the point of dissolution, took up the work of conversion. Islam, though it proselytized by fits and starts, had no separate machinery for carrying its message to the people. The Christian missionaries were different. They used no physical force, which Islam did not hesitate to do at intervals and in limited areas.

Brahmo Samaj

The first result of the Christian attack on Hinduism was a movement among educated Hindus in favour of a social reform of religion. The leader of this was Ram Mohan Roy (1772-1833), who may be called the father of the Hindu Reformation.

Born in a Brahmin family, Ram Mohan was brought up as a strict Hindu, but educated, as all Hindus who hoped to enter public service had perforce to be at that time, in Islamic culture. He was a deep student of Arabic and Persian when he entered the East India Company's service, where also he rose to some distinction. During this period he took to the study of English, which opened to him the whole range of Western liberal thought.

It was the time when the mellowed glow of the Great European Enlightenment had cast on European intellectual life an amazing serenity and sense of certainty. The light of D'Holbach, Condorcet, Diderot and the great Encyclopaedists had not died down and the dawn of the great nineteenth century thinkers, especially Bentham and the Utilitarians in England, which was destined to have so powerful an influence in the development of ideas in India, had not begun.

What Ram Mohan witnessed around him in India was a scene of utter devastation and ruin. The old order of Muslim rule had disappeared overnight, leaving behind it utter chaos in every walk of life. Hinduism in Bengal, once the centre of a devotional Vaishnava religion of great vitality, had sunk to a very low level of superstition, extravagance and immorality. A seeker after truth, Ram Mohan turned to the new religion which the missionaries were preaching. He studied Hebrew and Greek to understand Christianity better. But his scholarship was taking him at the same time to the well of European liberalism. Ram Mohan Roy was in fact the last of the Encyclopaedists. Thus he came to reject Christ, while accepting the wide humanism of European thought, its ethics and its general approach to the problems of life.

His book, The Precepts of Jesus, the Guide to Peace and Happiness, is an interpretation of Christianity in this new light, a reply to the missionaries rather than a call to Indians.

While Ram Mohan Roy thus rejected the Christian claims, he realized that Hinduism had to be re-interpreted. That interpretation he attempted in the Brahmo Samaj, a new reformed sect of

Hinduism, which he founded. The Samaj was not in its essence a Christian dilution of Hinduism, as has often been said, but a synthesis of the doctrines of the European Enlightenment, with the philosophical views of the Upanishads. As a religion Brahmo Samaj was based firmly on the Vedanta of genuine Hindu tradition, but its outlook on life was neither Christian nor Hindu, but European, and derived its inspiration from the intellectual movements of the eighteenth century.

Thus it may be said that as early as 1820 India had come into the direct current of European thought and had begun to participate in the fruits of Europe's intellectual quest. The Brahmo Samaj lived up to this ideal. Its social message was Westernization, to purge Hinduism of the customs and superstitions with which it was overlaid, to raise the status of women, to bridge the yawning gulf between popular and higher Hinduism, to fight relentlessly against caste, social taboo, polygamy and other well entrenched abuses. To the educated Hindu, who felt unsettled in mind by the attack of the missionaries, the Brahmo Samaj provided the way out.

The Brahmo tradition has become so much a part of the Indian way of life now, that one is inclined to overlook its distinctive contribution. It does not lie primarily in the fact that it enabled Hinduism to withstand the onslaught of the missionaries, but in that it introduced the modern approach to Indian problems. India started on her long adventure in building up a new civilization as a synthesis between the East and the West in the 1820s, and in that sense Ram Mohan is the forerunner of new India.

It has been well stated that 'he embodies the new spirit, its freedom of inquiry, its thirst for science, its large human sympathy, its pure and sifted ethics along with its reverent but not uncritical regard for the past and prudent disinclination towards revolt.'

Macaulay, English Education & Christian Missionaries...

The spirit of reform was entering Hinduism from other sources also. In 1835 the Government of India declared that 'the great object of the British Government ought to be the promotion of European literature and science among the natives of India', and embarked on a policy of Western education...

It was the devout hope of Macaulay, who was the champion of the scheme, and of many others, that the diffusion of the new learning among the higher classes would see the dissolution of

Hinduism and the widespread acceptance of Christianity. The missionaries were also of the same view, and; they entered the educational field with enthusiasm, providing schools and colleges in many parts of India, where education in the Christian Bible was compulsory for Hindu students.

The middle classes accepted Western education with avidity and willingly studied Christian scriptures, but neither the dissolution of Hindu society so hopefully predicted nor the conversion of the intellectuals so devoutedly hoped for showed any signs of materialisation.

On the other hand, Hinduism assimilated the new learning, and the effects were soon visible all over India in a revival of a universalized religion based on the Vedanta.

It is necessary to remember that, though the Hindu religion has innumerable cults and sects, the philosophic background of all of them-including Buddhism-is the Vedanta. The doctrine of the Vedanta is contained in three authoritative texts-which are not scriptures-the Brahma Sutras, the Upanishads and the Gita.

Every orthodox sect in India derives its authority directly from these and, as has been stated in the previous chapter, the protagonists of each new religious sect have had to demonstrate how their own teachings flowed directly from these three sources. Thus it was, that Sankara, the reformer of Hinduism in the eighth century, had to write his commentary on all the three. It is to the doctrines of the Vedanta, as embodied in the Upanishads, that Ram Mohan Roy turned when he also felt the need of a new religious interpretation.

Arya Samaj, Dayananda Saraswati...

The demand of new India was not for a new sect. It was for a universal religion acceptable to all Hindus. The first effort to provide such a basis was by Dayananda Saraswati who saw in the Vedas the revealed Word of God and felt that, as the Vedas were accepted by all who claimed to be Hindus, a religion based on the Vedas should have universal appeal in India.

The Muslims had a revealed book, the Holy Quran. The Christians had the Bible, and Swami Dayananda felt that the amorphous and indefinable nature of Hinduism, which exposed it to so much weakness, could be remedied by providing the

Hindus also with a revealed book. This seemed all the more the right path since the Vedas gave no authority to the usages and superstitions that had come to be accepted by the masses as Hinduism.

There was no sanction in the Vedas for caste, for the prohibition of the marriage of widows, for untouchability, for the taboo on food and the other characteristics of popular Hinduism which had been seized upon by the missionaries in their campaign and were being widely rejected by Hindu intelligentsia.

Swami Dayananda in his Satyartha Praksah, or the Light of True Meaning, made a brave and ingenious attempt to see in the Vedas all that the Christians and the Muslims were claiming to be the basis of their religions, universal brotherhood and a direct and non-metaphysical approach to God.

His Arya Samaj, however successful as a militant organization for the protection of Hinduism from the onslaughts of Islam and Christianity, never appealed to the Hindus outside the Punjab. The reasons were simple.

The attempt to go back to the Vedas involved a denial of the Hindu culture of the last three thousand years, a refusal to see any good in the puranic religion, in the variegated traditions which had enriched Hindu thought in the Middle Ages, all of which the Arya Samajists rejected without hesitation and attacked without reservation.

Secondly, the Vedic religion had long ago ceased to be related to the religious experience of Hindus. The Gita had poured scorn on Vedic sacrifices and held up the Veda-vadaratas (those who delight to argue on the basis of the Vedas) to contempt. The exclusiveness of the Arya Samaj, amounting to the intolerance of other religious practices though but a reflection of its prolonged fight against the proselytizing faiths and therefore essentially defensive, was also against the tradition of Hinduism which held firmly to the doctrine that the Gita preached, 'men worship Me in different ways, I give them the fruits appropriate to their worship'.

The Hindu does not deny the truth of any religion, or reject the validity of another's religious experience.

But the Arya Samajists, at least in their polemical days, were rigidly exclusive. The movement, therefore, did not spread to other parts of India and its influence was limited mainly to the Delhi and Punjab areas.

Theosophical Society, Annie Besant...

The urge of educated Hindus to find a common denominator for their various sects, which neither of these movements provided, was for a time fulfilled by the activities of the Theosophical Society, of which Colonel Olcott, the American, and Madame Blavatsky, the Russian, were the founders. Educated Hindus all over the country turned to the Theosophical Society, which introduced into India the organization and propagandist methods of European religious activity. Its interpretation of Hinduism followed the more orthodox lines, and many of its Indian leaders, like Dr. Bhagwan Das, of Benares, and Sir S. Subramania Aiyar, of Madras, were also leaders of Hindu Orthodoxy. Its social doctrines, however, were progressive and more important, and it cut through the sectarian lines of Indian religious organization.

Theosophic Hinduism was an All-India movement and it profoundly affected the outlook of the new generation. When Mrs. Annie Besant, an extremely gifted, persuasive and dynamic personality, became the President of the Society, its propaganda for a reformed universal Hinduism became more marked and was carried on incessantly through schools, colleges and an enormous output of popular literature. Mrs. Besant.had become steeped in Indian culture and her popular approach was Vedantic, as her translation of the Gita would testify.

Swami Vivekananda...

The Vedantic reformation which was thus in the air found its most widely accepted exponent in Swami Vivekananda. Vivekananda was a Western-educated Bengali who came under the influence of Ramakrishna, a mystic whose personality had made a deep impression on the Bengali society of his day. Vivekananda was fired by a desire to revive Hinduism and purify its religious and social teachings. Initiated a Sanyasi, he toured the length and breadth of India spreading the gospel of Vedanta. A prolonged visit to America and a tour in England inflamed his patriotism, his desire to rejuvenate Hindu society and to give Hinduism a social purpose. His fervent declaration that he did not 'believe in a religion that does not wipe out the widow's tears or bring a piece of bread to the orphan's mouth' expresses clearly the changed temper of Hinduism. His own mission he described as follows. Answering the question: 'What do you consider to be the function of your movement as regards India?' the Swami said: 'To find the common bases of Hinduism and to awaken the national consciousness to them.' That common basis he found in the Vedanta which he interpreted in popular phraseology and preached untiringly all over India.

'All the philosophers of India who are orthodox have to acknowledge the authority of the Vedanta and all our present-day religions, however crude some of them may appear to be, however inexplicable some of their purposes may seem, one who understands them and studies them can trace them back to the ideas of the Upanishads. So deeply have these Upanishads sunk into our race that those of you who study the symbology of the crudest religion of the Hindus will be astonished to find sometimes figurative expressions of the Upanishads. Great spiritual and philosophical ideas in the Upanishads are today with us, converted into household worship in the form of symbols. Thus the various symbols now used by us, all come from the Vedanta, because in the Vedanta they are used as figures.'

Again: 'Thus the Vedanta, whether we know it or not, has, penetrated all the sects in India and what we call Hinduism, that mighty banyan tree, with its immense and almost infinite rami fications, has been throughout interpenetrated by the influence J the Vedanta. Whether we are conscious of it or not, we think that Vedanta, we live in the Vedanta, we breathe the Vedanta and we die in the Vedanta, and every Hindu does that.'

He not only preached this gospel, but trained up a body of missionaries, men of education, pure life and religious zeal to carry this message to the villages.

There were innumerable other Sanyasis and learned men who, though belonging to no particular sect, were preaching the same principles all over India. In fact, the revival of Vedanta in Hindu thought at the end of the nineteenth century constitutes a religious movement of national significance. It was at the end of this period that Aurobindo gave what may be called the classic exposition of the entire Vedanta doctrine in his Essays on the Gita and later his Life Divine. By this, Vedanta may be said to have been restored to its place as the common background of all Hindu religious thought.

Vedanta, Popular Hinduism and the Law...

The unifying doctrine was the Vedanta, but the abstract conceptions of this philosophical approach could only appeal to the elite. Popular Hinduism continued in the old way, sectarian, devotional and based on daily rituals. But it also underwent extraordinary changes. The gnarled branches of this ancient tree either fell away by themselves or were chopped off by legislative action promoted by the reformers.

Child marriage, which many Hindu communities considered as an essential part of their religion, was abolished by law through the insistence of popular agitation. The remarriage of widows was permitted.

Social disabilities based on caste vanished by themselves, and the occupational basis of caste communities was weakened. Temples were thrown open to the untouchables, and in the most orthodox province of Madras, Hindu religious endowments were placed under the control of public bodies. The movement for the regeneration of the depressed classes assumed a national character, and their participation in social and political life became a major factor in the last days of British rule.

Popular Hinduism had a more vigorous life than it ever had in the immediately preceding times, but it had in the course of a hundred years changed its character and temper, though it had kept much of its form.

The major difficulty of Hinduism which had made it a wild jungle growth of widely varying customs, usages and superstitions was its lack of a machinery of reform and unification. The institutions of Hinduism, which in a large measure got identified with 'the religion itself, were the results of certain historical factors. They were upheld by law and not by religion. Vivekananda put the point well when he wrote:

> *'Beginning from Buddha down to Ram Mohan Roy, everyone made the mistake of holding caste to be a religious institution.... But in spite of all the ravings of the priests, caste is simply a crystallized social institution, which after doing its service is now filling the atmosphere of India with stench.'*

The caste organization, the joint family, the rights of inheritance and the relationships arising out of them, which in the main are the special features of Hindu society, are legal and not religious.

They are man-made institutions which do not claim Divine origin or religious sanction, and are upheld by man-made laws and not by any church or priesthood. It is a truism to say that legislation of today meets the social needs of yesterday and, unavoidably, law, as a conservative force, lags one step behind social necessities.

When the great codes of Hindu Law were evolved, no doubt they represented the social forces of the time, but soon they had become antiquated. The succession of authoritative commentaries would show that the urge for modifications was widely felt and, in the absence of a legislative authority, the method of a progressive interpretation in each succeeding generation was the only one available to Hindu thinkers.

The immutability of Hindu law and customs was never a principle with the authors of the great codes or their commentators. In fact, the monumental volumes of Dr. Kane's History of Dharma Sastra would demonstrate clearly that in every age social thinkers tried to adjust Hindu institutions to the requirements of the time.

If the laws are changeable it follows that the institutions which were based on such laws are equally changeable. The great weakness of Hindu society was not that the laws had remained immutable but that the changes introduced had been spasmodic, local and dependent to a large extent on the ingenuity of individual commentators. They were not in any sense a continuous renovation of legal principles, nor a legislative approximation to changing conditions.

The reason for this lack of direction of social ideas and the failure to prevent the growth of anti-social customs was undoubtedly the loss of political power. Not only was India as a whole never under a single sovereign authority, but even the political unity of North India which existed with occasional breaks from the time of the Mauryas (320 B.C.) to that of Harsha (A.D, 637) was broken up by the political conditions of the eighth century and lost for a period of 700 years with the Muslim invasion of the twelfth century. As a result, the Hindu community continued to be governed by institutions moulded by laws which were codified over 2,000 years ago and which were out of date even when they were codified.

The Muslim State had no legislative machinery, and when for the first time India was united under the British and the entire

Hindu community lived under a common administration, the authorities of the East India Company after a first effort at social reform withdrew, under the pretext of religious neutrality, from activities which they thought might cause popular upheaval. Perhaps it was a wise step, as the motive force of large-scale social reforms must come from the people themselves and legislation can only give statutory sanction to principles which have already gained wide acceptance. The reformation of the Hindu religion was therefore an essential prerequisite of social legislation.

It was only after the Great War that the legislating State came into existence in India. Under the scheme of partial self-government introduced in 1921, there was established a central legislative authority with a majority of non-official elected Indians, which; was both competent to change the laws of Hindu society and to enforce obedience to such laws through the length and breadth of India. In the provinces the direction of government passed in a large measure to elected legislatures.

The legislative achievements of the Central and Provincial Governments in the field of social reform have been fundamental, though they did not go anywhere as far as the public demanded. The Civil Marriage Act and the Age of Consent Act (raising the marriageable age of girls to I4) were among the more important pieces of legislation which the Central Indian Legislative Assembly enacted.

The Civil Marriage Act validates marriages between men and women of different castes of Hinduism. It strikes at the very root of the orthodox Brahminical conception of caste, and annuls the laws of Manu and the other orthodox codes of Hinduism.

'The immutable law', prohibiting Varna-Samkara or the mixture of castes, ceased by this single piece of legislation to operate through the length and breadth of India.

The Age of Consent Act was equally revolutionary. It was the custom for over two thousand years at least for large sections of people to have girls married before the age of puberty. There was not only long tradition behind the custom, but it was considered compulsory at least for Brahmins in the light of certain authoritative texts. The Indian legislature made this custom illegal, though it had so much religious authority behind it, and the performance of such marriages became a penal offence.

Thus by the end of the third decade, the Hindu reformation had made enough progress to enable the new society to direct its social forces towards general betterment.

The reformation of Hinduism has been treated in some detail, because without an appreciation of its consequences the effects of Western education on Indian society will not be fully clear.

Based on the Thought of Ram Mohan Roy

Hindu Sects

All religions, including Hinduism, have sects. A brief survey of Sects (past and present) in other religions produced the following results:

(Religions listed in alphabetical order)

Some Buddhist sects: Mahayana, Hinayana, Vajrayana, or the Diamond Vehicle, the Theravada School. By the time of King Ashoka the Great, there were eighteen or twenty different cults of Buddhism.

Some Christian Sects: Christian Science, Jehovah's Witnesses, Mormonism, Rasfatarianism, Unification Church, Protestant Church, Roman Catholic Church, Seventh Day Adventists, Baptist, Lutheran, Methodist, Orthodox, Pentecostal, Presbyterian, Universal Church from Brazil, Awakening Churches, etc.

Islamic sects: Ahmadia, Ismail, Salafi, Shia, Sufi, Sunni, Nizari Isma'ilis, Wahhabism, The Submitters, Nation of Islam etc.

Some sects in Judaism: Conservative, Hasidic, Humanistic, Karaite, Orthodox, Reconstructionist, Reform, Sephardic, Traditional, Essenes, Sadducees, Pharisees, Temple Israel, Zealots etc.

Some Shinto Sects: Tenrikyo, Konkokyo, Kurozumikyo, Shinto Taikyo, Fuso-kyo (which included Omoto-kyo), Izumo-oyashiro-kyo, Jikko-kyo, Misogi-kyo, Shinshu-kyo, Shinto-shuseiha, Shinri-kyo, Shinto Taisei-kyo, Ontake-kyo. etc

Some sects in Taoism: The Heavenly (or Celestial) Masters sect, The Supreme Peace sect, The Mao-shan (Mount Mao) sect, The Ling-pao (Marvellous Treasure) sect, The Ch'uan-chen (Completely Real) sect.

Hinduism is extremely catholic, liberal, tolerant, and elastic. This is the wonderful feature of Hinduism. A foreigner (visiting

India) is struck with astonishment when he hears about the diverse sects and creeds of Hinduism. But these varieties are really an ornament to Hinduism. They are certainly not its defects.

There are various types of minds and temperaments. So there should be various faiths also. This is but natural. This is the cardinal tenet of Hinduism. There is room in Hinduism for all types of souls-from the highest to the lowest-for their growth and evolution.

The term 'Hinduism' is most elastic. It includes a number of sects and cults, allied, but different in many important points. Hinduism has, within its fold, various schools of Vedanta; Vaishnavism, Shaivism, Shaktism, etc. It has various cults and creeds. Hinduism accommodates all types of men. It prescribes spiritual food for everybody, according to his qualification and growth. This is the beauty of this magnanimous religion.

This is the glory of Hinduism. Hence there is no conflict among the various cults and creeds. The Rig-Veda declares: "Truth is one; sages call it various names-Ekam Sat Vipra Bahudha Vadanti." The Upanishads declare that all the paths lead to the same goal, just as cows of variegated colours yield the same white milk. Lord Krishna says in the Gita: 'Howsoever men approach Me, even so do I welcome them, for the path men take from every side is Mine." All diversities are organized and united in the body of Hinduism.

Hinduism provides food for reflection for the different types of thinkers and philosophers all over the world. All sorts of philosophy are necessary. What appeals to one may not appeal to another, and what is easy for one may be difficult for another. Hence the need for different standpoints. All philosophies of Hinduism are points of view. They are true in their own way. They take the aspirant step by step, stage by stage, till he reaches the acme or the pinnacle of spiritual glory. Sanatana-Dharmists, Arya-Samajists, Deva-Samajists, Jainas, Buddhists, Sikhs and Brahmo-Samajists are all Hindus only, for they rose from Hinduism, and emphasized one or more of its aspects.

The Hindus are divided into three great classes, *viz.*,

1. Vaishnavas: Who worship the Lord as Vishnu;
2. Shaivas: Who worship the Lord as shiva; and
3. Saktas: Who adore Devi or the Mother aspect of the Lord.

In addition, there are the Sauras, who worship the Sun-God; Ganapatyas who worship Ganesh as supreme; and Kumaras who worship Skanda as the godhead.

The Vaishnavas-Sri Sampradaya

The Vadagalai School and The Tengalai School

The Vaishnavas are usually distinguished into four principal Sampradayas or sects. Of these, the most ancient is the Sri Sampradaya founded by Ramanuja Acharya about the middle of the twelfth century. The followers of Ramanuja adore Vishnu and Lakshmi, and their incarnations. They are called Ramanujas or Sri Sampradayins or Sri Vaishnavas. The teachers are Brahmins. The disciples may be of any caste. They all recite the Ashtakshara Mantra: "Om Namo Narayanaya." They put on (display) two white lines and a central red line on the forehead.

Vedantacharya, a follower of Ramanuja, made some reform in the Vaishnava faith. This gave rise to the formation of two antagonistic parties of Ramanujas, one called the Northern School (Vadagalai) and the other the Southern School (Tengalai). The Tengalais regard Prapatti or self-surrender as the only way to salvation. The Vadagalais think that it is only one of the ways. According to them, the Bhakta or the devotee is like the young one of a monkey which has to exert itself and cling to its mother (Markata-Nyaya or Monkey Theory); whereas, according to the Southern School, the Bhakta or the devotee is like the kitten which is carried about by the cat without any effort on its own part (Marjala-Nyaya or Cathold Theory). The Northern School accept the Sanskrit texts, the Vedas. The Southerners have compiled a Veda of their own called 'Nalayira Prabandha' or 'Four Thousand Verses', in Tamil, and hold it to be older than the Sanskrit Vedas. Really, their four thousand verses are based on the Upanishad portion of the Vedas. In all their worship, they repeat sections from their Tamil verses.

The Vadagalais regard Lakshmi as the consort of Vishnu, Herself infinite, uncreated and equally to be adored as a means (Upaya) for release. The Tengalais regard Lakshmi as a created female being, though divine. According to them, she acts as a mediator or minister (Purushakara), and not as an equal channel of release.

The two sets have different marks on their foreheads. The Vadagalais make a simple white line curved like the letter U to represent the sole of the right foot of Lord Vishnu, the source of the River Ganga (Ganges). They add a central red mark as a symbol of Lakshmi. The Tengalais make a white mark like the letter Y that represents both the feet of Lord Vishnu. They draw a white line half way down the nose.

Both the sects brand the emblems of Vishnu-the discus and the conch-on their breasts, shoulders and arms.

The Tengalais prohibit their widows from shaving their heads.

The usual surnames of the Ramanuja Brahmins are Aiyangar, Acharya, Charlu and Acharlu.

Ramanandis

The followers of Ramananda are the Ramanandis. They are well-known in upper Hindusthan (India). They are branch of the Ramanuja sect. They offer their worship to Lord Rama, Sita, Lakshmana and Hanuman. Ramananda was a disciple of Ramanuja. He flourished at Varanasi about the beginning of the fourteenth century. His followers are numerous in the Ganga (Ganges) valley of India. Their favourite work is the 'Bhakti-Mala.' Their sectarian marks are like those of the Ramanujas. The Vairagis are the ascetics among the Ramanandis.

Vallabhacharins or Rudra Sampradayins

The Vallbhacharins form a very important sect in Mumbai, Gujarat and the Central India. Their founder was born in the forest Camparanya in 1479. He is regarded as an incarnation of Krishna. The Vallabhacharins worship Krishna as Baba-Gopala. Their idol is one representing Krishna in his childhood till his twelfth year. The Gosains or teachers are family men. The eight daily ceremonials for God in the temples are Mangala, Sringara, Gvala, Raja Bhoga, Utthapana, Bhoga, Sandhya and Sayana. All these represent various forms of adoration of God.

The mark on the forehead consists of two red perpendicular lines meeting in a semicircle at the root of the nose and having a round dot of red between them. The necklace and rosary are made of the stalk of the Tulasi (holy Basil plant).

The great authority of the sect is the Srimad Bhagavata as explained in the Subodhini, the commentary thereon of

Vallabhacharya. The members of the sect should visit Sri Nathdvara, a holy shrine, at least once in their lives.

The Chaitanyas (Hare Krishna Movement)

This sect is prominent in Bengal and Orissa. The founder Chaitanya Mahaprabhu or Lord Gouranga, was born in 1485. He was regarded as an incarnation of Lord Krishna. He took sannyasa (monkhood) at the age of twenty-four. He went to Jagannath where he taught Vaishnava doctrines.

The Chaitanyas worship Lord Krishna as the Supreme Being. All castes are admissible into the sect. The devotees constantly repeat the Name of Lord Krishna.

Chaitanya's Charitamrita by Krishna Das is a voluminous work. It contains anecdotes of Chaitanya and his principal disciples and the expositions of the doctrines of this sect. It is written in Bengali.

The Vaishnavas of this sect wear two white perpendicular streaks of sandalwood paste or Gopichandan (a kind of sacred clay). Down the forehead uniting at the root of the nose and continuing to near the tip. They wear a close necklace of small Tulasi beads of three strings.

[Note: During the twentieth century, Swami Prabhupada, A.C. Bhaktivedanta became the founder Acharya of the International Society for Krishna Consciousness with branches all over the world. This movement urges devotees to recite with faith and devotion the following Hare-Krishna Mantra:

"Hare Krishna Hare Krishna Krishna Krishna Krishna Hare Hare,

Hare Rama Hare Rama Rama Rama Hare Hare"

'Rama' in the above mantra of the Hare-Krishna movement does not refer to Sri Rama from the Ramayana but to Balarama, the elder brother of Sri Krishna.]

You interestingly add in your text on Chaitanya philosophy that the Rama in the Maha-Mantra does not refer to the Sri Ramachandra from the Ramayana, but to Lord Balarama (Krishna's brother).

I'll just quote a little from Srila Prabhupada:

"We may mention an incident that took place between two of our Sannyasis (monks).

While we were preaching the Hare Krsna Maha-Mantra in Hyderabad, one of them stated that "Hare Rama" refers to Sri Balarama, and the other protested that "Hare Rama" means Lord Rama. Ultimately the controversy came to me (Srila Prabhupada), and I gave the decision that if someone says that "Rama" in "Hare Rama" is Lord Ramacandra and someone else says that the "Rama" in "Hare Rama" is Sri Balarama, both are correct because there is no difference between Sri Balarama and Lord Rama.... Those who are aware of the Vishnu-tattva do not fight over all these details".

Sri Caitanya Caritamrita Adi Lila 5.132 purport

Hoping this is of some help.

Ys,

Yashoda Dulal Das

(TKG)]

The Nimbarkas

The founder of this sect was Nimbarka or Nimbaditya. He was originally named Bhaskara Acharya. He is regarded as an incarnation of the Sun-God (Surya). The followers worship Krishna and Radha (Krishna's consort) conjointly. Their chief scripture is the Srimad Bhagavata Purana.

The followers have two perpendicular yellowish lines made from Gopichandan clay and applied from the root of the hair to the commencement of each eye-brow and there meeting in a curve. This represents the footprint of Lord Vishnu.

The Nimbarkas or Nimavats are scattered throughout the whole of upper India. They are very numerous around Mathura. They are also the most numerous of the Vaishnava sects in Bengal.

The Madhavas

The Madhavas are Vaishnavas. They are known as Brahma Sampradayins. The founder of the sect was Madhavacharya, otherwise called Ananda Tirtha and also called Purna-Prajna. He was born in 1200 ad. He was a great opponent of Sankaracharya's Advaita system of philosophy. He is regarded as an incarnation of Vayu or the Wind-God. He erected and consecrated at Udipi the image of Lord Krishna.

The Gurus of the Madhava sect are Brahmins and Sannyasins. The followers bear the impress of the symbols of Vishnu upon their breasts and shoulders. They are stamped with a hot iron. Their marks on the foreheads consist of two perpendicular lines made with Gopichandana and joined at the root of the nose. They make a straight black line (using charcoal from incense offered to Krishna), which terminates in a round mark made with tumeric. The Madhavas are divided into two classes called the Vyasakutas and the Dasakutas. They are found in Karnataka. Truthfulness, study of scriptures, generosity, kindness, faith and freedom from envy form the moral code of Madhavas. They give the Lord's names to their children (Namakarana Sanskar), and mark the body with His symbols (Ankana). They practise virtue in thought, word and deed (Bhajana).

Radha Vallabhis

Radha Vallabhis worship Krishna as Radha-Vallabha, the Lord or the Lover of Radha. Harivans was the founder of this sect. Seva Sakhi Vani gives a detailed description of the notion of this sect and more of their traditions and observances.

Charana Dasis, Dadu Panthis, Hari Chandis, Kabir Panthis, Khakis, Maluk Dasis, Mira Bais, Madhavis, Rayi Dasis, Senais, Sakhi Bhavas, Sadma Panthis, are all Vaishnava sects.

The Shaivas

Smarta Brahmins of the South

The Shaiva Brahmins of the Tamil India have their title Aiyer. They are called Smartas. They all wear three horizontal lines of Bhasma or Vibhuti (holy ash) on their forehead. They all worship Lord Shiva. The different sects are:

1. *Vadamas:* Vada Desa Vadamas, Chola Desa Vadamas and Inji Vadamas
2. *Brihatcharanam:* Mazhainattu Brihatcharanam, Pazhamaneri Brihatcharanam, Milaghu Brihatcharanam and Kandramanikka Brihatcharanam
3. Vathimars
4. Ashtasahasram
5. *Choliyas:* Otherwise called Pandimars and inhabitants of Tiruchendur, and
6. *Gurukkal:* A sub-sect of Vadamas not recognized as one amongst them and whose duties are to worship at temples.

They are also known by the name of Oattar in southern districts of Madras. These are different from Archaks. Archaks belong to any of the above sub-sects and intermarry with persons of other professions, but not Gurukkal or Pattar. While Gurukkal is used only for Saivites, Pattar and Archak are used for Vaishnavites also.

Shaiva Brahmins of Malabar

1.Nambuduri 2.Muse, and 3.Embrantiri

Shaiva Brahmins of Bengal

1.Chakravarti 2.Chunder 3.Roy 4.Ganguli 5.Choudhury 6. Biswas 7. Bagchi 8. Majumdar, and 9.Bhattacharji

Shaiva Brahmins of Karnataka

1.Smarta 2. Haviga 3.Kota 4.Shivalli 5.Tantri 6.Kardi 7.Padya

Telugu Smartas

1.Murukinadu, 2.Velanadu 3.Karanakammalu 4.Puduru Dravidis

5.Telahanyam 6.Konasima Dravidi and 7.Aruvela Niyogis

Lingayats

They are called Vira Shaivas. They are found in Mysore and Karnataka. They wear on their neck a Linga of Lord Shiva that is placed in a small silver box.

Other Shaiva sects

Akas Mukhis, Gudaras, Jangamas, Karalingis, Nakhis,

Rukharas, Sukharas, Urdhabahus, Ukkaras are all Shaiva sects.

The Saktas

The saktas are worshippers of Devi, the Universal Mother. Dakshinis, Vamis, Kancheliyas, Kararis are all Sakta sects.

Miscellaneous

The Sauras adore the Sun, the Ganapatyas adore Ganesh, and the Kaumaras adore Skanda.

The non-Brahmins of South India are Naidu, Kamma Naidu, Chetty, Mudaliar, Gounder, Pillai, Nair, Nayanar and Reddy.

Nanak Shahis of seven classes (*viz.*, Udasis, Ganj-bhakshis, Ramrayis, Sutra Shahis, Govinda Sinhis, Nirmalas, Nagas), Baba Lalis, Prana nathis, Sadhus, Satnamis, Shiva Narayanis are other miscellaneous sects.

The Arya Samaj

The founder of the Arya Samaj was Swami Dayananda Saraswati, who was born in Kathiawar in 1824. This Samaj is more of a social institution, with a religious background. It has Gurukulas, schools, and Pathshalas. The Suddhi Sabha is a proselytizing branch of the Arya Samaj.

[Note: The followers of the Arya Samaj do not perform idol worship. Swami Dayanand Saraswati wrote "Satyarth Parkash" (Light of Truth). This volume serves as the principal guiding light of the Arya Samaj. Some of the principles of the Arya Samaj are: God is the primary source of true knowledge and of all that is known by its means. The Vedas are the scriptures of all true knowledge. All acts ought to be performed in conformity with Dharma *i.e.* after due consideration of right and wrong. The primary object of the Arya Samaj is to do good to the world *i.e.* to ameliorate physical, spiritual and social standards of all men. All ought to be treated with love, justice, righteousness and due regard to their merits.]

The Brahmo Samaj

The Brahmo Samaj was founded originally by Raja Ram Mohan Roy, early in the nineteenth century. The Brahmo Samajists do not perform idol worship. Keshab Chandra Sen introduced some changes in the year 1860. There are now two branches within the Samaj, *viz.*, Adi Brahmo Samaj which holds to the tenets laid down by Raja Ram Mohan Roy and the Sadharana Barahmo Samaj which is somewhat modern and which follows Keshab Chandra Sen more closely. This Samaj has followers in Bengal.

The Jains

The first founder of the sect was Parsvanatha. Its first active propagator was Mahavira. The Jains are found in great numbers especially in the western coast of India. They are divided into two principal sects-the Svetambaras (clothed in white garments) and the Digambaras (sky-clad or naked).

The Jains do not admit the divine origin of the Vedas. They do not believe in any Supreme Deity. They pay reverence to holy men or saints who are styled Tirthankaras, who dwell in the heavenly abode and who, by long discipline, have raised themselves to divine perfection. The images of one or more of these Tirthankaras are placed in every Jain temple.

The Jains are strict vegetarians. They attach great sanctity to life. They practise Ahimsa (non-killing, non-violence). Strict Jains strain water before drinking, sweep the ground with a brush before treading on it or before sitting, never eat or drink at night and sometimes cover their mouths with muslin to prevent the risk of swallowing minute organisms.

There are two classes of Jains, *viz.*, Sravakas who engage themselves in secular occupations and Yatis or monks who lead an ascetic life.

The Sikhs

"Sikhism, while some of its' founding Guru's were Hindu, was created as a response to Hinduism and the reign of the Muslim Mughal empires."-KS Gidda 'Obedience to the Guru brings release from future births' this is a firm conviction of the Sikhs. Sikhs adopt the five Kakas, *viz.*, 1. The Kes (uncut hair), 2. The Kachhca (short drawers), 3. The Kara (iron bangle), 4. The Kirpan (steel dagger), and 5. The Kangha (small-tooth comb worn in the hair).

The Udasis are an ascetic order of the Nanaksahi Sikhs. Srichand, son of Guru Nanak, embraced Sannyasa. Udasis are his followers. Lakshmichand, another son of Guru Nanak, led the life of a house-holder. Vedis are his followers. Nirmalas are ascetic followers of Guru Govind Singh.

The Akalis are brave warriors. The Akalis wear a distinctive dress of blue, and a black turban.

The teachings of Guru Nanak are contained in the first book of the Adi Granth.

No Sikh smokes tobacco.

Sadhus and Sannyasins

Salutations unto the ancient Rishis, seers, saints, paramhansa sannyasins and sadhus, who are the repositories of divine knowledge and wisdom and who guide the destiny of the world in the past, present and future. Every religion has a band of anchorites who lead the life of seclusion and meditation. There are Bhikshus in Buddhism, Fakirs in Mohammedanism (Islam), Sufistic Fakirs In Sufism, and Fathers and Reverends in Christianity. The glory of a religion will be lost absolutely if you remove these hermits or Sannysins or those who lead a life of renunciation and divine contemplation. It is these people who maintain or preserve the religions of the world. It is these people who give solace to the householders when they are in trouble and distress. They are the messengers of the Atman-knowledge and heavenly peace. They are the harbingers of divine wisdom and peace. They are the disseminators of Adhyatmic science and Upanishadic revelations. They heal the sick, comfort the forlorn and nurse the bedridden. They bring hope to the hopeless, joy to the depressed, strength to the weak and courage to the timid, by imparting the knowledge of the Vedanta and the significance of the ""Tat Tvam Asi" Mahavakya (great saying).

Dasanama Sanyasins

Sanaka, Sanandana, Sanat-Kumara and Sanat-Sujata were the four mind-born sons of Lord Brahma. They refused to enter the Pravritti Marga or worldly life and entered the Nivritti Marga or the path of renunciation. The four Kumaras were the pioneers in the path of Sannyasa. Sri Dattatreya also is among the original Sannyasins. The Sannyasins of the present day are all descendants of the four Kumaras, Dattatreya and Sankaracharya.

Sri Sankaracharya, regarded as an Avatara of Lord Shiva and the eminent exponent of Kevala Advaita philosophy, established four Maths (monasteries) one at Sringeri, another at Dvaraka, a third at Puri and a fourth at Joshi Math in the Himalayas, on the way to Badrinarayana shrine.

Sri Sankara had four Sannyasin disciples, *viz.*, Suresvara, Padmapada, Hastamalaka and Totaka. Suresvara was in charge of Sringeri Math, Padmapada was in charge of Puri Math, Hastamalaka was in charge of Dvarka Math and Totaka was in charge of Joshi Math.

The Sannyasins of Sringeri Math, the spiritual descendants of Sri Sankara and Suresvacharya, have three names, *viz.*, Sarasvati, Puri and Bharati. The Sannyasins of the Dvaraka Math have two names, *viz.*, Tirtha and Asrama. The Sannyasins of the Puri Math have two names, *viz.*, Vana and Aranya. The Sannyasins of the Joshi Math have three names, *viz.*, Giri, Parvata and Sagara.

The Dasanamis worship Lord Shiva or Lord Vishnu, and meditate on Nirguna Brahman. The Dandi Sannyasins, who hold staff in their hands, belong to the order of Sri Sankara. Paramhansa Sannyasins do not hold staff. They freely move about as itinerant monks. Avadhutas are naked Sannyasins. They do not keep any property with them.

The Sannyasins of the Ramakrishna Mission belong to the order of Sri Sankara. They have the name Puri.

Then, there are Akhada Sannyasins, *viz.*, Niranjana Akhada and Jhuni Akhda. They belong to the order of Sri Sankara. They are Dasanamis. They are found in the Uttar Pradesh State only.

Rishikesh and Haridwar are colonies for Sannyasins. Varanasi also is among the chief abodes of Sannyasins.

Shaivas

In South India, there are Tamil Sannyasins who belong to the Kovilur Math and Dharmaputram Adhinam. They do not belong to the Sri Sankara order. They are Shaivas.

Nagas

Nagas are Shaiva Sannyasins. They are in a naked state. They smear their bodies with ashes. They have beard and matted locks.

Udasis

Guru Nanak's order of ascetics is called Udasis. They correspond to Sannyasins and Vairagis. They are indifferent to the sensual pleasures of this world (Udasina). Hence they are called Udasis.

Vairagis

A Vairagi is one who is devoid of passion. Vairagis are Vaishnavas. They worship Lord Rama, Sita and Hanuman. They read the Ramayana of Tulasidas. The mendicant Vaishnavas of the Ramanandi classs are the Vairagis. Sri Ananda, the twelfth disciple of Ramananda, instituted this ascetic order.

Rama Sanehis

The founder of this order was Ramcharan who was born in

the year 1718 in a village near Jaipur in Rajasthan. The Rama Sanehi mendicants are of two classes, *viz.*, the Videhis who are naked and the Mihinis who wear two pieces of cotton cloth dyed red in ochre. Their monastery is in Shahapur in Rajasthan. The Rama Sanehi sect has the largest following in Mewar and Alwar. They are found also in Mumbai and Poona (in Maharashtra State), Surat, Ahmedabad in Gujarat State), and Hyderabad and Varanasi.

Kabir Panthis (panthi=followers)

Kabir Panthis are the followers of saint Kabir. They are numerous in all the provinces of Upper and Central India. There are twelve branches. Kabir Chaura is at Varanasi. It is a big monastery of Kabir Panthis. Dharamdas was the chief disciple of Kabir. The followers are expected to have implicit devotion to the Gurus, in thought, word and deed. They should practise truthfulness, mercy, non-injury and seclusion. The followers of Kamal, son of Kabir, practise Yoga.

Dadu Panthis

The Dadu Panthis form one of the Vaishnava cults. Dadu, the founder of this sect, was a disciple of one of the Kabir Panthi teachers. The followers worship Lord Rama. Dadu was a cotton cleaner. He was born at Ahmedabad. He flourished about the year 1600. The Dadu Panthis are of three classes, *viz.*, the Viraktas who are bareheaded (clean shaven head) and have one cloth and one water-pot, the Nagas who carry arms and who are regarded as soldiers and the Vistar Dharis who do the avocations of ordinary life.

The Dadu Panthis are numerous in Marwar and Ajmer. Their chief place of worship is at Naraina, which is near Sambhur and Jaipur. Passages from the Kabor writings are inserted in their religious scriptures.

Gorakhnath Panthis

Gorakhnath was a contemporary of Kabir. He is regarded as the incarnation of Lord Shiva. He calls himself as the son of Matsyendranath and grandson of Adinath. There is a temple of Gorakhnath at Gorakhpur in Uttar Pradesh. Bhartrihari was a disciple of Gorakhnath.

Gorakhnath wrote Goraksha-Sataka, Goraksha-Kalpa and Goraksha-Nama. They are in Sanskrit.

The followers of Gorakhnath are usually called Kanphatas, because their ears are pierced and rings are inserted in them, at the time of their initiation. They worship Lord Shiva.

Nimbarka Sampradayis and Ramanuja Sampradayis

These are Sadhus of the Nimbarka Sampradaya. They are Vaishnavas. The Sannyasins of the Ramanuja Sampradaya wear orange coloured cloth, a holy thread and tuft and Tri-danda or three-staff. At present, they are very few in number.

Parinami Sect

Sri Pirannath was the founder of this sect. He was born in 1675 at Jamnagarh, district Rajkot, in Kathiawar. He was the Devan (chief minister) of Raja Jam Jasa. The followers are to practise Ahimsa, Satya and Daya-non-violence, truthfulness and compassion. They study the sacred book, Kul Jam Svarup or Atma-Bodha, in Hindi, which contains the teachings of Sri Pirannath. It contains 18000 Chaupais. They worship Bala-Krishna, *i.e.*, Krishna as a small child.

The followers are found mostly in the Punjab, Gujarat, Assam, Nepal and Mumbai. There are two Maths or monasteries-one at Jamnagarh and the other at Pamna.

Smarta Sect

What is the universalistic Smarta Sect?

Smartism is an ancient brahminical tradition reformed by Shankara in the ninth century. Worshiping six forms of God, this liberal Hindu path is monistic, nonsectarian, meditative and philosophical. Aum Namah Shivaya.

Smarta means a follower of classical smriti, particularly the Dharma Shastras, Puranas and Itihasas. Smartas revere the Vedas and honour the agamas. Today this faith is synonymous with the teachings of Adi Shankara, the monk-philosopher, known as shanmata sthapanacharya, "founder of the six-sect system." He campaigned India-wide to consolidate the Hindu faiths of his time under the banner of Advaita Vedanta. To unify the worship, he popularized the ancient Smarta five-Deity altar-Ganapati Surya, Vishnu, Shiva and Shakti-and added Kumara. From these, devotees may choose their "preferred Deity," or Ishta Devata. Each God is but a reflection of the one Saguna Brahman. Shankara organized hundreds of monasteries into a ten-order, dashanami system, which now has five pontifical centres. He wrote profuse commentaries on the Upanishads, Brahma Sutras and Bhagavad Gita. Shankara proclaimed, "It is the one Reality which appears to our ignorance as a manifold universe of names and forms and changes. Like the gold of which many ornaments are made, it remains in itself unchanged. Such is Brahman, and That art Thou." Aum Namah Shivaya.

Modern Hinduism

Following the decline of the Mughal Empire during the late 17th century, the British gradually succeeded in establishing themselves as the paramount power in India during the next century. The process began with a British victory in the Battle of Plassey in 1757, followed by the defeat of the Marathas in 1818. British victory over the Sikhs in 1846 completed the process. By this time the British had made two decisions of far-reaching importance for the future of Hinduism: to allow Christian missionaries to operate within the British dominions, in 1813; and to introduce English as the language of public instruction, in 1835. These decisions forced Hinduism to confront Christianity and Western modernity. At the same time, the Western world was exposed to Hindu scriptures translated into European languages.

Movements for Reform

One response to the encounter with Europe was reform. The Bengali scholar Ram Mohan Roy set the tone for reform in the early 19th century. Roy campaigned against medieval or regional Hindu practices that were objectionable in the modern world. He advocated allowing widows to remarry and abolition of the relatively rare practice of sati (self-immolation of a wife after her husband's death; see suttee). In 1828 Mohan Roy founded the Brahmo Samaj (Society of Brahma) to spread his ideas.

Another movement kept India from moving too far toward imitation of the modern Christian West. The movement was named after Ramakrishna, a Hindu spiritual leader who served as a priest at the Dakshineshwar Temple in the city of Kolkata (Calcutta). His reputation as a mystic drew many to him, including Swami Vivekananda, who founded the Ramakrishna movement after Ramakrishna's death in 1886. Vivekananda, a representative Hindu product of India's new English-language education system, became a devotee of Ramakrishna and renounced the world after the priest's death. His message was a return to the timeless wisdom of the Vedas. As an unknown swami, he turned up uninvited at the Parliament of World Religions in Chicago in 1893 to present Ramakrishna's teachings. He won instant celebrity and was hailed as a hero in India for his vigorous advocacy of Hinduism. In 1895 he founded the Vedanta Society in New York City to promote Hindu ideas.

Vivekananda primarily used English in his work of reforming Hinduism and stressing the inclusive aspects of Hindu spirituality over ritual and rules. Another reform-minded leader of the 19th century, Dayananda Sarasvati, used Hindi in responding to the challenges of Christianity and modernity. Sarasvati founded the Arya Samaj, a movement also dedicated to modernizing Hindu practices and asserting the universality of the Hindu tradition. These movements helped revitalize Hinduism.

Another issue that engaged Hindu reformers was the plight of the lowest social class, the panchama jatis who are also known as untouchables. Local movements, such as one led by Sri Narayana Guru in Kerala, were most successful at reform. Narayana, who was born in 1856, believed that education and greater self-esteem, rather than confrontation and blame, would elevate the untouchables. He established temples where all castes could pray together.

Hindu Reformers and Indian Nationalism

Brahmo Samaj

In 1828, a man named Raja Ram Mohan Roy (1772-1833) founded an organization called 'Brahmo Samaj'. Indian historians consider this organization forerunner which paved the way for reformation in India and its establisher as the 'father of modern India'. Raja Ram was a Brahman from Bengal. He was a British civil servant in India. He saw in British rule of India the best things that were benefical to India. He adored the west European philosophy of democracy, liberalism and humanism. He had a great interest in non-Indian cultures and religions. He was especially impressed by Christianity and other religions which preached the existence of one Almighty God.

Raja Ram tried to create a new Hindu religion philosophy and enfolded in it the existence of one God and other beliefs, which were then not the predominant features in Hinduism. He attacked some Hindu traditions and features among them caste system, child marriages, Sati-burning of the live wife over her dead husband's pyre, idolatry and other beliefs. He tried to change the popular Hindu traditions and claimed that the popular Hindu traditions were different from the real Hindu beliefs.

Raja Ram and his organization 'Brahmo Samaj' tried to change the social order of India. He established newspapers and schools all around India. He convinced the British in 1829 to outlaw Sati. But during that period there wasn't yet an Indian ethos among the Indians. Indians were never one nation but always a collection of different entities. They were used to different rulers including non-Indians. From their point of view the British were just another ruler over them (see India in the past). But the main contribution of the Brahmo Samaj to the society of India was that it evoked issues that were common to people all around the Indian sub-continent. The notions of this organization were the inspiration for other organizations and various secular political parties, like the Indian National Congress, which were later on created in India (see Creating the Indian identity).

Sati-The Burning of the Widow

Sati is described as a Hindu custom in India in which the widow was burnt to ashes on her dead husband's pyre. Basically the custom of Sati was believed to be a voluntary Hindu act in which the woman voluntary decides to end her life with her husband after his death. But there were many incidences in which the women were forced to commit Sati, sometimes even dragged against her wish to the lighted pyre.

Though Sati is considered a Hindu custom, the women, known as Sati in Hindu religious literature, did not commit suicide on their dead husband's pyre. The first woman known as Sati was the consort of Lord Shiva. She burnt herself in fire as protest against her father who did not give her consort Shiva the respect she thought he deserved, while burning herself she prayed to reborn again as the new consort of Shiva, which she became and her name in the new incarnation was Parvati. Other famous woman in Hindu literature titled Sati was Savitri. When Savitri's husband

Satyavan died, the Lord of death, Yama arrived to take his soul. Savitri begged Yama to restore Satyavan and take her life instead, which he could not do. So Savitri followed Lord Yama a long way. After a long way in which Yama noticed that Savitri was losing strength but was still following him and her dead husband, Yama offered Savitri a boon, anything other than her husband's life. Savitri asked to have children from Satyavan. In order to give Savitri her boon, Lord Yama had no choice but to restore Satyavan to life and so Savitri gained her husband back.

These two women along with other women in Hindu mythology who were exceptionally devoted to their husbands symbolized the truthful Indian wife who would do everything for their husband and they were named Sati. The meaning of the word sati is righteous. But as written earlier the women named Sati, in Hindu religious literature, did not commit suicide on their dead husband's pyre. Therefore the custom of burning the widow on her dead husband's pyre probably did not evolve from religious background but from social background.

There are different theories about the origins of Sati. One theory says that Sati was introduced to prevent wives from poisoning their wealthy husbands and marry their real lovers. Other theory says that Sati began with a jealous queen who heard that dead kings were welcomed in heaven by hundreds of beautiful women, called Apsaras. And therefore when her husband died, she demanded to be burnt on her dead husband's pyre and so to arrive with him to heaven and this way to prevent the Apsaras from consorting with her husband. There are also other theories about the origins of Sati.

Even though Sati is considered an Indian custom or a Hindu custom it was not practiced all over India by all Hindus but only among certain communities of India. On the other hand, sacrificing the widow in her dead husband's funeral or pyre was not unique only to India. In many ancient communities it was an acceptable feature. This custom was prevalent among Egyptians, Greek, Goths, Scythians and others. Among these communities it was a custom to bury the dead king with his mistresses or wives, servants and other things so that they could continue to serve him in the next world. Another theory claims that Sati was probably brought to India by the Scythians invaders of India. When these Scythians arrived in India, they adopted the Indian system of funeral, which was cremating the dead. And so instead of burying their kings and his servers they started cremating their dead with his surviving lovers. The Scythians were warrior tribes and they were given a status of warrior castes in Hindu religious hierarchy. Many of the Rajput clans are believed to originate from the Scythians. Later on other castes who claimed warrior status or higher also adopted this custom.

This custom was more dominant among the warrior communities in north India, especially in Rajasthan and also among the higher castes in Bengal in east India. Among the Rajputs of Rajasthan, who gave lot of importance to valor and self sacrifice, wives and concubines of the nobles even committed suicide, when they came to know that their beloved died in battlefield. In other parts of India it was comparatively low. And among the majority of Indian communities it did not exist at all.

A few rulers of India tried to ban this custom. The Mughals tried to ban it. The British, due to the efforts of Hindu reformers like Raja Ram Mohan Roy outlawed this custom in 1829.

There aren't exact figures about the number of Sati incidences. In general, before this custom was outlawed in 1829, there were a few hundred officially recorded incidences each year. Even after the custom was outlawed, this custom did not vanish completely. It took few decades before this custom almost vanished. But still there are rare incidences in which the widow demands to voluntary commit Sati. In 1987 an eighteen years old widow committed Sati in a village of Rajasthan with the blessing of her family members. In this incidence the villagers took part in the ceremony, praising and supporting the widow for her act. In October 1999 a woman hysterically jumped on her husband's pyre surprising everyone. But this incidence was declared suicide and not Sati, because this woman was not compelled, forced or praised to commit this act.

In different communities of India, Sati was performed for different reasons and different manners. In communities where the man was married to one wife, the wife put an end to her life on the pyre. But even in these communities not all widows committed Sati. Those women who committed Sati were highly honoured and their families were given lot of respect. It was believed that the woman who committed Sati blessed her family for seven generations after her. Temples or other religious shrines were built to honour the Sati.

In communities were the ruler was married to more than one wife; in some cases only one wife was allowed to commit Sati. This wife was normally the preferred wife of the husband. This was some kind of honour for the chosen wife and some kind of disgrace for the other wives. In other communities some or all of the wives and mistresses were immolated with the husband. And in some cases even male servants were immolated with the kings. This kind of Sati in which the wives and servants were treated as the ruler's property intensifies the theory that Sati was introduced to India by the Scythian invaders of India.

In some very rare incidences mothers committed Sati on their son's pyre and in even more rare cases husbands committed Sati on their wives pyres.

Raj Ram Mohan Roy vs. Dayananda

Hindu Renaissance, which is referred to as a religious and political movement, is closely related to a burgeoning Indian Nationalism. Hindu revivalism is of vital importance in the development of Hinduism as a world religion. The Hindu Renaissance had a tendency to play down the difference between theological traditions and to regulate ritual level, below the ethical spirituality of the Upanishads and the Gita. Hindu reform movement developed to restore the perceived greatness of Hinduism's ancient past, to adopt rationalist elements form within Christianity, and to pay particular attention to social and ethical concerns. The leaders of Hindu renaissance like Raja Ram Mohan Roy and Dayananda Saraswati played an important role in the awakening of social and religious reforms. Raja Ram Mohan Roy (1772-1833) was born of a distinguished Brahmin family in Bengal. He was educated at the Muslim University at Patna where he studied Arabic and Persian philosophical literature. He also studied Sanskrit in Varanasi, as well as English, Hebrew and Greek with a view to translating Bible into Bengali. Because of the Muslim influence, particularly Sufi, Roy was a St...

The main contribution of Brahmo Samaj to the society of India was that it evoked issues that were common to the people all around the Indian sub continent.

They make faith in the doctrines of Karma and Rebirth optional. He wanted to return to the "Sanatana Dharma", the eternal law, which Hindus have moved away from by worshipping icons and reading Epics and Purans. He also supported remarriage of widows, if their previous marriage had not consummated. marriage by choice? the most ancient form of marriage in India-is the best form of marriage. He lost his faith in the Shaiva religion of image worship, when he saw mice climbing over the temple icon, eating the food which had been offered to the deity.

Dayananda Saraswati (1824-1883) was born in Saurashtra in Gujarat to a Shaiva Brahman family.

Raja Ram Mohan Roy, through his services, was considered the true leader of Renaissance and known as the "father of Renaissance". He believed that people should not be discriminating by their birth but by their Karma, actions. It was not a seperate religion but a reform movement within Hinduism.?

Dayananda Saraswati opposed the Varna system. The four Vedas are; Rig Veda, Yajur Veda, Sama Veda, & Atharva Veda.?

Roy founded the Atmiya Sabha in 1815.

Beliefs of the Brahmo Samaj

Fundamental Principles of the Brahmo Religion and Universalism

The fundamental principles of the Brahmo Samaj, founded by Raja Ram Mohan Roy in 1828 are:

1. There is only one God, who is the creator, and the saviour of this world. He is spirit, infinite in power, wisdom, love, justice and holiness, omnipresent, eternal and blissful.
2. The human soul is immortal and capable of infinite progress, and is responsible to God for its doings.
3. Man's happiness in this and the next world consists in worshipping God in spirit and in truth.
4. Loving God, holding communion with Him, and carrying out His will in all the concerns of life, constitute true worship.
5. No created object is to be worshipped as God, and God alone is to be considered as infallible.

To this, Raja Ram Mohan Roy added "The true way of serving God is to do good to man." Since no one person is considered to be infallible, the Brahmos hold all the great religious leaders of the world in respect, and believe that truth is to be gleaned from all the scriptures of the world. To that extent, the Brahmo religion is truly eclectic. Universalist in nature, it is "dogmatically undogmatic". The Brahmo Samaj has a great deal in common with the other free churches of the world, and is one of the founding members of the "The International Association for Religious Freedom". Rationalist in everything, it does not deny the possibility of Divine Revelation, but reserves the right to test the validity of what is supposed to be revelation. The connection between the Brahmo Samaj and the other liberal churches of the world is best understood when we considered the basics of Universalism, which are dealt with in the following paragraphs:

Duncan Howlett has aptly described Universalism as a doctrine of "Testing, Questing and never Resting, with Open Mind and Open Heart."

Each of these items bears detailed examination. The root question is how can we be sure about the truth of our beliefs? After all, there is no doubt that we human beings are fallible. The only way we can surmount our human fallibility is by continually testing the validity of our assumptions. We have to accept that we are prone to making mistakes and deceiving one another all the time. Even in the age of computers, there is always the possibility of mistakes being made in programming or worse still, valuable data being lost on account of viruses deliberately planted by misguided souls. We must therefore check everything by all the means at our disposal. This is true even in the case of religion, where we can no longer be certain of the infallibility of scriptures or prophets.

If our human capacity for error is a severe limitation, then our imagination and probing curiosity are surely among our greatest assets. It is the human spirit of inquiry and questing, in other words, seeking for the truth, which is behind all advances in Philosophy or Religion. The enquiring mind pushes beyond ideas that we already have, in order to discover new perfections. In this process of Questing, we are never really satisfied until we feel that we have gone as far as is humanly possible. This is what is meant by "never Resting". On the path of discovery we are bound to meet like-minded souls also engaged in the same search for truth. We must be open to dialogue with them, and at least listen to them even if we do not agree. The spirit of the "open mind" is a safeguard against dogma, which has no place in Universalism.

While the open mind enlarges our own frontiers, it is not enough to merely be open to other ideas. Acceptance of the other person as a brother and a comrade makes religion truly universal. Merely accepting that "In the Father's house there are many mansions" does not better our human lot the way "Love thy neighbour as thyself" does. True Universalism is based on the "Fatherhood of God and the Brotherhood of Man" more than anything else. Universalists believe that religion should be dynamic and not static. Everything in this world is evolving, and religion too, changes with time. Any religion that adheres to a set of unchanging beliefs is a dead religion. Of course, any change has to be tested for validity by applying our God given powers of logic and reasoning, and must be acceptable to our conscience. The Brahmos believe that God reveals Himself in His own creation, and speaks to man through his conscience. The relationship between God and man is one of loving and giving. Our life is a gift from God. What we do with our life is our gift to God.

History of the Brahmo Samaj

As British rule consolidated in India during the 18th century, two factors contributed to the formation of the Brahmo Samaj in the following century. Firstly the Hindu social system had begun to stagnate and placed too much of an emphasis on traditional rituals. Secondly an English educated class of Indians began to emerge to fulfil the administrative and economic needs of British rule. Raja Ram Mohan Roy, a Bengali, was a product of the latter trend. What made Raja Ram Mohan Roy stand out from his peers was his questioning mind. Apart from knowing several languages he was a Sanskrit and an Arabic scholar, and studied several religions. He campaigned for social reform and women's education. He founded the Brahma Samaj at Calcutta in 1828, which was initially known as the "Brahmo Sabha." Later in 1868 it was changed to the "Adi" (Original) Brahmo Samaj. It rejected idol worship and the worship of multiple gods and goddesses of the traditional Hindu beliefs. Raja Ram Mohan Roy was much influenced by western thought, especially Christianity. He was one of the first Hindus to visit Europe, where he was much admired by the intellectuals. He died in Bristol.

He was friendly with another famous Bengali, Dwarakanath Tagore. Prior to his departure to Europe, Raja Ram Mohan Roy had asked Dwarakanath Tagore's son, Debendranath Tagore, to continue his work in his absence. Debendranath Tagore took an active interest in the Brahmo Samaj, and began to transform the Brahmo Samaj into a spiritual fraternity. He formulated the "Brahmo-upadesa" which were a set of readings from the ancient Hindu book, the "Upanishads."

Debendranath Tagore's successor was Keshab Chandra Sen. He sought to incorporate Christian ideals into the Brahmo Samaj movement. He began the compilation of a scripture including passages from the Holy Books of many religions-Hindu, Buddhist, Christian and Muslim. Gradually, due to differences in certain areas of religious beliefs, three institutions arose:

- The Adi (Original) Brahmo Samaj-founded by Debendranath Tagore
- The Naba-Bidhan (New Dispensation) Samaj-founded by Keshab Chandra Sen
- The Sadharan (Common) Brahmo Samaj-founded by Pandit Shivanath Shastri

The Sadharan Brahmo Samaj sought to provide a more rational and monotheistic interpretation of the Upanishads. A "mandir" (prayer house) was built in Cornwallis Street, (now re-named "Bidhan Sarani") Calcutta. Eventually these three Samajes united to form the "Brahmo Sammilan Samaj," and a "mandir" was built in Bhowanipur, Calcutta. This celebrated its centenary in 1997.

The Brahmo Samajes grew in several Indian cities and abroad. There are records of one being present in Rangoon and in London as far back as 1911.

Social Welfare

Removing the Caste System: The caste system has been a part of Hindu society for hundreds of years. It's inherent divisive nature and social injustices were abhorrent to the early Brahmos. Therefore an important reform that the early Brahmos campaigned for was the removal of the caste system.

Many of the early Brahmos came from the Brahmin caste, who wore a sacred thread around their body to signify their caste superiority. From the 1850's onwards the renunciation of the sacred thread came to symbolise this break with tradition. The equality of all men was fundamental to the Brahmo movement, and to them it did not matter what caste or indeed religion someone was born into. For example even in 1865 there was a case of a Muslim boy being attracted into the religion. Given the polarization of society between Hindus and Muslims at the time, this was revolutionary in those days.

Widow Remarriage: Despite Iswar Chandra Vidyasagar's campaign that led to the legalisation of widow remarriage (1856) in India, Hindu society had many reservations on this issue. The Brahmos campaigned against such pre-judices. To reinforce their commitment to this many young men of the Brahmo movement made a positive point of marrying widows.

Saving of Upper Caste Unmarried Women: It wasn't just the lower castes who suffered in the caste system. Despite their caste status, the girls from the upper caste families suffered because of their position. If a suitable bridegroom could not be found for such a girl in their caste, their options were limited, as marriage to lower caste men was not permitted. These girls often found themselves being married off to very old men who were already married several times over. Or worse still, sometimes these girls would be poisoned to death. Again the Brahmos campaigned against such unjust practices and saved the lives of many such girls.

Women's Education and Status: Traditionally education had been primarily for the men. However during the 1860's and the 1870's the attitude of the Brahmos started to change. Education was encouraged among the Brahmo women. At the same time their equal status in society was emphasised by allowing women to pray with men at the prayer halls. In 1881 the Brahmo Samaj at Barishal (Bengal) appointed the first woman Brahmo preacher (Manorama Mazumdar).

This article was written by Dr. Sumit Chanda, based on source material provided by the Brahmo Sammilan Samaj at Calcutta. The drawings originally formed part of the Poster Exhibition held in August-September, 1997, on the occasion of the Centenary celebration of the Brahmo Sammilan Samaj. These have been reproduced with the kind permission of Mr. P.R. Das Gupta, the Secretary of the Brahmo Sammilan Samaj.

Brahmo Wedding: In a Brahmo wedding, the bride and the groom, as adults, declare in an open house that each is willing to accept the other as a partner for life. Thus a Brahmo wedding has no tradition of "giving away" the daughter by her parents. The bride and the groom pray to God together and take their nuptial vows. The minister and the other fellow Brahmos pray for their welfare and future happiness. The bride and groom typically exchange garlands and rings, and the prayers are complemented by singing of hymns.

Millennium Sermon: On the first Maghotsav of this century and in the new millennium I would like to share with you some thoughts that have crossed my mind.

The word January comes from the Roman God Janus, who had two heads-one pointing to the past, and one pointing to the future.

As we are celebrating Maghotsav in January at the beginning of the century, it is befitting that we first take a look at the past, and then into the future. A look at the past takes us to the Renaissance in India, and in Bengal in particular. In 1828 the Brahmo Samaj was established by Raja Ram Mohan Roy, who was followed by other leaders like Keshab Chandra Sen and Shivanath Shastri. It was a time of great spiritual social reforms against casteism and the emancipation of women. It was a period when superstitious and evil customs like the suttee were abolished. It an era when great educational institutions were established in Calcutta. That era has also seen the birth of men like Ramakrishna and Rabindranath and preachers of a non-violence like Mahatma Gandhi. We have seen the birth of the largest democratic nation when India achieved independence in 1947.

During the last century we have seen tremendous advances in the field of science and medicine. We have made great strides in developing transport-faster cars, trains and planes. Men have landed on the moon and we have watched it sitting in our own homes on TV. The past century has made enormous progress in the field of computers and satellite communication-the mobile phones and telecommunications by way of videoconferences in distant lands has brought the world closer. The world has become smaller and closer. Countries no longer think individually. They take a global view of trade and commerce.

However in spite of all the scientific achievements and material comforts have we made any real progress in moral and human values? Are human hearts and minds now closer to each other than 500 years ago? The 1900s have seen two World Wars-the people of the past century have experienced fighting and bloodshed and the horrific destruction of Nagasaki with the atom bomb. In spite of modern communications systems, communities seem to have grown apart and divided, as we have seen in Bosnia and very recently in the atrocities of Kosovo and now in Chechnya. At present and there are many wars going on in Africa and Asia with the devastating consequences of land mine injuries long afterwards.

Our social structure and family life has also changed. The extended family is on the brink of extinction. The advances in medicine have increased longevity, but are we able to provide a reasonable quality of care? Can we spare a little time for visiting elderly friends? Do we as human beings care for other humans and the plants and animals of this beautiful world? Today at the beginning of the 21st century let us attempt to try to look at the future. We do not know what the future holds for us; but we can hope that the world will be a better place for all of us.

The world, we can hope, will be a peaceful place-not only will there be peace among nations, but also in the hearts all men who will fulfil their duties towards the old, the sick and hungry. Societies and nations will not just think of their own survival but will work for the benefit of others, which is one of the ideals of the promise of the Brahmo Samaj, and that the other principles-"truth, justice and love" shall prevail in the hearts of men and women of the 21st century. We hope that the hearts and the minds of all the people in the world will be united and the century will be a happier place for all of us. It may seem like a dream but it is up to each one of us to make an effort, however small towards achieving this dream-and making this place a better place. May we find the world in the 21st century as Tagore has described in one of his poems.

The New India and Raja Ram Mohan Roy

In spite of political convulsions and economic retrogression the first century of British rule in India (1757-1858) is in certain respects a memorable epoch in her history. The period witnessed a remarkable outburst of intellectual activity in India and a radical transformation in her social and religious ideas. The impetus to these changes came from the introduction of English education. Through this channel came the liberal ideas of the West which stirred the people and roused them from the slumber of ages.

Reason and judgment took the place of faith and belief; superstition yielded to science. This great change affected at first only a small group of persons, but gradually the ideas spread among larger sections of the people, and ultimately their influence reached, in greater or les degree even the masses. The new spirit of this age is strikingly illustrated by the life and career of Raja Ram Mohan Roy, a remarkable personality, a great political and social reformer.

Raja bagan his reforming activity by preaching the unity of God, assailing the prevalent Hindu belief in many gods, and the worship of their images with elaborate rituals. He tried to demonstrate that the views were in accordance with the old and true scriptures of the Hindus, and that the modern deviations from them due to superstitions of a later age without any moral and religious sanction behind them. Ram Mohan's views stirred Hindu society to its depths, and bitter controversies followed. Ram Mohan published translations of ancient scriptures in order to defend his thesis, and carried on the contest, almost single-handedly, by the publication of a large number of Bengali tracts. Towards the close of his life he founded, in 1828, an organization for furthering his religious views. The organization ultimately developed into Brahma Samaj. It was meant to be an assembly of all who believed in the unity of God and discarded the worship of images. A house was built and handed over to a body of trustees. The Trust Deed which the Raja executed on 8th January 1830, directed that the building was to be used "as for a place of public meeting of all sorts of descriptions of people, without distinction ", for the worship of the one Great God, but that no image should be admitted or rituals permitted therein. The Raja however never regarded himself to be somebody else but a Hindu, and stoutly denied, up to the last day of his life that he was founding a different sect.

Ram Mohan was a great pioneer of English education. Not only did he himself found several institutions for that purpose, but he always lent a helping hand to others who endeavored to do so. He along with the active participation of the English man David Hare founded the Hindu College in Kolkata in the year 1817, which later on came to be called as the Presidency College. Ram Mohan's reforming activity was also directed against social abuses of Hindu society, notably the rigours of caste and the degradation of the position of women.

Those days a custom was prevailing in the society, known as the Sati daha prahta. According to this custom, a widow was forcibly immolated to death in the pyre of her husband. The word Sati means a chaste and virtuous woman but has by a curious process applied to the practice of burning chaste women along with the dead bodies of their husbands. This actually finds origin in the religious belief that there is a life after death and if the wife is burnt along with the husband, they will lead the life together after death. Such hopes and encouragements both to the victim and her natural protectors produced the inevitable consequences. In many cases the material interests of the male relations, added to religious faith induced them to persuade the unhappy victim to the tragic course. The British government tried to do away with this practice, but was bolted from the civil population. Thanks to the unwearied efforts of Raja Ram Mohan Roy. He stood firmly against the orthodox Hindus and supported the Government in its attempt. In a counter petition submitted by the Raja and his coadjutors against the petition of the orthodox Hindu section. After describing the horrors of the Sati in vivid terms, they declared that "all these instances are murders, according to every Shastra as well as to the common sense of all nations". To educate public opinion Raja Ram Mohan wrote a pamphlet on the subject and organized a vigilance committee in order to ensure that the Government regulations were followed in each instance. The Raja was bitterly opposed by the orthodox Hindus under the leader ship of Raja Radhakanta Deb. Feelings at last ran so high that even Raja Ram Mohan's life was threatened. Ultimately on 4th December 1829. The famous Regulation was passed, in which Sati was declared illegal and punishable by courts.

He also endeavoured to ameliorate the fate of helpless widows by many other ways, notably by changing the Hindu laws of inheritance about women giving them proper education. He was opposed to polygamy and various other abuses in the social system of Bengal. He also advocated remarriage of widows under specified circumstances. His ideals of womanhood and man's duty towards them, preached in forceful language in various tracts, were far ahead of his age and were inspired by the memories of the golden age of India.

In the field of Indian politics also Raja Ram Mohan was the prophet of the new age. He laid down the lines of political agitation in a constitutional manner which ultimately led to the birth of Indian National Congress half a century later. The Raja was a great champion of the liberty of the Press. Ever since 1799 there had been a strict censorship in the publication of journals. In 1817 Lord Hastings abolished the censorship, but laid down regulations, which among other things, prohibited the discussion of certain matters. Raja Ram Mohan presented petitions against the new Press Regulations both to the Supreme Court and to the King-in-Council. Though the petition was rejected but they form a noble landmark in the progress of Indian culture.

The Raja similarly drew up petitions against the Jury Act of 1827 The Raja had a clear grasp of the political machinery by which India was ruled and fully realized the importance of presenting India's case before the home authorities when the questions of the renewal of the Company's Charter in 1833 was being considered by Parliament. This was one of his main objects in under taking the voyage to England. These documents enable us to gather the view-point of Raja Ram Mohan and of the advanced Indian thinkers of his time, on the burning questions of the day. The Raja strongly championed the cause of the peasants. He pointed out that under the Permanent Settlement, the zaminders had increased their wealth, but the exorbitantly high rents exacted from their tenants had made the lots of the riots a miserable one. He advocated a reduction of the rent to be paid by the tenants by means of a reduction in the revenue payable by the zaminders. The consequent loss of revenue, he suggested, should be met by a tax upon luxuries or by employing low-salaried Indians as collectors instead of high-salaried Europeans. He favoured the Permanent Settlement but he rightly urged that the Government should fix the maximum rent to be paid by each cultivator.

Among the other measures advocated by the Raja may be mentioned the Indianisation of the British-Indian army, trial by jury, separation of the offices of judge and magistrate, codification of civil and criminal laws, consultation with the Indian leaders before enactment of new laws and the substitution of English for Persian as the official language of the courts of law.

3

Prarthana Samaj

Prarthana Samaj, or also called "Prayer Society" in Sanskrit, is a movement for religious and social reform in Maharashtra based on previous reform movements and traditions of Maharashtra. The direct predecessor of the Prarthana Samaj in Mumbai was the Paramahamsa Sabha, a secret society for the furtherance of liberal ideas formed in 1849 by Ram Balkrishna Jaykar and others in Mumbai. It was secret in order to avoid the wrath of the powerful and orthodox elements of society. Meetings were for discussion, the singing of hymns, and the sharing of a communal meal prepared by a low-caste cook. Members ate bread baked by Christians and drank water brought by Moslems.

Religious Reform

Like the parallel Brahmo Samaj of Bengal, the Prarnatha Samaj represented an Indian response to European liberalism, including the ideals of rational or theistic belief and social reform. The Prarthana Samaj(ists) are followers of the great religious tradition of the Maratha Sant Mat like Namdev, Tukaram and Ramdas (the guru of Shivaji). The Brahmo Samaj founders examined many world religions including ancient Vedic texts which subsequently were not accepted to be infallible or divine. Although the adherents of Prarthana Samaj were devoted theists, they also do not regard the Vedas as divine or infallible. They drew their nourishment from the Hindu scriptures and used the hymns of the old Marathi "poet-saints" in their prayers. Their ideas trace back to the devotional poems of the Vitthalas as part of the Vaishnava bhakti devotional movements of the thirteenth century in southern Maharashtra. The Marathi poets had inspired a movement of resistance to the Mughals. But, beyond religious concerns, the primary focus of the Prarnatha Samaj was on social and cultural reform.

Social Reform

Prarthana Samaj critically examined the relations between contemporary social and cultural systems and religious beliefs and gave priority to social reform as compared with the political changes already initiated by the British government. Their comprehensive reform movement has led many impressive projects of cultural change and social reform in Western India, such as the improvement of the lot of women and depressed classes, an end to the caste system, abolition of child marriages and infanticide, educational opportunites for women, and remarriage of widows. Its success was guided by Sir Ramakrishna Gopal Bhandarkar, a noted Sanskrit scholar, Dr. Atmaram Pandurang, Narayan Chandavarkar, and Justice Mahadev Govinda Ranade. Ranade emphasized that "the reformer must attempt to deal with the whole man and not to carry out reform on one side only". "The social organism in India," according to Ranade, "shows a growth which should not be ignored and cannot be forcibly suppressed." Later Prarthana Samaj, in Pune, continued the reforms of the caste system and untouchability. Maharshi Vithal Ramji Shinde championed the complete eradication of caste and untouchability. He founded the first depressed classes mission.

Manav Dharma Sabha

Manav Dharma Sabha was one of the earliest socio-religious reform movements in Gujarat and British India. It was founded on 22 June 1844 in Surat by Mehtaji Durgaram Manchharam, Dadoba Panderung Tarkhad and a few others. The goals of the Sabha were to expose the hypocritical arts present in Christian, Muslim and Hindu religions. It had a very short life span and ceased to exist as Dadoba left for Bombay in 1846 and Durgaram left for Rajkot in 1852. It acted as a secret society and is believed that the revealation of its existence compounded to its demise.

Paramahansa Mandali

Paramahansa Mandali was a secret socio-religious group in Bombay and is closely related to Manav Dharma Sabha. It was started by Dadoba Panderung and a group of his friends in 1849.

Dadoba Panderung assumed leadership of this organisation after he left Manav Dharma Sabha. He outlined his principles in *Dharma Vivechan* in 1843.

Ramakrishna Gopal Bhandarkar

Ramakrishna Gopal Bhandarkar (July 6, 1837–August 24, 1925) was an Indian scholar, orientalist, and social reformer.

Early Life

Bhandarkar was born in Malvan in Ratnagiri district of Maharashtra. After his early schooling in Ratnagiri, he studied at Elphinstone College in Bombay. Along with Mahadev Govind Ranade, Bhandarkar was among the first graduates in 1862 from Bombay University. He obtained his Master's degree the next year.

Scholarly Career

Bhandarkar taught at Elphinstone College and Deccan College during his distinguished teaching career. He was involved in research and writing throughout his life. He retired in 1894 as the Vice Chancellor of Bombay University. He participated in international conferences on Oriental Studies held in London (1874) and Vienna (1886), making invaluable contributions. Historian R. S. Sharma wrote of him: "He reconstructed the political history of the Deccan of the Satavahanas and the history of Vaishnavism and other sects. A great social reformer, through his researches he advocated widow marriages and castigated the evils of the caste system and child marriage."

Social Reformer

In 1853, while a student, Bhandarkar became a member of the Paramhansa Sabha, an association for the furtherance of liberal ideas which was then secret to avoid the wrath of the powerful and orthodox elements of the contemporary society. Visits of Keshub Chunder Sen during 1864 had inspired the members of the Sabha. In 1866, some of the members held a meeting in the house of Atmaram Pandurang and publicly pledged to certain reforms, including (1) denunciation of the caste system, (2) encouragement of widow remarriage, (3) encouragement of female education, and (4) abolition of child marriage.

The members concluded that religious reforms were required as a basis for social reforms. They held their first prayer meeting on 31 March 1867, which eventually led to the formation of the Prarthana Samaj. Another visit by Keshub Chunder Sen and visits of Protap Chunder Mozoomdar and Navina Chandra Rai, founder of Punjab Brahmo Samaj, boosted their efforts. World-renowned Bhandarkar Oriental Research Institute at Pune is named after Ramakrishna Gopal Bhandarkar.

N. G. Chandavarkar

Sir Narayan Ganesh Chandavarkar (December 2, 1855-May 14, 1923) was an early Indian National Congress politician and Hindu reformer. He was regarded by some as the "leading Hindu reformer of western India"

Early Life

Narayan Ganesh Chandavarkar was born in Honavar in the Bombay Presidency on December 2, 1855. His maternal uncle was Shamrao Vithal Kaikini, another notable reformer from the Saraswat community. He served as a Dakshina Fellow in Elphinstone College for some time before earning a law degree in 1881. Shortly before the Indian National Congress was founded in 1885, N. G. Chandavarkar went to England as a member of the three-man delegation.

The group was sent to educate public opinion about India right before general elections took place in England. G.L. Chandavarkar writes, "His visit to England in 1885 carved out for Chandavarkar a political career, and he threw himself whole-heartedly into the work of the Indian National Congress which was founded in Bombay in 1885 on December 28, the day on which he and the other delegates returned to India."

Career

He was elected the president of the annual session of the Indian National Congress in 1900 and one year later he was promoted to the high bench at the Bombay High Court. He took a break from politics for the next twelve years and devoted his time to the judicial system and various social groups. The main social group he worked with was the Prarthana Samaj ("Prayer Society"). He took the leadership reins from Mahadev Govind Ranade after the death of the latter in 1901. The organization was inspired by the Brahmo Samaj and was involved in the modernization of Hindu society.

Return to Politics

He returned to the realm of Indian politics in 1914. A schism in the Congress in 1918 came to separate the organization into two camps. Chandavarkar became the head of the *All-India Moderates Conference* in 1918 along with Surendranath Banerjea and Dinshaw Wacha. In 1920 "he presided over the public meeting held in Bombay to protest against the report of the Hunter Committee on the Jallianwala Bagh atrocities which was appointed by the Government of India." Mahatma Gandhi was inspired by this to move a resolution on the topic. Later, on Chandavarkar's advice, Gandhi called off his Civil Disobedience campaign in 1921.

Mahadev Govind Ranade

Justice Mahadev Govind Ranade (16 January 1842–16 January 1901) was a distinguished scholar, great social reformer, and an author from India. He was a founding member of the Indian National Congress and owned several designations as member of the Bombay legislative council, member of the finance committee at the centre, and the judge of Bombay High Court..

Professional Career

Ranade was born in a small town in Nasik district named Niphad. Ranade began studies at the Elphinstone College in Mumbai, at the age of fourteen. He belonged to Bombay University, one of the three new British universities, and was part of the first batches for both the B.A. (1862) and the LLB. (Government Law School, 1866) where he graduated at the top of his class. Great scholar and founder of BORI Mr.. Bhandarkar was his classmate.

He was appointed Presidency magistrate, fourth judge of the Bombay Small Causes Court in 1871, first-class sub-judge at Pune in 1873, judge of the Poona Small Causes Court in 1884, and finally to the Bombay High Court in 1893. From 1885 until he joined the High Court, he belonged to the Bombay legislative council. He was a well known public figure, who's personality as a calm and patient optimist would influence his attitude towards dealings with Britain, as well as with reform in India. During his life he helped establish the Poona Sarvajanik Sabha, the Prarthana Samaj, and would edit a Bombay Anglo-Marathi daily paper, the Induprakask, founding all on his ideology of social and religious reform.

In 1897, Ranade served on a committee charged with the task of enumerating imperial and provincial expenditure and making recommendations for financial retrenchment. This service won him the decoration of Companion of the Order of the Indian Empire. Ranade also served as a special judge under the Deccan Agriculturists' Relief Act from 1887.

In addition, Ranade held the offices of syndic and dean in arts at Bombay University, where he displayed much organizing power and great intimacy with the needs of the student class. Himself a thorough Marathi scholar, he encouraged the translation of standard English works, and tried, with some success, to introduce vernacular languages into the university curriculum. He published books on Indian economics and on Maratha history. He stated the requirement of heavy industries such as Steel as necessity for economic progress. He believed in Western education as a vital element to the foundation of an Indian nation. He felt that by understanding the mutual problems of India and Britain, both reform and independence could be achieved to the benefit of all. He insisted that an independent India could only be stable after such reforms were made. Reform of Indian culture and use of an adaptation of Western culture, in Ranade's view, would bring about "common interest... and fusion of thoughts" amongst all men."

Activism

Religious: With his friends Dr. Atmaram Pandurang, Bal Mangesh Wagle and Vaman Abaji Modak, Ranade founded the Prarthana Samaj, a Hindu movement inspired by the Brahmo Samaj, espousing principles of enlightened theism based on the ancient Vedas. Prarthan samaj was started by Keshav Chandra Sen, a staunch Brahma Samajist, with the objective of carrying out religious reforms in Maharashtra.

Political

Ranade founded the Poona Sarvajanik Sabha and later was one of the originators of the Indian National Congress. He has been portrayed as an early adversary of the politics of Bal Gangadhar Tilak and a mentor to Gopal Krishna Gokhale.

The 1911 *Encyclopedia Britannica* stated that the Poona Sarvajanik Sabha "frequently helped the government with sound advice". Not everyone agreed. In a letter to Henry Fawcett, Florence Nightingale wrote:

"[T]he Poona Sarvajanik Sabha (National Association) [...] again pretends to represent the people and merely represents the money lenders, officials, and a few effete Mahratta landlords."

In 1943, B. R. Ambedkar praised Ranade and rated him favourably against Gandhi and Jinnah:

"Ranade never received the honours of apotheosis as these great men of India today are destined to receive. How could he? He did not come with a message hot from Senai. He performed no miracles and promised no speedy deliverance and splendour. He was not a genius and he had no superhuman qualities. But there are compensations. If Ranade did not show splendour and dominance, he brought us no catastrophe. If he had no superhuman qualities to use in the service of India, India was saved from ruin by its abuse. If he was not a genius, he did not display that perverse super-subtlety of intellect, and a temper of mind which is fundamentally dishonest and which has sown the seeds of distrust and which has made settlement so difficult of achievement.

There is nothing exuberant and extravagant in Ranade. He refused to reap cheap notoriety by playing the part of an extremist. He refused to mislead people by playing upon and exploiting the patriotic sentiments of the people. He refused to be a party to methods which are crude, which have volume but no effect, and which are neither fool-proof nor knave-proof, and which break the back even of the most earnest and sincere servants of the country and disable them from further effort. In short, Ranade was like the wise Captain who knows that his duty is not to play with his ship clever and masterful tricks, just for effect and show in the midst of the ocean, but to take it safely to its appointed port. In short, Ranade was not a forged bank note and in worshipping him we have no feeling of kneeling before anything that is false."

Social

Ranade was a founder of the Social Conference movement, which he supported till his death, directing his social reform efforts against child marriage, the shaving of widows' heads, the heavy cost of marriages and other social functions, and the caste restrictions on travelling abroad, and he strenuously advocated widow remarriage and female education. Ranade attempted to work with the structure of weakened traditions, reforming, but not destroying the social atmosphere that was India's heritage. Ranade valued India's history, having had a great interest in Shivaji and the Bhakti movement, but he also recognized the influence that British rule over India had on its development. Ranade encouraged the acceptance of change, believing traditional social structures, like the caste system, should accommodate change, thereby preserving India's ancient heritage. An overall sense of national regeneration was what Ranade desired.

Though Ranade criticised superstitions and blind faith, he was conservative in his own life. He chose to took *prayaschitta* (religious penance) in case of *Panch-houd Mission Case* rather than taking a strong side of his opinions.

Family

Ranade belonged to an orthodox Chitpavan Brahman family. He was born in Niphad and spent much of his childhood in Kolhapur where his father was a minister. Upon the death of his first wife, his reform-minded friends expected him to marry (and thereby rescue) a widow. However, he adhered to his family's wishes and married a child bride, Ramabai Ranade, whom he subsequently provided with an education. After his death, she continued his social and educational reform work. He had no children.

Ramabai Ranade in her memoirs has stated that when one equally prominent Pune personality Vishnupant Pandit married a widow, Ranade entertained him and a few guests at his home. This was not liked by his orthodox father who decided to leave Ranade's home in Pune and go to Kolhapur. It was only after he(i.e Mahadev G. Ranade) told the father that he would resign from his government job that the father relented and cancelled his plans to go to Kolhapur. Ranade decided never to do any such thing in future.

Pandita Ramabai

Pandita Ramabai (23 April 1858, Maharashtra- 5 April 1922) was an eminent Indian Christian social reformer and activist.

She was a poet, a scholar, and a champion of improvement in the plight of Indian women. As a social reformer, she championed the cause of emancipation of Indian women. A widely travelled lady, she visited most parts of India, and even went to England (1883) and the U.S. (1886-88). She wrote many books including her widely popular work titled *The High Caste Hindu Woman*, which showed the darkest of subject matter relating to the life of Hindu women, including child brides and the treatment they receive by the government. She had a strong view of what should be accomplished so women would be able to have more freedom, including protection of widowed women and child brides and she was also against the practice of suttee. Pandita Ramabai was born into an intellectual Brahmin family. Her father believed that women should have an education and against traditional Hindu social structure he taught Ramabai as well as his second wife, Ramambai's mother Puranic and how to read and write Sanskrit. As well as how to interpret vedic texts. She was raised by her father in the year 1880 the late Shri V. K. Chiplunkar with Lokmanya Tilak and M. B. Namjoshi started 'New English School' in Pune with the objective of 'cheapening and facilitating education'. In course of time Shri V. S. Apte, (M. A.), Shri. G. G. Agarkar, (M. A.), Shri V. B. Kelkar, (B. A.), Shri M. S. Gole, (M. A.), and Shri. N. K. Dharap, (B. A.) joined them.

This was a revolutionary step because Government Institutions and Christian missionaries were the only agencies involved in educating the masses and the education provided failed to generate leadership for industrial regeneration of a self-governing nation. Private enterprises in education were discouraged. With the idea of providing education to rouse the intellect, drooping will and slumbering conscience of the fallen countrymen, Deccan Education Society came into existence.

Theosophical Society

The Theosophical Society was an organization formed in 1875 to advance the spiritual principles and search for Truth known as Theosophy. Theosophy is an active belief system today, and through a process of schism has also given rise to many other mystical beliefs and organisations.

History

Formation

The Theosophical Society was founded in New York City, USA, in 1875 by Helena Blavatsky, Henry Steel Olcott, William

Quan Judge and others. Its initial objective was the investigation, study and explanation of mediumistic phenomena. After a few years Olcott and Blavatsky moved to India and established the International Headquarters at Adyar, Madras (Chennai). There, they also became interested in studying Eastern religions, and these were included in the Society's agenda. After several iterations the Society's objectives have evolved to be:

1. to form a nucleus of the universal brotherhood of humanity without distinction of race, creed, sex, caste, or colour.
2. to encourage the study of comparative religion, philosophy, and science.
3. to investigate the unexplained laws of nature and the powers latent in man.

In addition to the stated objectives, as early as 1889 Blavatsky purportedly had told a group of Theosophical students that the real purpose of establishing the Society was to prepare humanity for the reception of the World Teacher when he appeared again on earth. This was repeated again more publicly by Annie Besant in 1896, five years after Blavatsky's death. In Blavatsky's own writings, the only reference to a similar idea indicated that it would not be for at least a century.

Schisms

After Helena Blavatsky's death in 1891, the Society's leaders seemed at first to work together peacefully. This did not last long. Judge was accused by Olcott and Annie Besant of forging letters from the Mahatmas; he ended his association with Olcott and Besant in 1895 and took most of the Society's American Section with him. The original organisation led by Olcott and Besant remains today based in India and is known as the Theosophical Society-Adyar. The group led by Judge further splintered into a faction led by Katherine Tingley, and another associated the Judge's secretary Ernest Temple Hargrove. While Hargrove's faction no longer survives, the faction led by Tingley is today known simply as the Theosophical Society, but often with the clarifying statement, "international headquarters, Pasadena, California". A third organization, the United Lodge of Theosophists or ULT, in 1909 split off from the latter organization.

In 1902, Rudolf Steiner became General Secretary of the German/Austrian division of the Theosophical Society. He maintained a Western-oriented course, relatively independent from the Adyar headquarter led by Besant and Olcott. After serious philosophical conflicts, primarily on the spiritual significance of Christ and on the status of the young boy Krishnamurti, most of the German and Austrian members split off in 1913 and formed the Anthroposophical Society. The latter remains very active and influential today and has branches in almost all western communities, including the US and Canada.

Controversy/Racial Beliefs

Blavatsky posited that humanity had descended from a series of non-human "Root Races" (Cosmologically on par with the Christian sacraments, Cabalistic Tree of life, the eastern phylosophy of the chakras) naming the fifth root race (out of seven) the Aryan race. The Root Races were evolutionary stages, each new Root Race being more evolved than the previous one. She thought that the Aryans originally came from Atlantis,, who were part of the fourth Root Race. The Aryan Root Race was only one more step in the evolutionary progress and it would eventually be superseded by a more spiritual Root Race, the sixth. She believed that "The Semites, especially the Arabs, are later Aryans — degenerate in spirituality and perfected in materiality. To these belong all the Jews and the Arabs. The former are a tribe descended from the Tchandalas of India, the outcasts, many of them ex-Brahmins, who sought refuge in Chaldea, in Scinde, and Aria (Iran), and were truly born from their father A-bram (No Brahmin) some 8,000 years B.C.

The latter, the Arabs, are the descendants of those Aryans who would not go into India at the time of the dispersion of nations, some of whom remained on the borderlands thereof, in Afghanistan and Kabul,* and along the Oxus, while others penetrated into and invaded Arabia. But this was when Africa had already been raised as a continent. We have meanwhile to follow, as closely as limited space will permit, the gradual evolution of the now truly human species. It is in the suddenly arrested evolution of certain sub-races, and their forced and violent diversion into the purely animal line by artificial cross-breeding, truly analogous to the hybridization, which we have now learned to utilize in the vegetable and animal kingdoms, that we have to look for the origin of the anthropoids."

She did not encourage any feeling of superiority by any person or race, spreading the idea of the common origin and destiny of all humanity, and establishing the principle of universal brotherhood as the First Object of the Theosophical Society: "To form the nucleus of a Universal Brotherhood of Humanity without distinction of race, colour, or creed.". Thus, she declares "Theosophists, collectively, respect the Bible as much as they do the sacred scriptures of other people, finding in it the same eternal truths as in the Vedas, the Zend-Avesta, the Tripitakas, etc."

Guido von List (and his followers such as Lanz von Liebenfels) later took up some of Blavatsky's ideas, mixing her ideology with nationalistic and fascist ideas; this system of thought became known as Ariosophy.

Some researchers, when tracing the links between Ariosophy and Theosophy, tried to portray the latter as relying mostly on "intellectual expositions of racial evolution". However, in The Key to Theosophy Helena Blavatsky had clearly pointed out that "The Society is a philanthropic and scientific body for the propagation of the idea of brotherhood on practical instead of theoretical lines.".

"***Enquirer.*** Can you attain the "Secret Wisdom" simply by study? Encyclopaedias define Theosophy pretty much as Webster's Dictionary does, i.e., as "supposed intercourse with God and superior spirits, and consequent attainment of superhuman knowledge by physical means and chemical processes." Is this so?

Theosophist: I think not. Nor is there any lexicographer capable of explaining, whether to himself or others, how superhuman knowledge can be attained by physical or chemical processes. Had Webster said "by metaphysical and alchemical processes," the definition would be approximately correct: as it is, it is absurd. Ancient Theosophists claimed, and so do the modern, that the infinite cannot be known by the finite — i.e., sensed by the finite Self — but that the divine essence could be communicated to the higher Spiritual Self in a state of ecstasy. This condition can hardly be attained, like hypnotism, by "physical and chemical means."

Unlike Theosophists (whose first objective was "to form the nucleus of a Universal Brotherhood of Humanity without distinction of race, colour, or creed"), "The Thule Society preached Aryan supremacy and acted to achieve it. It provides the final link between occult racial theories and the racial ideology of Hitler, who skewed the fundamental principles of and understandings for sociological and economic control by the emerging Nazi party."

Krishnamurti

In 1909, C.W. Leadbeater, one of the leaders of this movement, proclaimed J. Krishnamurti, an adolescent Hindu boy, as the vehicle for a new indwelling of the Maitreya. Krishnamurti's family had relocated to live on the site of the Theosophical Society headquarters in Adyar India in January 1909, a time when Annie Besant was the head of the organization in India.

By 1925 J. Krishnamurti had begun his movement away from the organization, and in 1931 he disavowed his status and left the Theosophical Society altogether. He spent the rest of his life as an independent spiritual teacher, though he remained on friendly terms with some individuals of the Theosophical Society. Leadbeater was not among these: Krishnamurti much later described him as "an evil man."

Helena Blavatsky

Helena Blavatsky, (born as Helena von Hahn 12 August [O.S. 31 July] 1831, Yekaterinoslav, Yekaterinoslav, Russian Empire (today Dnipropetrovsk, Ukraine) – died 8 May, 1891, London), was a founder of Theosophy and the Theosophical Society.

Biography

Family: Her parents were Colonel Peter von Hahn of the ancient von Hahn family of German nobility (German: *uradel*) from Basedow (Mecklenburg) and Helena Fadeyeva, the author, under the pen-name "Zeneida R-va", of a dozen novels. Described by Belinsky as the "Russian George Sand", she died at the age of 28, when Helena was eleven. Helena's sister Vera Zhelikhovsky was a writer of occult/fantastic fiction. Helena's first cousin was Sergei Witte, who was Russian Minister, and then Prime Minister in the reign of Tsar Nicholas II. In his memoirs, Count Witte recalls his encounters with Helena.

Helena's maternal grandparents were Andrey Mikhailovich Fadeyev, Governor of Saratov, later of Tbilisi, and his wife Princess Helene Dolgoruki prominent figures of the age of Russian enlightenment. Helena grew up amid a culture rich in spirituality and traditional Russian mythologies, which introduced her to the realm of the supernatural. Helena's great-grand nephew Boris de Zirkoff was an active member of the Theosophical Society and editor of the Blavatsky Collected Writings; her great-grand niece, also Helena (b. 1935), lives in Moscow and her resemblance to HPB is striking.

First Marriage

She was married four weeks before she turned seventeen, on July 7, 1848, to the forty-year old Nikifor (also Nicephor) Vassilievich Blavatsky, vice-governor of Erivan. After three unhappy months, she stole a horse and escaped back over the mountains to her grandfather in Tiflis. Her grandfather decided that she should be shipped off immediately to her father, who was retired and living near Saint Petersburg. Although her father travelled two thousand miles to meet her at Odessa, she was not there. She had missed the steamer, and sailed away with the skipper of an English bark bound for Istanbul. According to her account, they never consummated their marriage, and she remained a virgin her entire life.

Wandering Years

According to her own story as told to a later biographer, she spent the years 1848 to 1858 travelling the world, and is said to have visited Egypt, France, Canada (Quebec), England, South America, Germany, Mexico, India, Greece and especially Tibet to study for two years with the men she called Brothers. She claimed to have become Buddhist while in Sri Lanka and to have been initiated in Tibet. She returned to Russia in 1858 and went first to see her sister Vera, a young widow living in Rugodevo, a village which she had inherited from her husband.

Agardi Metrovitch

About this time, she met and left with Agardi Metrovich, an Italian opera singer. While unconfirmed gossip of that time referred about a child named Yuri, whom she loved dearly, she clarified it in writing that Yuri was a child of her friends the Metroviches. To balance this statement, Count Witte, her first cousin on her mother's side, stated in his memoirs (as quoted by G. Williams), that her father read aloud a letter in which Metrovich signed himself as "your affectionate grandson". This is evidence that Metrovich considered himself Helena's husband at this point. Yuri died at the age of five, and Blavatsky said that she ceased to believe in the Russian Orthodox God at this point.

Two different versions of how Agardi died are extant. In one, G. Williams states that Agardi had been taken sick with a fever and delirium in Ramleh, and that he died in bed on April 19, 1870. In the second version, while bound for Cairo on a boat, the *Evmonia*, in 1871, an explosion claimed Agardi's life, and Blavatsky continued on to Cairo alone. During her stay in Cairo in the early 1870s, Blavatsky established herself as a medium, and began to hold seances.

Another unfounded account is that while in Cairo she formed the *Societe Spirite* for occult phenomena with Emma Cutting (later Emma Coulomb), which is said to have closed after dissatisfied customers complained of fraudulent activities.

To New York

It was in 1873 that she emigrated to New York City. Impressing people with her professed psychic abilities, she was spurred on to continue her mediumship. Mediumship (among other psychical and spiritual sciences of the time), based upon the belief known as Spiritualism which began at Rochester, NY, was a widely popular and fast-spreading field upon which Blavatsky based her career.

Throughout her career she claimed to have demonstrated physical and mental psychic feats which included levitation, clairvoyance, out-of-body projection, telepathy, and clairaudience. Another claim of hers was materialization, that is, producing physical objects out of nothing, though in general, her interests were more in the area of 'theory' and 'laws' rather than demonstration. In 1874 at the farm of the Eddy Brothers, Helena met Henry Steel Olcott, a lawyer, agricultural expert, and journalist who covered the Spiritualist phenomenon. Soon they were working together in the "Lamasery" (alternate spelling: "Lamastery") where her book *Isis Unveiled* was written.

Blavatsky married her second husband, Michael C. Betanelly on April 3, 1875 in New York City. She separated from Betanelly after a few months, and their divorce was legalized on May 25, 1878. On July 8, 1878, she became a naturalized citizen of the United States, but after leaving for India later that year she never returned to the country.

Foundation of Theosophical Society

Living in New York City, she helped found the Theosophical Society in September 1875, with Henry Steel Olcott, William Quan Judge and others.

Blavatsky wrote that all religions were both true in their inner teachings and problematic or imperfect in their external conventional manifestations. Her writings connecting esoteric spiritual knowledge with new science may be considered to be the first instance of what is now called New Age thinking, "the hippy movement of the last quarter of the twentieth century".

She also lived in Philadelphia for part of 1875, where she resided at 3420 Sansom Street, now home of the White Dog Cafe. While living on Sansom Street, Madame Blavatsky became ill with an infected leg. She claimed to have undergone a "transformation" during her illness which inspired her to found the Theosophical Society. In a letter dated June 12, 1875, she described her recovery, explaining that she dismissed the doctors and surgeons who threatened amputation. She is quoted as saying "Fancy my leg going to the spirit land before me!", and had a white dog sleep across her leg by night.

To India

She had moved to India, landing at Bombay on February 16, 1879, where she first made the acquaintance of A. P. Sinnett. In his book *Occult World* he describes how she stayed at his home in Allahabad for six weeks that year, and again the following year.

Sometime around December 1880, while at a dinner party with a group including A. O. Hume and his wife, she is claimed to have been instrumental in causing the materialization of Mrs Hume's lost brooch.

By 1882 the Theosophical Society became an international organization, and it was at this time that she moved the headquarters to Adyar near Madras, India (now Chennai).

The society headquartered here for some time, but she later went to Germany for a while, in between she stayed at Ostend (July 15, 1886 – May 1, 1887) where she could easily meet her English friends. She wrote a big part of the *Secret Doctrine* in Ostend and there she claimed a revelation during an illness telling her to continue the book at any cost. Finally she went to England.

A disciple put her up in her own house in England and it was here that she lived until the end of her life.

Final Years

In August, 1890 she formed the "Inner Circle" of 12 disciples: "Countess Constance Wachtmeister, Mrs Isabel Cooper-Oakley, Miss Emily Kislingbury, Miss Laura Cooper, Mrs Annie Besant, Mrs Alice Cleather, Dr. Archibald Keightley, Herbert Coryn, Claude Wright, G. R. S. Mead, E. T. Sturdy, and Walter Old".

Suffering from Bright's disease and complications from influenza, Blavatsky died in her home at 19 Avenue Road, St. Johns Wood, London, on May 8, 1891. Her last words in regard to her work were: "Keep the link unbroken! Do not let my last incarnation be a failure." Her body was cremated at Woking on May 11; one third of her ashes were sent to Europe, one third with William Quan Judge to the United States, and one third to India where her ashes were scattered in the Ganges River. May 8 is celebrated by Theosophists, and it is called White Lotus Day.

Following Blavatsky's death, the Theosophical Society split in two, each part claiming her as its "rightful progenitor". One branch was headed by her protege, Annie Besant, and the other, the American Section, by her friend W. Q. Judge.

Controversies of Authenticity, Plagiarism, Influence, and Aryanism

Well-known and controversial during her life, Blavatsky was influential on spiritualism and related subcultures: "the western esoteric tradition has no more important figure in modern times." She wrote prolifically, publishing thousands of pages, and debate continues about her claims.

Throughout much of Blavatsky's public life, her work drew harsh criticism from some of the learned authorities of her day, who accused her of being a charlatan, an impostor, and a fraud.

In *The New York Times* Edward Hower wrote, "Theosophical writers have defended her sources vehemently. Skeptics have painted her as a great fraud."

The authenticity and originality of her writings were questioned. Blavatsky was accused of having plagiarized a number of sources, copying the texts crudely enough to misspell the more difficult words.

In his 1885 report to the Society for Psychical Research (SPR), Richard Hodgson concluded that Blavatsky was a fraud. However, in a 1986 press release to the newspapers and leading magazines in Great Britain, Canada and the USA the same SPR retracted the Hodgson report, after a re-examination of the case by the Fortean psychic Dr. Vernon Harrison, past president of The Royal Photographic Society and formerly Research Manager to Thomas De La Rue, an expert on forgery, as follows: "Madame Blavatsky, co-founder of the Theosophical Society, was unjustly condemned, new study concludes."

Blavatsky famously favoured an Aryan race and for her advocation of a superior race, based on Indian culture. Blavatsky argued that all humanity descended from seven root races, with the fifth one being the Aryan race.

Since her death, Blavatsky's work has shown its influence in the works of dictators, political leaders, new religion leaders, writers, musicians, and other public figures.

Blavatsky argued that humanity had descended from a series of "Root Races", naming the fifth root race (out of seven) the Aryan Race. She thought that the Aryans originally came from Atlantis and described the Aryan races with the following words:

"The Aryan races, for instance, now varying from dark brown, almost black, red-brown-yellow, down to the whitest creamy colour, are yet all of one and the same stock — the Fifth Root-Race — and spring from one single progenitor, (...) who is said to have lived over 18,000,000 years ago, and also 850,000 years ago — at the time of the sinking of the last remnants of the great continent of Atlantis."

Blavatsky used "Root Race" as a technical term to describe human evolution over the large time periods in her cosmology. However, she also claimed that there were modern non-Aryan peoples who were inferior to Aryans. She regularly contrasts "Aryan" with "Semitic" culture, to the detriment of the latter, asserting that Semitic peoples are an offshoot of Aryans who have become "degenerate in spirituality and perfected in materiality." She also states that some peoples are "semi-animal creatures". These latter include "the Tasmanians, a portion of the Australians and a mountain tribe in China." There are also "considerable numbers of the mixed Lemuro-Atlantean peoples produced by various crossings with such semi-human stocks — e.g., the wild men of Borneo, the Veddhas of Ceylon, classed by Prof. Flower among Aryans (!), most of the remaining Australians, Bushmen, Negritos, Andaman Islanders, etc."

Despite this, Blavatsky's admirers claim that her thinking was not connected to fascist or racialist ideas, asserting that she believed in a Universal Brotherhood of humanity and wrote that "all men have spiritually and physically the same origin" and that "mankind is essentially of one and the same essence". On the other hand, in *The Secret Doctrine*, Blavatsky states: "Verily mankind is 'of one blood,' but not of the same essence."

Blavatsky connects physical race with spiritual attributes constantly throughout her works:

"Esoteric history teaches that idols and their worship died out with the Fourth Race, until the survivors of the hybrid races of the latter (Chinamen, African Negroes, & c.) gradually brought the worship back. The Vedas countenance no idols; all the modern Hindu writings do".

"The intellectual difference between the Aryan and other civilized nations and such savages as the South Sea Islanders, is inexplicable on any other grounds. No amount of culture, nor generations of training amid civilization, could raise such human specimens as the Bushmen, the Veddhas of Ceylon, and some African tribes, to the same intellectual level as the Aryans, the Semites, and the Turanians so called. The 'sacred spark' is missing in them and it is they who are the only inferior races on the globe, now happily — owing to the wise adjustment of nature which ever works in that direction — fast dying out. Verily mankind is 'of one blood,' but not of the same essence. We are the hot-house, artificially quickened plants in nature, having in us a spark, which in them is latent".

According to Blavatsky, "the MONADS of the lowest specimens of humanity (the "narrow-brained" savage South-Sea Islander, the African, the Australian) had no Karma to work out when first born as men, as their more favoured brethren in intelligence had".

She also prophecies of the destruction of the racial "failures of nature" as the future "higher race" ascends:

"Thus will mankind, race after race, perform its appointed cycle-pilgrimage. Climates will, and have already begun, to change, each tropical year after the other dropping one sub-race, but only to beget another higher race on the ascending cycle; while a series of other less favoured groups — the failures of nature — will, like some individual men, vanish from the human family without even leaving a trace behind".

It is interesting to note that the second subrace of the Fifth or Aryan root race, the Arabian, is regarded by Theosophists as one of the Aryan subraces. It is believed by Theosophists that the Arabians, although asserted in traditional Theosophy to be of Aryan (i.e., Indo-European) ancestry, adopted the Semitic language of the people around them who had migrated earlier from Atlantis (the fifth or (original) Semite subrace of the Atlantean root race). Theosophists assert that the Jews originated as an offshoot of the Arabian subrace in what is now Yemen about 30,000 BC. They migrated first to Somalia and then later to Egypt where they lived until the time of Moses. Thus, according to the teachings of Theosophy, the Jews are part of the Aryan race.

Works

The books written by Madame Blavatsky included:

- Blavatsky, H P (1877), *Isis unveiled,* J.W. Bouton
- Blavatsky, H P (1880), *From the Caves and Jungles of Hindostan*
- Blavatskaja, Elena Petrovna (1888), *The secret doctrine*
- Blavatsky, H P (1933) [1889], *The voice of the silence*
- Blavatsky, H P (1889), *The key to theosophy*
- Blavatsky, H P (1892), *Nightmare tales,*
- Blavatsky, H P; Neff, Mary Katherine (1937),
- Blavatsky, H P; Goodrick-Clarke, Nicholas (2004), *Helena Blavatsky.*

Her many articles have been collected in the Collected Writings of H. P. Blavatsky. This series has 15 numbered volumes including the index.

Henry Steel Olcott

Colonel Henry Steel Olcott (August 2, 1832 – February 17, 1907) was an American military officer, journalist, lawyer and the co-founder and first President of the Theosophical Society.

He was the first well-known person of European ancestry to make a formal conversion to Buddhism. His subsequent actions as president of the Theosophical Society helped create a renaissance in the study of Buddhism. He is still honoured in Sri Lanka today for these efforts. He is considered a Buddhist modernist for his efforts in interpreting Buddhism through a Westernized lens.

Olcott has been called by Sri Lankans "one of the heroes in the struggle for our independence and a pioneer of the present religious, national and cultural revival." More ardent admirers have claimed that Olcott was a bodhisattva, a reincarnation of the third century B.C.E. Buddhist emperor Ashoka, and/or a reincarnation of Gautama Buddha himself.

Biographical Overview

Olcott was born in 1832 in Orange, New Jersey. Henry was the oldest son of six children born to a Presbyterian businessman Henry Wyckoff Olcott and his wife Emily Steel Olcott. As a child, Olcott lived on his father's New Jersey farm.

During his teens he attended first the College of the City of New York and then Columbia University, where he joined the St. Anthony Hall fraternity, a milieu of well-known people, until his father's business failed during 1851. Unfortunately, he had to leave the university since his father could not afford the tuition.

In 1860 he married Mary Epplee Morgan, daughter of the rector of Trinity parish, New Rochelle, New York. They had four children, two of which died in infancy. Olcott was the agricultural correspondent for the New York Tribune and The Mark Lane Express from 1858 to 1860, and he sometimes submitted newspaper articles on various other subjects. He also published a genealogy of his family that traced him back to Thomas Olcott, one of the founders of Hartford, Connecticut in 1636.

He served in the US Army during the Civil War and afterward was admitted as the Special Commissioner of the War Department in New York. He was later promoted to the rank of Colonel and transferred to the Navy Department in Washington, DC. He was well respected, and in 1865 when Abraham Lincoln was assassinated, Olcott assisted in the investigation. In 1868 he became a lawyer specializing in insurance, revenue, and fraud.

In 1874 he became aware of the seances of the Eddy brothers of Chittenden, Vermont. His aroused interest motivated Olcott to commission an article from the New York Sun, allowing him to investigate the Eddy Farms. His article was popular enough that other papers, such as the New York Daily Graphic, ran it. His 1874 publication of *People from the Other World* began with his these early articles concerning the Spiritualist movement.

In 1874, while writing this series of articles, Olcott met Helena Blavatsky when both of them visited the Eddy farm. His foundational interest in the Spiritualist movement and his budding relationship with Blavatsky helped foster his development of spiritual philosophy. Olcott official conversion to Buddhism is considered the first American Buddhists. Olcott once described his adult faith as "pure, primitive Buddhism," but his was a unique sort of Buddhism.

Olcott continued to act as a lawyer during the first few years of the establishment of the Theosophical Society, in addition to being the financial supporter of the new religious movement. In early 1875 Olcott was asked by important Spiritualists to investigate an accusation of fraud against the mediums Jenny and Nelson Holmes, who had claimed to materialize the famous spirit control Katie King (Doyle 1926: volume 1, 269-277).

Theosophical Society

From 1874 on, Olcott's spiritual growth and development with Blavatsky and other spiritual leaders would lead to the founding of the Theosophical Society.

In 1875, Olcott, Blavatsky, and others, notably William Quan Judge, formed the Theosophical Society. Olcott financially supported the earliest years of the Theosophical Society and was acting President while Blavatsky served as the Society's Secretary. In December 1878 they left New York in order to move the headquarters of the Society to India.

They landed at Bombay on February 16, 1879.. Olcott set out to experience the native country of his spiritual leader, the Buddha. The headquarters of the Society were established at Adyar, as the Theosophical Society (Adyar). While in India, Olcott strove to receive original translations of texts which had grown in popularity as a result of colonialist collections of sacred Oriental texts. His intent was to avoid the Westernized interpretations often encountered in America, and to discover the pure message of texts from the Buddhist, Hindu, and Zoroastrian religions, in order to properly educate Westerners.

Olcott's main religious interest was Buddhism, and he is commonly known for his work in Ceylon. On 16 May 1880, they arrived in Colombo, in what was then known as Ceylon, currently known as Sri Lanka. On May 25th, Olcott and Blavatsky were formally acknowledged as Buddhists, although Olcott noted that they had previously declared themselves Buddhists, while still living in America. During his time in Ceylon, Olcott strove to revive Buddhism within the region, while compiling the tenets of Buddhism for the education of Westerners. It was during this period that he wrote the *Buddhist Catechism* (1881), which is still used today.

The Theosophical Society built several Buddhist schools in Ceylon, most notably Ananda College, Dharmaraja College, Maliyadeva College, and Mahinda College. After his death, Blavatsky's protege Annie Besant became the manager of the Society.

Olcott acted as adviser to the committee appointed to design a Buddhist flag. Blavatsky eventually went to live in London where she died, but Henry stayed in India and pursued the work of the Society there. Olcott's role in the Theosophical Society would still be as President, but the induction of Annie Besant sparked a new era of the movement. Upon his death, the Society elected her to take over as President and leader of the movement.

Buddhist Catechism

The Buddhist Catechism, composed by Olcott in 1881, represents one of his most enduring contributions to the revival of Buddhism in Sri Lanka, and it remains in use there still today. The text outlines what Olcott saw to be the basic doctrines of Buddhism, including the life of the Buddha, the message of the Dharma, the role of the Sanga. The text also treats how the Buddha's message correlates with contemporary society. Olcott was considered by South Asians and others as a Buddhist revivalist.

Olcott's *Buddhist Catechism* is presented in the same format of question and answer used in the Christian Catechism. Here are a few examples from that text:

Q. Would you call a person a Buddhist who has merely been born of Buddhist parents?

A. Certainly not. A Buddhist is one who not only professes belief in the Buddha as the noblest of Teachers, in the Doctrine preached by Him, and in the brotherhood of Arhats, but practices his Precepts in daily life.

Q. What is Karma?

A. A causation operating on the moral, as well as physical and other planes. Buddhists say there is no miracle in human affairs: what a man sows that he must still reap.

Q. What other good words have been used to express the essence of Buddhism?

A. Self-culture and universal love.

Concerning the Four sights and how they impacted the Buddha:

Q: Why should these sights, so familiar to everybody, have caused him to go into the jungle?

A. We often see such signs. He had not; and they made a deep impression on his mind.

Q: Why had he not also seen them?

A: The astrologers had foretold at his birth that he would one day resign his kingdom and become a Buddha. The King, his father, not wishing to loose his son, had carefully prevented his seeing any sights that might suggest to him human misery and death. No one was allowed even to speak of such things to the Prince. He was almost like a prisoner in his lovely palaces and flower gardens. They were surrounded with high walls; and inside everything was made as beautiful as possible, so that he might not want to go and see the sorrow and distress that are in the world.

Q: Was he so kind hearted that his father feared he might really want to sacrifice himself for the world's sake?

A: Yes; he seems to have felt for all being so strong a pity and love as that.

Q. Why does ignorance cause suffering?

A. Because it makes us prize what is not worth prizing, grieve for that we should not grieve for, consider real what is not real but only illusory, and pass out lives in the pursuit of worthless objects, neglecting what is in reality most valuable.

Q. And what is that which is most valuable?

A. To know the whole secret of man's existence and destiny, so that we may estimate at no more than their actual value and this life and its relations; so that we may live in a way to insure the greatest happiness and the least suffering for our fellow-men and ourselves

Olcott's Catechism reflects a new, Protestant interpretation of traditional Buddhist tenets. As David McMahan stated, "[Olcott] allied Buddhism with scientific rationalism in implicit criticism of orthodox Christianity, but went well beyond the tenets of conventional science in extrapolating from the Romantic-and Transcendentalist-influenced 'occult sciences' of the nineteenth century."

Olcott's Science and Theosophy

The Theosophists combination of spiritualism and science to investigate the supernatural reflected the society's desire to combine of religion and reason and to produce a rationally spiritual movement. This "occult science" within the Theosophical Society was used to find the "truth" behind all of the world's major religions. Through their research, Olcott and Blavatsky concluded that Buddhism best embodied elements of what they found significant in all religions.

Olcott utilized Western scientific reasoning in his synthesis and presention of Buddhism. This is clearly seen in a chapter of the Buddhist Catechism, entitled "Buddhism and Science." Notably, his efforts represent one of the earliest attempts to combine the scientific understanding and reasoning of the West with the Buddhist religion of the East. The interrelationship he saw between Buddhism and Science paralleled his Theosophical approach to show the scientific bases for supernatural phenomena such as auras, hypnosis, and Buddhist "miracles."

Death and Legacy

Olcott was President of the Theosophical Society until his death on February 17, 1907.

Olcott Mawatha, a major street in Colombo, has been named after him. A statue of him has been built in front of Colombo Fort Railway Station. Many other schools that he helped to found or were founded in memory of him have commemorative statues in honour of his contribution to Buddhist education. He is still remembered fondly by many Sri Lankans today.

The date of his death is often remembered by Buddhist centres and Sunday schools in present-day Sri Lanka, as well as in

Theosophical communities around the globe. Olcott believed himself to be Asia's savior, the outsider hero who would sweep in at the end of the drama to save a disenchanted subcontinent from spiritual death.

The effort to revitalize Buddhism within Ceylon was successful and influenced many native Buddhist intellectuals. Ceylon was dominated by colonial power and influence at the time, and many Buddhists heard Olcott's interpretation of the Buddha's message as socially motivating and supportive of efforts to overturn colonialist efforts to suppress Buddhism and Buddhist tradition. As David McMahan wrote, "Henry Steel Olcott saw the Buddha as a figure much like the ideal liberal freethinker – someone full of 'benevolence,' 'gratitude,' and 'tolerance,' who promoted 'brotherhood among all men' as well as 'lessons in manly self-reliance'" His view of Buddha influenced Sri Lankan leaders, such as Anagarika Dharmapala.

Olcott and Anagarika Dharmapala were associates, which reflects both men's awareness of the divide between East and West-as seen in their presentation of Buddhism to the West. Olcott helped financially support the Buddhist presence at the World Parliament of Religions in Chicago, 1893. The inclusion of Buddhists in the Parliament allowed for the expansion of Buddhism within the West in general and in America specifically, leading to other Buddhist Modernist movements.

As Stephen Prothero wrote,

It was Olcott who most eloquently articulated and most obviously embodied the diverse religious and cultural traditions that shaped Protestant Buddhism, who gave the revival movement both its organizational shape and its emphasis on education-as-character-building.

The most Protestant of all early Protestant Buddhists, Olcott was the liminoid figure, the griot who because of his awkward standing betwixt and between the American Protestant grammars of his youth and the Asian Buddhist lexicon of his adulthood was able to conjure traditional Sinhalese Buddhism, Protestant modernism, metropolitan gentility, and academic Orientalism into a decidedly new creole tradition. This creole tradition Olcott then passed on to a whole generation of Sinhalese students educated in his schools.

Olcott is probably the only major contributor to the nineteenth-century Sinhalese Buddhist revival who was actually born and raised in the Protestant fold. As such, he can be credited him with influencing the start of Protestant Buddhism.

Works

- *Sorgho and Imphee, the Chinese and African sugar canes;* A. O. Moore, New York 1857
- *Outlines of the first course of Yale agricultural lectures;* C. M. Saxton, Barker & Co., New York 1860
- *Descendents of Thomas Olcott,* 1872
- *Human Spirits and Elementaries;* 1875
- *People from the other world;* American Publishing Co., Hartford 1875
- *A Buddhist catechism;* Madras 1881
- *Theosophy, Religion, and Occult Science;* New York 1885
- *Old Diary Leaves* (6 volumes)
- *The Hindu Dwaita Catechism;* 1886
- *The Golden Rules of Buddhism;* 1887
- *The kinship between Hinduism and Buddhism;* The Maha-Bodhi society, Calcutta 1893
- *The Poor Pariah;* Addison & Co., Madras 1902
- *The Life of the Buddha and its Lessons;* 1912
- *Old diary leaves, Inside the occult, the true story of Madame H. P. Blavatsky*

William Quan Judge

William Quan Judge (April 13, 1851 – March 21, 1896) was a mystic, esotericist, and occultist, and one of the founders of the original Theosophical Society. He was born in Dublin, Ireland. When he was 13 years old, his family emigrated to the United States. He became a naturalized citizen of the USA at age 21 and passed the New York state bar exam, specializing in commercial law.

Although merely a young man, he was among the seventeen people who first put the Theosophical Society together. Like H.P. Blavatsky and Henry Steel Olcott, he stayed in the organization when others left. When Olcott and Blavatsky left the United States for India, Judge stayed behind to manage the Society's work, all the while working as a lawyer.

Judge wrote theosophical articles for various theosophical magazines, and also the introductory volume, *The Ocean of Theosophy* in 1893. He became the General Secretary of the American Section of the Theosophical Society in 1884, with Abner Doubleday as President.

After Blavatsky died in 1891, Judge became involved in a dispute with Olcott and Annie Besant over his allegedly forging letters from the Mahatmas. As a result, he ended his association with Olcott and Besant during 1895 and took most of the Society's American Section with him. He managed his new organization for about a year until his death in New York, whereupon Katherine Tingley became manager. The organization originating from the faction of Olcott and Besant is based nowadays in India and known as the Theosophical Society-Adyar, while the organization managed by Judge is known nowadays simply as the Theosophical Society, but often with the specification, "international headquarters, Pasadena, California". In 1898, Ernest Temple Hargrove, who had initially supported Tingley, left with other members to form the Theosophical Society in America (Hargrove) Branch. Other new organizations fissioned from his, including the Temple of the People (whose library bears his name) during 1898 and the United Lodge of Theosophists or ULT during 1909.

Annie Besant

Annie Besant was a prominent Theosophist, women's rights activist, writer and orator and supporter of Irish and Indian self rule.

In 1873 she married Frank Besant and moved to London where she became a prominent speaker for the National Secular Society and writer and a close friend of Charles Bradlaugh. In 1877 they were prosecuted for publishing a book by birth control campaigner Charles Knowlton. The scandal made them famous and Bradlaugh was elected MP for Northampton in 1880.

Annie became involved with Union organisers including the Bloody Sunday riot and the London matchgirls strike of 1888 and a leading speaker for the Fabian Society and the (Marxist) Social Democratic Federation and was elected to the London School

Board for Tower Hamlets, topping the poll even though few women were qualified to vote at that time.

In 1890 Annie Besant met Helena Blavatsky and over the next few years her interest in Theosophy grew and her interest in left wing politics waned. She travelled to India and in 1898 helped establish the Central Hindu College in India.

In 1902 she established the International Order of Co-Freemasonry in England and over the next few years established lodges in many parts of the British Empire.

In 1908 Annie Besant became President of the Theosophical Society and began to steer the society away from Buddhism and towards Hinduism. She also became involved in politics in India, joining the Indian National Congress. When war broke out in Europe in 1914 she helped launch the Home Rule League to campaign for democracy in India and dominion status within the Empire which culminated in her election as president of the India National Congress in late 1917. After the war she continued to campaign for Indian independence until her death in 1933.

Early Life

Annie Wood was born in 1847 in London into a middle-class family of Irish origin. She was always proud of being Irish and supported the cause of Irish self-rule throughout her adult life. Her father died when she was five years old, leaving the family almost penniless. Her mother supported the family by running a boarding house for boys at Harrow. However, she was unable to support Annie and persuaded her friend Ellen Marryat to care for her. Marryat made sure that Annie had a good education. She was given a strong sense of duty to society and an equally strong sense of what independent women could achieve. As a young woman, she was also able to travel widely in Europe. There she acquired a taste for Catholic colour and ceremony that never left her.

In 1867, at age nineteen she married 26-year-old clergyman Frank Besant, younger brother of Walter Besant. He was an evangelical Anglican clergyman who seemed to share many of her concerns. Soon Frank became vicar of Sibsey in Lincolnshire. Annie moved to Sibsey with her husband, and within a few years they had two children: Digby and Mabel. The marriage was, however, a disaster. The first conflict came over money and Annie's independence. Annie wrote short stories, books for children and articles. As married women did not have the legal right to own property, Frank was able to take all the money she earned. Politics further divided the couple. Annie began to support farm workers who were fighting to unionise and to win better conditions. Frank was a Tory and sided with the landlords and farmers. The tension came to a head when Annie refused to attend Communion. She left him and returned to London. They were legally separated and Annie took her daughter with her.

Annie began to question her own faith. She turned to leading churchmen for advice. She even went to see Edward Bouverie Pusey, leader of the Catholic wing of the Church of England. He simply told her she had read too many books. Annie returned to Frank to make one last effort to repair the marriage. It proved useless. She finally left for London. Divorce was unthinkable for Frank, and was not really within the reach of even middle-class people. Annie was to remain Mrs Besant for the rest of her life. At first, she was able to keep contact with both children and to have Mabel live with her. She got a small allowance from Frank. Her husband was given sole custody of their two children.

Birkbeck

For a time she undertook part-time study at the Birkbeck Literary and Scientific Institution, where her religious and political activities were to cause alarm. At one point the Institution's governors sought to withhold the publication of her exam results.

Reformer and Secularist

She fought for the causes she thought were right, starting with freedom of thought, women's rights, secularism (she was a leading member of the National Secular Society alongside Charles Bradlaugh), birth control, Fabian socialism and workers' rights.

Once free of Frank Besant and exposed to new currents of thought, Annie began to question not only her long-held religious beliefs but also the whole of conventional thinking. She began to write attacks on the churches and the way they controlled people's lives. In particular she attacked the status of the Church of England as a state-sponsored faith.

Soon she was earning a small weekly wage by writing a column for the National Reformer, the newspaper of the National Secular Society. The Society stood for a secular state: an end to the special status of Christianity. The Society allowed her to act as one of its public speakers. Public lectures were very popular entertainment in Victorian times. Annie was a brilliant speaker, and was soon in great demand. Using the railway, she criss-crossed the country, speaking on all of the most important issues of the day, always demanding improvement, reform and freedom.

For many years Annie was a friend of the Society's leader, Charles Bradlaugh. It seems that they were never lovers, but their friendship was very close. Bradlaugh, a former seaman, had long been separated from his wife. Annie lived with Bradlaugh and his daughters, and they worked together on many issues.

Bradlaugh was an atheist and a republican. He was working to get himself elected as MP for Northampton to gain a better platform for his ideas.

Besant and Bradlaugh became household names in 1877 when they published a book by the American birth-control campaigner Charles Knowlton. It claimed that working-class families could never be happy until they were able to decide how many children they wanted. It suggested ways to limit the size of their families. The Knowlton book caused great offence to the Churches, but Annie and Bradlaugh proclaimed in the National Reformer: "We intend to publish nothing we do not think we can morally defend. All that we publish we shall defend."

The pair were arrested and put on trial for publishing the Knowlton book. They were found guilty, but released pending appeal. As well as great opposition, Annie and Bradlaugh also received a great deal of support in the Liberal press. Arguments raged back and forth in the letters and comment columns as well as in the courtroom. For a time, it looked as though they would be sent to prison. The case was thrown out finally only on a technical point: the charges had not been properly drawn up.

The scandal lost Annie her children. Frank was able to persuade the court that she was unfit to look after them, and they were handed over to him permanently.

Bradlaugh's political prospects were not damaged by the Knowlton scandal. He got himself into Parliament at last in 1881. Because of his atheism, he refused to swear the oath of loyalty. Although many Christians were shocked by Bradlaugh, others (like the Liberal leader Gladstone) spoke up for freedom of belief.

It took more than six years before the whole issue was sorted out (in Bradlaugh's favour) after a series of by-elections and court appearances.

Meanwhile Besant built close contacts with the Irish Home Rulers and gave them support in her newspaper columns. These were crucial years, in which the Irish nationalists were forming an alliance with Liberals and Radicals. Annie met the leaders of the movement. In particular, she got to know Michael Davitt, who wanted to mobilise the Irish peasantry through a Land War: a direct struggle against the landowners. She spoke and wrote in favour of Davitt and his Land League many times over the coming decades.

However, Bradlaugh's parliamentary work gradually alienated Annie. Women had no part in parliamentary politics. Annie was searching for a real political outlet: politics where her skills as a speaker, writer and organiser could do some real good.

Socialist

For Annie, politics, friendship and love were always closely intertwined. Her decision in favour of Socialism came about through a close relationship with George Bernard Shaw, a struggling young Irish author living in London, and a leading light of the Fabian Society. Annie was impressed by his work and grew very close to him too in the early 1880s. It was Annie who made the first move, by inviting Shaw to live with her. This he refused, but it was Shaw who sponsored Annie to join the Fabian Society. In its early days, the Society was a gathering of people exploring spiritual, rather than political, alternatives to the capitalist system.

Annie now began to write for the Fabians. This new commitment-and her relationship with Shaw-deepened the split between Annie and Bradlaugh, who was an individualist and opposed to Socialism of any sort. While he would defend free speech at any cost, he was very cautious about encouraging working-class militancy.

Unemployment was a central issue of the time, and in 1887 some of the London unemployed started to hold protests in Trafalgar Square. Annie agreed to appear as a speaker at a meeting on 13 November. The police tried to stop the assembly. Fighting broke out, and troops were called. Many were hurt, one man died, and hundreds were arrested. Annie offered herself for arrest, but the police refused to take the bait.

The events created a great sensation, and became known as Bloody Sunday. Annie was widely blamed-or credited-for it. She threw herself into organising legal aid for the jailed workers and support for their families. Bradlaugh finally broke with her because he felt she should have asked his advice before going ahead with the meeting.

Socialists saw the trade unions as the first real signs of working people's ability to organise and fight for themselves. Until now, trade unions had been for skilled workers-men with a craft that might take years to acquire and which gave them at least a little security. The Socialists wanted to bring both unskilled men and women into unions to fight for better pay and conditions.

Her most notable victory in this period was perhaps her involvement in the London matchgirls strike of 1888. Annie was drawn into this first really important battle of the "New Unionism" by Herbert Burrows, a young socialist with whom she was for a time in love. He had made contact with workers at Bryant and May's match factory in Bow, London, who were mainly young women. They were very poorly paid. They were also prey to horrendous industrial illnesses, like the bone-rotting Phossy jaw, which was caused by the chemicals used in match manufacture. Some of the match workers asked for help from Burrows and Annie in setting up a union.

Annie met the women and set up a committee, which led the women into a strike for better pay and conditions. The action won enormous public support. Annie led demonstrations by "match-girls". They were cheered in the streets, and prominent churchmen wrote in their support. In just over a week they forced the firm to improve pay and conditions. Annie then helped them to set up a proper union and a social centre.

At the time, the matchstick industry was an immensely powerful lobby, since electric light was not yet widely available, and matches were essential for lighting candles, oil lamps, gas lights and so on. (Only a few years earlier in 1872, lobbyists from the match industry had persuaded the British government to change its planned tax policy.) Besant's campaign was the first time anyone had successfully challenged the match manufacturers on a major issue, and was seen as a landmark victory of the early years of British Socialism.

Marxist

During 1884, Annie had developed a very close friendship with Edward Aveling, a young socialist teacher, who lived in her house for a time. Aveling was a scholarly figure and it was he who translated the important works of Marx into English for the first time. Annie seems to have fallen in love with Aveling, but it is not clear that he felt the same way. He was certainly a great influence on her thinking, and she was a great support to his work. However, Aveling left Annie to live with Eleanor Marx, daughter of Karl Marx. This led to permanent ill-feeling between Annie and Eleanor and probably pushed Annie towards the rival Fabians at that time. Aveling and Eleanor joined the Marxist SDF but they distrusted its leader, Henry Hyndman. Soon they left the SDF to join the Socialist League, a small Marxist splinter group which formed around the artist William Morris.

It seems that Morris played a large part in converting Annie to Marxism, but it was to the SDF, not his Socialist League, that she turned in 1888. She remained a member for a number of years and became one of its best speakers. Strangely, she was still a member of the Fabian Society. Neither she nor anyone else seemed to think the two movements completely incompatible at the time.

Soon after joining the Marxists, Annie stood for election to the London School Board. Because women were not able to take part in parliamentary politics, it is often thought that they did not have the vote until 1918. In fact, women householders had been brought into the local electorate in 1881, and soon began to make a mark in local politics.

Annie drove about with a red ribbon in her hair, speaking at noisy meetings. "No more hungry children," her manifesto proclaimed. She made clear that her Socialism had a feminist side too: "I ask the electors to vote for me, and the non-electors to work for me because women are wanted on the Board and there are too few women candidates." Astonishingly, Annie came out on top of the poll in Tower Hamlets, with over 15,000 votes. Annie wrote in the National Reformer: "Ten years ago, under a cruel law, Christian bigotry robbed me of my little child. Now the care of the 763,680 children of London is placed partly in my hands."

Annie was also closely involved in the struggle for the "Dockers' Tanner". The dockers were poorly paid for hard and dangerous work. They were casual labourers, only taken on for one day at a time. Ben Tillett set up a union for dockers. Annie was crucial in this. She helped Tillett to draw up the union's rules and played an important part in the meetings and agitation which built up the organisation. Tillett led the dockers in a fight for better wages: sixpence an hour. Annie spoke for the dockers at public meetings and on street corners. Like the match-girls, the dockers won a lot of public support for their struggle. Even Cardinal Manning, the head of the Roman Catholic Church in England, came out on their side. After a bitter strike, the "dockers' tanner" was won.

Co-Freemasonry

Given Annie Besant's activity in pursuing the rights of women, humanitarian causes, the mysteries and occult teachings, her interest in freemasonry and subsequent leadership and activism comes as no surprise. She pursued freemasonry with equal vigour when it was mentioned to her that there was a masonry that "accepted women as well as men". She saw freemasonry, in particular co-freemasonry, as an extension of her interest in the rights of women and the greater brotherhood of man and saw co-freemasonry as a "movement which practised true brotherhood, in which women and men worked side by side for the perfecting of humanity. She immediately wanted to be admitted to this organisation", known now as The International Order of Co-Freemasonry, Le Droit Humain.

The link was made in 1902 by Francesca Arundale, who accompanied Annie Besant to Paris, along with six friends. "They were all initiated, passed and raised into the first three degrees and Annie returned to England, bearing a Charter and founded there the first Lodge of International Mixed Masonry, Le Droit Humain."

"In a very short time, Sister Besant founded new lodges: three in London, three in the south of England, three in the North and North-West; she even organised one in Scotland." Travelling in 1904 with her sisters and brothers she met in Holland, other brethren of a male obedience, who, being interested, collaborated in further expansion of Le Droit Humain. "Annie continued to work with such ardour that soon new lodges were formed Great

Britain, South America, Canada, India, Ceylon, Australia and New Zealand. The lodges in all these countries were united under the name of the British Federation." Annie Besant, therefore not only founded the British Federation of Le Droit Humain, of which she was eventually the Most Puissant Grand Commander, she was a major influence in the international growth of the Order-a truly committed freemason and an extraordinary person.

Theosophist

Besant was a prolific writer and a powerful orator. In 1889, she was asked to write a review for the *Pall Mall Gazette* on *The Secret Doctrine*, a book by H.P. Blavatsky. After reading it, she sought an interview with its author, meeting Blavatsky in Paris. In this way she was converted to Theosophy. Annie's intellectual journey had always involved a spiritual dimension, a quest for transformation of the whole person. As her interest in Theosophy deepened, she allowed her membership of the Fabian Society to lapse (1890) and broke her links with the Marxists. When Blavatsky died in 1891, Annie was left as one of the leading figures in Theosophy. Her most important public commitment to the faith came in 1893, when she went to present it at the Chicago World Fair.

Soon after becoming a member of the Theosophical Society she went to India for the first time (in 1893). After a dispute in which William Quan Judge, leader of the American section, was accused of falsifying letters from the Masters, the American section split away. The remainder of the Society was then led by Henry Steel Olcott and Besant and is today based in Chennai, India, and is known as the Theosophical Society Adyar. Thereafter she devoted much of her energy not only to the Society, but also to India's freedom and progress. Besant Nagar, a neighbourhood near the Theosophical Society in Chennai, is named in her honour.

President of Theosophical Society

She first met clairvoyant theosophist Charles Webster Leadbeater in London in April 1894. They became close co-workers in the theosophical movement and would remain so for the rest of their lives. Besant became clairvoyant in the following year. In a letter dated 25 August 1895 to Francisca Arundale, Leadbeater narrates how Besant became clairvoyant. Together they would investigate the universe, matter, thought-forms and the history of mankind through clairvoyance, and would co-author several books. In 1906 Leadbeater suddenly became the centre of controversy when it emerged that he was sleeping with young boys and engaging in mutual masturbation with them – Leadbeater explained that he had been offering them advice and guidance in order to keep them from sleeping with women. He was forced to resign from the Theosophical Society over this in 1906, but the next year Annie Besant became President of the Society and in 1908 he was taken back into the fold on her insistence. Leadbeater went on to face many more accusations of improper relations with boys, but Besant never deserted him.

Up until Besant's presidency, the society had as one of its foci Theravada Buddhism and the island of Ceylon, where Henry Olcott did the majority of his useful work. Under Besant's leadership there was a decisive turn away from this and a refocusing of their activities on "The Aryavarta", as she called central India. Besant actively courted Hindu opinion more than former Theosophical leaders. This was a clear reversal of policy from Blavatsky and Olcott's very public conversion to Buddhism in Ceylon, and their promotion of Buddhist revival activities on the subcontinent.

Annie set up a new school for boys at Varanasi: the Central Hindu College. Its aim was to build a new leadership for India. The boys lived like monks.

They spent 90 minutes a day in prayer and studied the Hindu scriptures, but they also studied modern science. It took 3 years to raise the money for the CHC. Most of the money came from Indian princes. In April 1911, Annie and Pandit Madan Mohan Malaviya met and decided to unite their forces and work for a common Hindu University at Varanasi. Annie and fellow trustees of the Central Hindu College also agreed to Government of India's precondition that the college should become a part of the new University. The Banaras Hindu University started functioning from 1 October 1917 with the Central Hindu College as its first constituent college.

As early as 1889, Blavatsky had told a group of Theosophical students that the real purpose of establishing the Society was to prepare humanity for the reception of the World Teacher when he appeared again on earth. This was repeated again more publicly by Besant in 1896, five years after Blavatsky's death.

Krishnamurti

Soon after Besant's inheritance of the presidency, in 1909, Leadbeater discovered Jiddu Krishnamurti on the private beach that was attached to the society's headquarters at Adyar. Krishnamurti had been living there with his father and brother for a few months prior to this. This discovery started years of upheaval in the Theosophical Society in Adyar, as the boy was proposed as the incarnate vessel for the Christ. Jiddu Krishnamurti and his brother Nitya were brought up by Theosophists from that moment on, with a subsequent lawsuit filed by his father for regaining custody of his children that was denied. Krishnamurti and Besant developed a close bond and he thereafter addressed Besant as 'amma' or mother.

Eventually, in 1929, Krishnamurti ended up disbanding the Order of the Star of the East, which had been founded to support him and of which he had been made the leader. However, she was concerned for his well being and purchased 6 acres (24,000 m) of land near the Theosophical Society headquarters which later became the headquarters of the Krishnamurti Foundation in India.

The Home Rule Movement

Along with her theosophical activities, Annie continued to participate in concrete political struggles. She had joined the Indian National Congress. As the name suggested, this was originally a debating body, which met each year to consider resolutions on political issues. Mostly it demanded more of a say for middle-class Indians in British Indian government. It had not yet developed into a permanent mass movement with local organisation. About this time she lost her clairvoyance, and co-worker C.W. Leadbeater felt called to move to Sydney, Australia.

In 1914 war broke out in Europe. Britain needed the support of its empire in the fight against Germany. Annie said: "England's need is India's opportunity," a clear echo of an Irish nationalist slogan. As editor of a newspaper called New India, she attacked the (British) government of India and called for clear and decisive moves towards self-rule. As with Ireland, the government refused to discuss any changes while the war lasted.

In 1916 Annie launched the Home Rule League, once again modeling demands for India on Irish models. For the first time India had a political party to fight for change. Unlike the Congress itself, the League worked all year round. It built a strong structure of local branches, enabling it to mobiiise demonstrations, public meetings and agitations. In June 1917 Annie was arrested and interned at a hill station. She flew a red and green flag in the garden to show her defiance. Congress and the Muslim League together threatened to launch protests if she were not set free. Annie's arrest had created a focus for protest, giving those who wanted long-term independence for India a chance to work together for a simple, achievable goal.

The government was forced to give way and to make vague but significant concessions. It was announced that the ultimate aim of British rule was Indian self-government, and moves in that direction were promised. Annie was freed in September to a tremendous welcome from crowds all over India. In December she took over as President of Congress for a year. It was perhaps the greatest honour she received in her lifetime.

After the war, there could be no going back. A new leadership emerged around Mohandas K. Gandhi-one of those who had written to demand Annie's release. He was a lawyer who had returned from leading Asians in a peaceful struggle against racism in South Africa. Jawaharlal Nehru, Gandhi's closest collaborator, had been educated by a Theosophist tutor.

The new leadership too was committed to action that was both militant and nonviolent, but there were differences between them and Annie. Despite her past, she was not happy with their socialist leanings.

Until the end of her life, however, she continued to campaign for India's independence, not only in India but also on speaking tours of Britain. In her own version of Indian dress, Mrs Besant remained a striking presence on speakers' platforms. She produced a torrent of letters and articles demanding independence.

Later Years

She tried to accommodate Krishnamurti's views into her life, but never really succeeded. The two remained friends, however, until the end of her life. Annie Besant died in 1933 and was survived by her daughter, Mabel. After her death, her colleagues, J. Krishnamurti, Aldous Huxley, Dr. Guido Ferrando, and Rosalind Rajagopal, built Happy Valley School, now renamed Besant Hill School in her honour.

Annie Besant's Descendants

The family history onward from the era in which Annie Besant lived became quite fragmented by the late 1940s. A number of Annie Besant's descendants have been traced in detail from her son Arthur Digby's side. One of Arthur Digby's daughters was Sylvia Besant, who married Commander Clem Lewis in the 1920s. They had a daughter, Kathleen Mary, born in 1934, who was given away for adoption within three weeks of the birth and had the new name of Lavinia Pollock. Lavinia married Frank Castle in 1953 and raised a family of five (Besant's great-great grandchildren)-James, Richard, David, Fiona and Andrew Castle-the last and youngest sibling being a former British professional tennis player and now television presenter and personality.

Selected Works

- *The Political Status of Women* (1874)
- *My Path to Atheism* (1877)
- *The Law Of Population* (1877)
- *Marriage, As It Was, As It Is, And As It Should Be: A Plea For Reform* (1878)
- *Autobiographical Sketches* (1885)
- "Why I became a Theosophist" (1889)
- *The Ancient Wisdom* (1898)
- *Thought Forms* (1901)
- *Bhagavad Gita* (translation) (1905)
- *Introduction to Yoga* (1908)
- *Australian Lectures* (1908)
- *Occult Chemistry*
- *The Doctrine of the Heart* (1920)
- *The Case for India by Annie Wood Besant* at Project Gutenberg The Presidential Address Delivered by Annie Besant at the Thirty-Second Indian National Congress Held at Calcutta 26 December 1917
- Besant, Annie. *Man and his bodies*. Theosophical Publishing House, London, 1911.
- Beasant, Annie and Blavatsky, H P-"Memory and Its Nature", Theosophical Publishing House, Madras, ca 1935.

4

A History of Child Marriage in India

Introduction: The Reform Movement 1860-1886

In India during the 1860's, marriage meant girls getting married below 8 or 9 years old. Socio-reform religious movements such as the Brahmo Samaj and the Arya Samaj pioneered work against child marriage. Late in the 1860's some success was met when the Indian Penal Code prohibited intercourse with a wife who had not reached ten years of age.

Nevertheless, it wasn't until 1880 that child marriage as a problem became a public issue in India during the debate on the Age of Consent Bill. Towards the end of the debate a child wife of eleven years old, Named Phulmani, died when her husband raped her. More than 500 women doctors sent a memorandum to the Viceroy requesting him to stop marriage of girls below 14 years of age. The resulting bill compromised at 12 years old.

On August 15, 1884 a Parsee reformist, Behramji Malabari, circulated two notes which highlighted the evils of child marriage and enforced widowhood. The Honourable J. Gibbs added his comments to Malabari's notes saying that, "Young mothers become stunted in growth, and often become invalids for life, while children were too often pony and weak." Kadhavdas added to the list of evils, "Early marriage is a great obstacle in the progress of female education."

Shortly thereafter, in 1886 the first petition against 'Hindu Infant Marriage' was proposed to the Government by the natives of Meerut. It was finally passed in 1927. It declared that no marriage would be valid unless the girl had completed her twelfth year. In spite of laws prohibiting the practice, child marriage continues to be a widespread custom in India. After looking at the debate which raged in the 1880's, I look at Hindu scriptures and their mandates for the practice.

The Malabari Letters-1887

Between 1884 and 1887 Behramji Malabari collected opinions for and against infant marriage and enforced widowhood from "representative Hindu gentlemen and official and other authorities." The "Hindu gentlemen" were mostly selected from Brahmins educated in English universities. The resultant letters, dedicated to the Duke and Duchess of Connaught were published in the Voice of India. Malabari argued that infant marriage was "a practice more evil than infanticide." His arguments against infant marriage can be summarized as a too early consummation of the nuptial troth, breaking down the constitutions and the ushering in of disease, the birth of sick children, the necessity of feeding too many mouths, poverty and dependence, and a disorganized household leading perhaps to sin.

A response by Ramanujchari's typifies the reformer's view of child marriage, an evil which he thought that even the reformers were unaware, ".the practice of the selling of girls by their parents has become so rife in these parts of the country that girls are disposed of in marriage to the highest bidders like goods at an auction sale. Girls are married, as a rule, before they attain their 8th or 9th birthday-an age when they are utterly incompetent to comprehend the contract they enter into." The authors included in Malabari's publication nearly universally condemned infant marriage as a "great physical and moral evil." Infant marriage was considered "one of two evils that, if not remedied in time, are sure to destroy the vitality of the whole native community of India." Infant marriage was not confined to the Hindus, but was also "practiced by Parsis and Mohamedans."

Two related issues were being discussed, child marriage and infant widowhood. Shirgaonkar, not so interested in child marriage, objected to child widowhood. He said, "I condemn infant marriages not because I think that they afterwards prove unhappy-which statement I will not accept unsupported by statistics-but because such marriages increase infant widows"

How child marriage works to increase infant widows and their misery is hinted at by Colonel E.W. West, "I have known many cases of old men marrying girls not yet emerged from childhood and it needs but little knowledge of human nature to realize the misery during the husband's lifetime, and of Hindu ways to realize the misery after his death, of the girl."

Many authors felt that government action was a necessity: "The reason for this is that for the last 2000 years the Hindus have lost the power of refection, and even that of following or imitating what is good.. The masses still grope in darkness. They are bound by their customs and the foolish teachings of their priests."

Of the eighty-seven respondents, only a few suggested that the evil wasn't as great as Malabari considered it to be. For example, Dr. Rajendralala Mitra from Calcutta said, "I have also yet to learn that disparity in age of marriage does more harm in India than it does in Europe."

Mozoomdar objected and offered some statistics, arguing that the problem of infant widowhood wasn't nearly so serious as propounded. According to the census there were only 28,369 widows between the ages of 14 and 19 out of twenty million total widows in India.

More than a few of the respondents objected to Malabari's proposal for prohibition of child marriage. Taleyar Khan from Baroda argued that, "Our English ideas actually jar with their (the Hindus) sympathies, the antipathies, and all important affections of their heart and mind."

He goes on to explain that 'marriage seasons' can be at intervals as many as twelve years apart. In the case cited a girl of four couldn't be married until she was sixteen, "A horrible purgatory, according to the Shastras, for the parents to keep her unmarried at that age."

He continues by saying, "It is a wonder how this nation has succeeded for ages in preserving such a marked harmony of their homes. If we have weakly children the homes are happy, contented, well regulated and economical."

Reformers Ignored Hindu Scriptures and Epics

Malabari claims that, "No Shastra enforces marriage proper on a girl under 12 years of age, when presumably the boy must be between 15 and 20." That being Malabari's only comment on the religious basis of the nearly universal custom of child marriage he concluded, "So much as to the social or so-called religious aspect of the practice."

The writers who supported Malabari, with one or two exceptions, also denied the religious-spiritual background of infant marriage. Lakshmiram, for example, said, "There is one foolish text, I know, which enjoins the marriage of every girl before she is eleven years old."

One exception to this denial is found in the letter of Keshaveal Madhavadas who says, "The Hindu law gives clear injunction not to keep a girl unmarried beyond 12 years old."

While it does appear to be arguable that the Vedic literature, written before 400 B.C. advised that children not be married before puberty, in the following compilation I show that the British and their Brahmin supporters ignored the long Hindu scriptural tradition of child marriage during Vedic times and after the fourth century BC. The citations also help us understand the point of view of a civilization that allowed for child marriage.

Child Marriage Before the Fourth Century B.C.

The Vedic mantras, such as the Rigveda mentioned that a girl could be married only when she was fully developed both physically and mentally and that she was to be fully developed physically before leaving her father's home. Men were advised to marry a girl with a fully developed body. One hymn mentions that a female should be married only "when she is not a child". One modern commentator, Sharma who wrote in 1993, argues that during the time of the great epics, the Ramayana and Mahabharata, the girls "used to be grown up at the time of marriage".

Sharma's reasoning is that, "In the Ramayana it is described that the brides came to Ayodhya and after paying due respect to the elders lived merrily with their husbands in seclusion which presupposes post-puberty marriages." Sharma also argues that the marriage rituals described in the Grihyasutras, the Baudhayana presuppose that the marriageable age was after puberty. The consummation of the marriage could take place directly after the marriage ceremonies or a few days afterwards. "Since consummation couldn't possibly take place before puberty," goes Sharma's reasoning, the bride must have reached maturity. It sounds as if Sharma considers pre-pubescent girls as being physically incapable of having intercourse and therefore not marriageable.

Malabari, more than century before Sharma, discussed the ability of pre-pubertal girls to consummate marriage willingly when he wrote A.O. Hume, "Mr. Hume is informed that consummation is deferred in many cases. Not so to my knowledge.it takes but little knowledge of human nature to see that infant marriage super-induces precocious development in the case of the boy. In the case of the girl it is worse, and almost all circumstances conspire to make her a willing accessory to what, on public grounds, I am constrained to denounce as a crime." According to Malabari, pre-pubescent sexual relationships while both common and consensual, were still a "crime".

Also suggestive that the Rigveda allowed for child marriage is a hymn that mentions that Indra gave a child-wife named Vrichaya to the old man Kashivan. Furthermore, in the epic Aranyakanda, the godess Sita is supposed to have told Ravana that when she was kidnapped by him, she was eighteen and her husband twenty five and that they had spent twelve years at Ayodhya. From this commentary, the age of Sita is known to have been six years old at the day of her marriage. Sharma (1993) argued this is not true because, "the Ramayana was recast many times and the verses in question are from later editions." He says the same concerning the Uttararamacharita Bhavabhuti which described Sita as a child bride playing at the knee of her mother-in-law.

Only in the Mahabharta is there a unequivocable injunction that a girl should be married after puberty. In fact this work decrees that she should wait three years after puberty to obtain a husband.

The Kamasutra on Courtship

The Kama Sutra is attributed to Vatsyayana who wrote his "profound discussion of love and sex" no later than 300 AD and perhaps as early as 300 BC. The work wasn't original, it was a summing up of ancient wisdom. Love and sex were considered as something a-moral, something which transcends ethics and has its own justifications.

According to the Kama Sutra the results of marrying a young girl is untarnished love, "When a girl of the same cast, and a virgin, is married in accordance with the precepts of the Holy Writ (Darma Shastras), the results of such a union are untarnished love."

Loving a girl that had been loved by others would be reproachful, "But at all events, says Ghotakamukha, a girl who has already been joined with others (that is, no longer a maiden) should never be loved, for it would be reproachful to do such a thing." A girl who has "fully arrived at puberty" should be avoided as a wife.

The Kama Sutra describes wooing, "When a boy has thus begun to woo a girl that he loves, he should spend his time with her and amuse her with various games and diversions fitted for their age and acquaintanceship, such as picking and collecting flowers, making garlands of flowers, playing parts of members of a fictitious family.. the game of odds and evens, the game of finding out the middle finger, the game of six pebbles. Hide-and-seek, playing with seeds, blind-man's bluff and other games of the same sort." In short, child's games.

If the wooer is a man he should, "attach himself to the daughter of the girl's nurse and. procure for her such playthings as may be hardly known to other girls. He should give her dolls made of cloth.."

We may wonder what the girl thinks of all this. According to the Kama Sutra, a girl always shows her love by outward signs and actions, "She never looks the man in the face and becomes abashed when she is looked at by him; under some pretext or another she shows her limbs to him; she looks secretly at him; hangs down her head when she is asked some questions by him, and answers in indistinct words and unfinished sentences, delights to be in his company for a long time; under some pretext or another she makes him look at different things, narrates to him tales and stories very slowly so that she may continue conversation with him for a long time; always wears anything that he may have presented to her, and becomes dejected when any other bridegroom is mentioned by her parents.."

That the attentions are being paid to pre-pubescent girls is shown clearly by the concluding paragraph on Kama Sutra courtship, "A man who has seen and perceived the feelings of the girl toward him, and who has noticed the outward signs and movements by which those feelings are expressed, should do everything in his power to effect a union with her. He should gain over a young girl by childlike sports."

Later, in the Yajnvalkya Smriri and its contemporary literature, we find that the fear of post-puberty marriages became so great that the Smitris brought the marriageable age of girls still lower. According to the Parashar Smitri and Sheeghrabodha the marriageable girls were divided into five categories:

1) Nagnika or naked. A girl seven years old or younger. This was regarded as best age for marriage.
2) Gauri. A girl eight years old.
3) Rohini. A girl of nine years old.
4) Kanya. A ten years old girl.
5) Rajaswala. A girl above ten years old.

According to Vaikhnasa, a Brahmin should marry a Nagnika since that is the best match. According to Marici the best age of marriage for a girl is five years old. Brahmapurana also prescribes marriage in childhood. Failure to do this will condemn the parents or gaurdian to utmost degradation.

Child Marriage from the 6th Century AD-1400 AD

After the sixth century the marriageable age of girls went down lower and lower. The stoppage of participation of girls in Vedic education, Upanayana rituals and the insistence of purity in *yajna* (sacrificial) ritual contributed to the lowering of the marriage age for girls.

All the literature of the epic clearly show the tendency to lower the age of marriage age of girls. The injunction in the Dharmasutra for a woman to wait three years after obtaining womanhood to select a mate was limited to three months by Guatama and Vishnu. Guatama said that a girl should be married before she attains womanhood, otherwise it would be a sin. According to the Baudhayana and Vashithat Dharmasutras a father who allowed his daughter to remain unmarried until after her first menstruation was considered guilty of the sin of abortion on each monthly period.

Later, the Manusmitri places stress on the suitability of the groom and makes it clear that marriage of a girl before her first menstruation was permissible. In the Baudhayana it is said that a girl should be given in marriage to a suitable groom even if she is immature, and that if she is mature she should be given in marriage even if the groom is unsuitable.

By the time of the Yajnavalkyasmitri and its contemporary literature, we find that the fear of post-puberty marriage became so great that the marriageable age was brought down even lower. Nagnika, girls seven years old or younger, were regarded as the best by Vaikknasa. Marichi considered the best age for marriage of girls to be five years old. It was said that if a father does not give her girls in marriage, then the ancestors of the girl would drink the menstrual flow of the girl.

The Ratirimanjeri of Jayadeva-1400 AD

About 1000 years (1400-1500 AD) after the Kamasutra, the Ratimañjari or "The Posy of Love' described the 125 *slokas*, or sexual positions. The work was dedicated to Lord Siva.

Young girls are mentioned in only two verses, Until sixteen years, a young girl was called *bala,* until thirty she was called *taruni,* or young woman. The Ratimanjari said, "The *bala* is a lover of flowers and sweet things, the young woman is given to love-play. The *bala* gives a man pleasure and the breath of life, *prana;* the *taruni* draws out the breath of life."

An allusion is made to hairlessness as being attractive. "Now the *queynt* of woman should be like the back of a tortoise, the cassia blossom, lotus-scented, hairless and well spread: these five are accounted desirable.

The Koka Shastra-1400 AD

The Koka Shastra also discusses courtship with young girls. "The *bala* can be won by giving betal fruit, promising her elaborate meals, by recounting all manner of wonders to her, by the arts and by games."

Young girls or young girl somatypes are preferred sexual partners, "A pretty girl of phlegmatic constitution; a mare-or gazelle-woman, *yaksi,* human or goddess-type; a young girl or one in the freshness of youth-this is the ideal for those who desire pleasure in the world."

In another verse we find that, "A young girl from a strange part of the country should be studied accordingly: her inborn inclinations can be found only from experience.. When you have considered this discrepancy between individual preference and local custom, and also somatype, speed of reaching orgasm, degree of response, age group, and constitutional type, you can proceed accordingly-first to appropriate 'outer forms'-the first of these are the embrace..Until her sixteenth year a girl is called *bala* a young girl who is not yet mature must be approached by way of the 'outer' forms of lovemaking."

The outer forms of love-making include embraces. There are two sorts of embrace for those who have not yet declared their love, four embraces by which they can make known their mind, and eight embraces for those who have shared love-pleasure already.

Children are to avoided for the inner form of love-making, as we can see from the following verse, "Woman who has been put out of her caste, a personal friend, a child, an invalid, a woman who makes love in public, a lunatic, or one who is ill-smelling, aged are always to be avoided as a matter of practice".

More Hindu Scriptual Sources-Nineteenth Century Opinions

Hindu religion enjoined parents not to keep a girl unmarried even at as small an age as 8 years. Puberty sets in among Indian females generally after 11 years, when any marriage is considered unholy. Jayal said that, "Hindu law gives clear injunction not to keep a girl unmarried beyond 12 years."

Keeping girls unmarried until their first menstruation would condemn the family to hell, as Paitinashi said, "A damsel should be given in marriage before her breasts swell. But if she has menstruated before marriage, both the giver and the taker fall into the abyss of hell; and her father, grandfather, and great grandfather are born insects in ordure."

In addition, Brahmins who married girls after their first period would become outcastes as spoken of in the Angirasmitri where it is said, "There is no atonement for man who has intercourse with a *Vrishali*, i.e, a woman who has her courses before marriage. It is also stated, ". the father, mother and elder brother who tolerate a girl in her courses before marriage go to hell.. A Brahmin who will marry such a girl is not to be spoken of or admitted to society." Hindu scriptures sanctioned both child marriage and early consummation, "the girl should be married before puberty and certainly immediately after her first menstruation. If a girl gets married after her first menses it would not be a *Kanya-dan* but *streedan*". *Kanyadan* can be consummated at the most at 11 years of her age." In one of the scenes in the Shastras a father addresses his father-in-law on giving her in marriage, "I have brought this girl up for eight years like a boy. I now give her away to your son, treat her with affection." (Nagi 1993:4).

Age at Marriage

The Manu, Mahabharata and the Vishnu Purana decreed that the man should be three times older than the girl, thus a man marrying a ten year old should be thirty, an eight year old girl should marry a man of twenty-four and so on. One pragmatical Hindu reformer suggested that a law be made prohibiting the marriage of a man over the age of 45 with a girl younger than twelve.

The practice of marrying girls between the age of two and eight years old was common, not only amongst the Hindus, but the Mohammedans and Parsees. Even the Prophet of Islam married a child as a first wife. Oman (No date) complained that, "it is undeniably true that throughout India the marriage of very young girls from 2 to 8 years old of age, with equally young boys, or often with adults of any age, is a very common practice amongst Hindus. The practice also prevails in lesser degrees amongst Parsees and Indian Mohammedans, but it cannot be repugnant to the religious sentiments of the later, since the Prophet of Islam married Ayishah when she was nine years old. She was his favourite wife, and lived to the age of sixty-nine." Abielle (No date) found that child marriage was prevalent even in the Christian areas of India. One of Abielle's more interesting findings was that their was a near unanimity of satisfaction of the couples involved with their experiences in child marriage. As for consummation Oman continues, "Equally true it is that even consummation of marriage has commonly taken place when the child-wife is perhaps not more than ten years of age."

Discussion

The East India Company's 17th century "looting spree" turned into a permanently profitable business by the 1800's. The British

Prime Minister Salisbury soberly decreed that India should be bled "judiciously". A flood of Christian preachers, missionaries and teachers were dispatched to Anglicize the "savages." While appearing to be judicious, they were vicious in their derision of Hindus and their customs. The Brahmin caste were eager for social acceptance by those in power and quick to adopt European ideas. According to the social historian Amrit Srinivasan, "Civilizing the Indians through enforcing a uniform adoption of the Victorian ethic for women" became a central goal of the reformers. Gradually the seeds of cultural shame were sown and an Indian clone of British mentality successfully bred. From then onwards, the most effective critics of Hindu tradition were Indians themselves.

The English, who were ignorant of the long tradition of Indian spiritual literature, declared that there was no religious basis for child marriage and found support for their beliefs from their supporters within the Brahmin caste. Nearly all British educated Indians of the era parroted the English position that child marriage was an insidious evil and destroying the fabric of Indian society.

The Indian populace disagreed. As K.N. Kane of Bombay said in 1884, "There cannot be two opinions about the evil effects which these customs produce in Hindu society, but the efforts of both high and low have been rendered futile owing to the majority of the Hindu population adhering tenaciously to the opposite views." If Kane is to believed, the majority of India's people thought child marriage to be beneficial and a source of pride. Larkshmiram, who considered child marriage a "curse", also said that, "The common saying, 'my children were betrothed while in the cradle yet' is the proud expression of the completely satisfied aspiration of a Gujurato parent."

At the time of the British reform movement in the 1880's scholars and politicians reported girls being married at 8 and 9 years old to men three times their age, an ancient Hindu, and apparently Mohammadan and Parsee custom. The practice of marrying girls before they were thirteen was all but universal. According to various authors many of the marriages were consummated before puberty. Malabari himself said that, "The nuptial ceremonies, I think, are a direct inducement in 95 out of 100 cases to a too early consummation. Even the utmost precaution taken by sensible parents fails to keep the pair from mischief." The

English called them "victims". Anglicized Hindus called them "willing victims in the vast majority of cases." Cross-generation marriage was both sanctioned and encouraged by at least two thousand years of scripture and literature, perhaps even longer if we accept that Sita was a "child-bride at the knee of her mother-in-law."

An unmigated evil as the English believed? Or beneficial as the Hindus believed? Shirgaonkar, would not accept that child marriages were unhappy and complained of a lack of statistics. Taleyarkhan noted Hindu families as "happy, contented, well regulated and economical." Former Government Secretary to India, Allan Octavian Hume who almost single-handedly establish the Indian National Congress told Malabari, "I must say that I think that you *somewhat* exaggerate the evil results of these traditional institutions. There are millions of cases in which early marriages are believed to be daily proving happy ones." Hume quotes a letter from a native friend, "Those ignorant of our inner life calls this a vile subjugation and say that we have made our wives our slaves, but those who live amongst us know, that it is the result of that deep seated affection that springs from early association. Where will you find a wife as true and contented as the Hindu women of a respected family?"

Gopal Hari Deshmukh

Gopal Hari Deshmukh (1823-1892) was a social reformer from Maharashtra, India.

Career

Deshmukh his career as a translator for the government then under British Raj. In 1867, the government appointed him a small cause judge in Ahmedabad, Gujarat. He retired as a sessions judge.

Social Work in Maharashtra

At age 25, Deshmukh started writing articles aimed at social reform in Maharashtra in the weekly *Prabhakar* under the pen name *Lokhitwadi*. In the first two years, he penned 108 articles on social reform. That group of articles has come to be known in Marathi literature as *Lokhitwadinchi Shatapatre*.

He promoted emancipation and education of women, and wrote against arranged child marriages, dowry system, and polygamy, all of which were prevalent in India in his times. He promoted nationalistic spirit in Maharashtra. He wrote against the evils of caste system which was strongly prevalent in India in his times, condemned harmful Hindu religious orthodoxy, and attacked the monopoly in religious matters and rituals which Brahmin priests had through a long tradition. (Noteworthily, Deshmukh belonged to the Brahmin class.) He enunciated certain 15 principles for bringing about religious reform in Hindu society.

Deshmukh founded a public library in Pune under the leadership of the then governor of the state of Bombay Henry Brown. He took a leadership role in founding *Dnyan Prakash, Indu Prakash*, and "*Lokhitwadi* periodicals in Maharashtra.

Social Work in Gujarat

While Deshmukh was serving as a judge in Ahmedabad, he organized in that city annual speech conferences on social issues under the sponsorship of Premabhai Institute, and also himself delivered speeches. He established in Ahmedabad a branch of Prarthana Samaj, founded an institute promoting remarriages of widows, and invigorated Gujarat Vernacular Society. He started a weekly *Hitechchhu* in both Gujarati and English.

Books

Deshmukh wrote 35 books on diverse topics, including religious, social, economic, political, historic, and literary matters. He further translated into Marathi some worthy English works.

Shiv Narayan Agnihotri

Shiv Narayan Agnihotri (1850-1929) was the founder of an atheist society in India called the *Deva Samaj* or "Society of God". Agnihotri enrolled in the state-sponsored Thompson Engineering College in Roorkee, and in 1873 he took up a job as a drawing master in Government School in Lahore. Later he and his wife became active members of the Brahmo Samaj until he broke off to form the rival Deva Samaj.

Behramji Malabari

Behramji Merwanji Malabari (1853 – 1912) was an Indian poet, publicist, author, and social reformer best known for his ardent advocacy for the protection of the rights of women.

Early Life

Behramji Merwanji Malabari was born in 1853 at Baroda (present-day Vadodara, Gujarat) the son of a poor Parsi employed by the British colonial government. His father of whom nothing more is known than "than that he was a mild, peace-loving man, with a somewhat feeble constitution and not overmuch force of character" died when the boy was six or seven. His mother then took him to Surat (on the coast, 140 km from Baroda), where Behramji was then educated in an Irish Presbyterian mission school. He was subsequently adopted by the childless owner of a drugstore who traded in sandalwood and spices from the Malabar Coast hence the name 'Malabari'.

Author and Editor

As early as 1875 Malabari published a volume of poems in Gujarati, followed in 1877 by *The Indian Muse in English Garb*, which attracted attention in England, notably from Alfred Tennyson, Max Muller, and Florence Nightingale. Müller and Nightingale would also play a role in his campaign for social reform, and the latter would also write the preface to an 1888/1892 biography of Malabari. At some point, Malabari relocated to the city of Bombay (now Mumbai), then centre of commerce and administration of the British possessions in Western India. In 1882 he published his *Gujarat and the Gujaratis: pictures of men and manners taken from life*, a book "of a somewhat satirical nature," that went through five editions.

Malabari's life work began in 1880 when he acquired the *Indian Spectator*, an English language daily, which he edited for twenty years until it was merged into the *Voice of India*, which Malabari had already been editing together with Dadabhai Naoroji and William Wedderburn since 1883.

It was under his editorship of the *Spectator* that the religious debates between the Parsis and John Wilson a Scottish Presbyterian missionary and vociferous critic of the Parsi's Zoroastrianism played out. In 1901 he became editor of the monthly *East and West*, a position he would hold until shortly before his death on July 12, 1912.

Malabari's account of his three visits to England, entitled *The Indian Eye on English, or, Rambles of a Pilgrim Reformer*, went through four editions.

Social Reformer

"What propelled Malabari to prominence across India and prompted his [first] visit to Britain in 1890 was what reformers in Victorian England and India called 'the problem of Hindu women,'" that is, his ardent advocacy for social reform with regards to child marriage and the remarriage of widows. In August 1884, Malabari published a set of *Notes on Infant Marriage and Enforced Widowhood,* that he sent to 4,000 leading Englishmen and Hindus. In it, Malabari deplored the "social evil" of "baby marriage" and demanded legislature to prevent it. Similarly on the issue of remarriage for widows, Malabari criticized the Hindu practice of prohibiting it, and he placed the blame squarely with that religion's "priestly class" and the "social monopolists" (i.e. the Brahmin caste) for their "vulgar prejudices." Although acknowledging that many educated Hindus deplored the practice, he repeatedly argued that it was due to inaccurate interpretation of scripture by "the greedy priests" and base Hindu "superstition" that caused "a girl after ten [to be treated as] a serpent in the parents' house." His "notes" were the prelude to an emotionally-charged discussion that occupied the press for over seven years and made Malabari "one of, if not the most influential" Indian social reformer of his time.

In 1885, a girl named Rukhmabai was ordered by a Judge Pinhey to return to her husband or be jailed. Malabari's editorials of the Rukhmabai case gave the issue a popular focus, and it "was largely by his efforts" and the agitation of William Thomas Stead in the *Pall Mall Gazette* that brought about the Criminal Law Amendment Act of 1885, and the Age of Consent Act (which regulated the age of consent for females in Britain and India) in 1891. In this, Malabari "was instrumental not just in refining the gendered dimensions of contests for cultural legitimacy and power in the western presidency, but in refiguring such contests for consumption by the British reform public at home as well." His agitation for reform in India "through the agitation of the British public at home was virtually unprecedented."

In his conviction that the Hindu priesthood were misinterpreting the Vedas and Upanishad, Malabari was also instrumental in the translation of Max Müller's *Hibbert Lectures* into Indian languages. On the insistence of Müller and assisted by one N. M. Mobedjina, Malabari himself undertook the translation into Gujarati. Malabari then attempted to have the lectures translated into other languages (including Marathi, Bengali, Hindi and Tamil), and to do so travelled extensively to find translators and the funding for them.

Although Malabari stayed away from the Indian National Congress as an organization, Malabari attended the Indian National Congress in Bombay in 1885, and "he was a nationalist" and he had a close relationship with Dadabahi Naoroji," one of the founders and leaders of the Congress. It was however to his advantage to not allow his name to be brought in connection with any specific political party or movement, and would have precluded support from British politicians in his campaign for social reform as well as from the Indian princes of Patiala, Gwalior and Bikaner upon whose financial generosity he depended.

1891 Age of Consent Act

The 1891 Age of Consent Act was legislation introduced in British India to raise the age of consent of consummation from ten to twelve years. While an 1880 case in a Bombay high court by a child-bride, Rukhmabai, renewed discussion of such a law, the death of an eleven-year-old Bengali girl, Phulomnee, due to forceful intercourse by her 35 year old husband in 1889, necessitated intervention by the British. The act was passed in 1891. It received support from Indian reformers such as Behramji Malabari and women social organisations and was opposed by Hindu nationalists including Bal Gangadhar Tilak. The law was never seriously implemented and it is argued that the real effect of the law was reassertion of Hindu patriarchal control over domestic issues as a nationalistic cause.

Passage of Legislation

In 1880, Rukhmabai, a 22-year-old woman was taken to Bombay high court by her husband Dadaji as she refused to recognise their marriage rights. She was married as a child to him and argued that their marriage is not binding after 11 years of separate living. She eventually lost the case. This trial is believed to be one of the precursors for the passage of this legislation. The death of an 11-year-old Bengali girl Phulomnee after being brutally raped by her 35-year-old husband Hari Mohan Maitee in 1889 served as a catalyst for its legislation. While Hindu law permitted intercourse with minors, colonial law considered sex with wives only under ten as rape. Therefore, Hari Mohan Maitee was acquitted on charges of rape, but found guilty on causing death inadvertently by a rash and negligent act.

A committee comprising of influential British and Anglo-Indian statesmen established in London had submitted recommendations to the colonial government including the change in age of consent. The law was signed on 19 March 1891 by the government of Lord Lansdowne raising the age of consent for consummation from ten to twelve years.

Support

Behramji Malabari, a Parsi reformer and a journalist from Bombay advocated for this legislation. He published his messages in "Notes on Infant marriage and enforced widowhood" in 1884. Although a Parsi, he claimed to be as critical of Hindu customs and domestic practices as the British.

Though women were not consulted for determining the effect of child-marriage, women in Bombay presidency including Rukhmabai and Pandita Ramabai made a cogent case for the ban on child-marriage in their magazines and social reform organisations. Anandi Gopal Joshi, a Maharashtrian woman who also happened to be the first female medical doctor in India advocated interference of the British Government in child marriage.

Opposition

The bill however provoked a powerful Hindu orthodox backlash. Opposition to the bill in Maharashtra was led by Bal Gangadhar Tilak and Poona Sarvajanik Sabha in alliance with Poona revivalists who often invoked Hindu, Brahman and Maratha glory. Tilak opposed the bill on the grounds that this was not an issue for the British but Hindus to decide. It was strongly opposed in Bengal as well and it is believed that the bill radicalised the nationalist movement in Bengal.

Orthodox Hindus argued that it violated Hindu rite "garbadhan," which obligated Hindu girls to have intercourse with her husband within sixteen days of her first period.

Dhondo Keshav Karve

Maharshi Dr. Dhondo Keshav Karve (April 18, 1858-November 9, 1962) was a preeminent social reformer of his time in India in the field of women's welfare. Karve was one of the pioneers of promoting women's education and the right for widows to remarry in India. The Government of India recognized his reform work by awarding him its highest civilian award, Bhârat Ratna, in 1958 (Incidentally his centennial year).

The appellation *Maharshi,* which the Indian public often assigned to Karve, means "a great sage". Those who knew Karve affectionately called him as *Anna Karve.* (In Marathi-speaking community, to which Karve belonged, the appellation *Annâ* is often used to address either one's father or an elder brother.)

Early Life

Annasaheb Karve was born on 18 April 1858 at *Sheravali, Khed Taluka* of Ratnagiri district in Maharashtra. He was a native of Murud in the Konkan region. He was born in a lower middle-class Chitpavan Brahmin family.

His father's name was *Keshav Bapunna Karve.* In his autobiography, he wrote of his struggle to appear in a certain *public service examination,* walking 110 miles in torrential rain and difficult terrain to the nearest city of Satara, and his shattering disappointment at not being allowed to appear for the examination because *he looked too young.*

Karve studied at Elphinstone College in Bombay (Mumbai) to receive a bachelor's degree in mathematics.

First Marriage

Karve's parents arranged his marriage when he was 14 to an 8 year old girl named *Radhabai.* Karve had written in his autobiography:

"... I was married at the age of fourteen and my wife was then eight. Her family lived very near to ours, and we knew each other very well and had often played together. However, after marriage, we had to forget our old relation as playmates and to behave as strangers, often looking toward each other but never standing together to exchange words.... We had to communicate with each other through my sister...... My marital life began under the parental roof at Murud when I was twenty...".

Radhabhai died in 1891 during childbirth at age 27, leaving behind a young son named Raghunath Karve. Raghunath became a visionary social reformer.

Second Marriage

Reformatory thoughts concerning the then prevalent harsh social mores against womankind, stated above, were already stirring up the mind of Karve by the time Radhabai died. Implementing his own reformatory thoughts with extraordinary courage, two years later he chose as his second wife a widow — a 23 year old widow named *Godubai*— rather than an unmarried girl whom he could have easily arranged to secure as his new wife according to the prevalent social mores. Godubai, who had been widowed at age 8 within three months of her marriage even before she knew, as she would say later, what it was to be a wife. Before marrying Karve, Godubai had started studying in her early twenties at Pandita Ramabai's pioneering Sharada Sadan as its first widow student, and had also displayed equal courage, like Karve, in defying social mores against remarriages by widows.

Concerning his marriage to Godubai, Karve described in his autobiography how he had asked for her hand in marriage to her father:

"I told him.....[that] I had made up my mind to marry a widow. He sat silent for a minute, and then hinted that there was no need to go in search of such a bride".

Career as a college professor

During 1891-1914, Karve taught mathematics at Fergusson College in Pune, Maharashtra. After marriage Dodhubai's name became Aanandibai.

Inspirations

The work of Pandita Ramabai inspired Karve to dedicate his life to the cause of female education, and the work of Pandit Vishnushastri and Pandit Ishwar Chandra Vidyasagar inspired him to work for uplifting the status of widows. Writings of Herbert Spencer had also highly influenced him.

Social Work

In 1893, Karve founded *Widhawa-Wiwahottejak Mandali*, which, besides encouraging marriages of widows, also helped the needy children of widows. In 1895, the institution was renamed as *Widhawa-Wiwaha-Pratibandh-Niwarak Mandali* (Society to Remove Obstacles to Marriages of Widows).

In 1896, Karve established a *Hindu Widows' Home Association* and started in Hingane, a village then in the outskirts of Pune in Maharashtra, *Mahilashram*, a shelter and a school for women, including widows. He started *Mahila Vidyalaya* in 1907; the following year, he started *Nishkam Karma Math* (Social Service Society) to train workers for the *Widows Home* and the *Mahila Vidyalaya*.

Later, *Widows Home* was renamed as *Hingane Stree Shikshan Sanstha*. Still later, as the institution flourished by leaps and bounds, it was renamed as Maharshi Karve Stree Shikshan Sanstha. When Karve had started his shelter and school for women, including widows, in 1896, he had to start it in the remote village of Hingane outside the city of Pune because the dominant orthodox Brahmin community in the city had ostracized him for his reformatory activitities. (Karve himself belonged to the Brahmin community.) With his meager resources, for many years Karve would walk several miles from Hingane to the city of Pune to teach mathematics at Fergusson College and also collect in his spare time paltry donations from a few progressive donors, even as some others from the orthodox community would openly hurl insulting epithets at him when he went around to spread the word of his emancipatory work and collect donations.

Karve's 20 year old widowed sister-in-law, *Parwtibai Athawale*, was the first widow to join his school. After finishing her education, she joined him as the first lady superintendent of the then *Hindu Widows' Home Association*.

After reading information about Japan Women's University in Tokyo, Japan, Karve felt inspired to establish in 1916 in Pune the first university for women in India, with just five students. The curriculum was tailored to the aptitudes of women. During 1917–1918, Karve established a *Training College for Primary School Teachers* and another school for girls, named *Kanya Shala*.

In 1920, an industrialist and philanthropist from Mumbai, Sir Vithaldas Thackersey, donated Karve's university 1.5 million Indian rupees —a substantial sum in those days— and the university was then renamed as *Shreemati Nathibai Damodar Thackersey Indian Women's University or SNDT Women's University*.

In March 1929, Karve left for a tour in England. He attended the *Primary Teachers' Conference* at *Malvern*, and spoke on *Education of Women in India* at a meeting of the *East India Association* at *Caxton Hall, London*. During 25 July-4 August 1929, he attended an educational conference in Geneva, and spoke on *The Indian Experiment in Higher Education for Women*. During 8-21 August, he attended in *Elsinor* the international meeting of educationists under the auspices of the *New Education Fellowship*.

During his subsequent tour of America, Karve lectured at various forums on women's education and social reforms in India. He also visited the Women's University in Tokyo. He returned to India in April 1930.

In December 1930, Karve left for a fifteen-month tour in Africa to spread information about his work for women in India. He visited Mombasa, Kenya, Uganda, Tanganayika, Zanzibar, Portuguese East Africa, and South Africa.

In 1931, the SNDT university established its first college in Mumbai, and moved its headquarters to Mumbai five years later.

In 1936, Karve started the *Maharashtra Village Primary Education Society* with the goal of opening primary schools in villages which had no schools run by the *District Local Boards*. He also encouraged maintenance of reading habits of adults in villages. In 1944, he founded the *Samata Sangh* (Association for the Promotion of Human Equality).

In 1949, the Government of India recognized SNDT University as a statutory university.

The SNDT University and other educational institutions for women started by Karve currently cover the spectrum ranging from pre-primary schools to colleges in humanities, sciences, engineering, architecture, and business management.

Besides dedicating his life to the emancipation of women in India, Karve stood for the abolition of the caste system and the curse of untouchability in the Hindu society.

Family

Karve had four sons: *Raghunath* (from his first marriage), *Shankar, Dinkar*, and *Bhaskar*. All of them rose to eminence in their own fields of work. Raghunath Karve was a professor of mathematics and a pioneer in sex education and birth control in India. Dinkar was a professor of chemistry and an eminent educationist. (Dinkar's wife, Irawati Karve, was a leading sociologist of India.) Bhaskar (and his wife *Kaveri*) worked in Hingane Stree Shikshan Sanstha in various leading capacities. His second son, Shankar Karve spent most of his professional life as an eminent doctor in the city of Mombasa, in the then British colony of Kenya. On his 80th birthday, the Kenyan government issued a postage stamp in his honour.

Raghunath published a health magazine, especially promoting sex education and birth control. Dinkar wrote a book titled "The New Brahmans: Five Maharashtrian Families" in which he profiled his father along with other Brahmin reformers, and coauthored a book titled *A History of Education in India and Pakistan (1964).* Irawati wrote a sociological book in Marathi and a compilation of her essays. A son, Anand, of Dinkar and Irawati, won at a ceremony in UK in 2002 the prestigious *Ashden Award* of two million Indian rupees which is given for innovative work concerning the environment in the Third World. The judges declared themselves as *excited* about Anand's work concerning an integrated fuel-from-waste system that can create thousands of rural entrepreneurs all over the world, while saving trees and reducing dependence on petroleum.

Annasaheb Karve often exhibited eccentricities which were not uncommon among men of his generation, was a man of extreme principles, and could be logical to excess. He used to pay for food whenever he had his meals at his son's place. He never accepted a gift from anybody for himself. A son tried to buy him warm clothes but had to accept money in return; he suggested the son donate money to his social work. On the flip side, Durga Bhagwat has written a devastating indictment of Karve, alleging that he preyed on young women who were facing hard times, and tried to put them under debt of gratitude so that they would be drawn into his coterie for life, looking heartlessly upon them as possible recruits in his social mission. But he was also capable of courage of thought. Karve was in his 90s when his eldest son Raghunath died. Visitors feared they may have to listen to the old man's terrible torment. But Karve calmly and courageously told them that Raghunath was old and death at that age wasn't unusual. 'Having to witness the death of your children is one of the hazards of living to a very long age, and that is my lot. Nothing can be done about it.'

5

Depressed Class Movement

Satyashodhak Samaj

Satyashodhak Samaj is a religion established by Mahatma Jyotirao Phule on September 24, 1873. This was started as a group whose main aim was to liberate the social Shudra and Untouchables castes from exploitation and oppression.

Through his writings and activities Mahatma Phule always condemned Hinduism and the privileged status of priests in it. He openly condemned the inequality in the religious books, orthodox nature of religion, exploitation of masses by the means of it, blind and misleading rituals, and hypocrisy in the prevalent religion.

While condemning the prevalent religion, Phule established *Satyashodhak Samaj* with the ideals of human well being in broader aspects, human happiness, unity, equality, and easy religious principles and rituals.

His movement was kept alive by Shahu Maharaj, Krantisinha Nana Patil and many other leaders after him. A H Salunkhe is one of the prominent activists related to this society today.

Jyotirao Phule

Mahatma Jotiba Govindrao Phule (April 11, 1827 – November 28, 1890), also known as Mahatma Jotiba Phule was an activist, thinker, social reformer, writer, philosopher, theologist, scholar, editor and revolutionary from Maharashtra, India in the nineteenth century. Jotiba Phule and his wife 'Krantijyoti' Savitribai Phule were the pioneer of women's education in India. His remarkable influence was apparent in fields like education, agriculture, caste system, women and widow upliftment and removal of untouchability. He is most known for his efforts to educate women and the lower castes as well as 'Bahujan people'. He, after educating his wife, opened the first school for girls in India in August 1848.

In September, 1873, Jotirao, along with his followers, formed the Satya Shodhak Samaj (Society of Seekers of Truth) with Jotirao as its first president and treasurer. The main objective of the organisation was to liberate the Bahujanas, Shudras and Ati-Shudras and to prevent them from 'exploitations' and 'artocites' created by the Brahmins, (he did however have a few Brahmin friends like Sadashiv Ballal Govande.) For his fight to attain equal rights for peasants and the lower caste and his contribution to the field of education he is regarded as one of the most important figures in Social Reform Movement in Maharashtra.

Early Life

Jotirao Govindrao Phule was born in Satara district of Maharastra in a family belonging to mali caste, a caste perceived to be inferior caste by certain sections of the society. His father, Govindrao, was a vegetable vendor. His mother died when he was 9 months old. After completing his primary education Jotirao had to leave school and help his father by working on the family's farm. He was married at the age of 12. His intelligence was recognised by a Muslim and a Christian neighbour, who persuaded his father to allow Jotirao to attend the local Scottish Mission's High School, which he completed in 1847. The turning point in Jotiba's life was in year 1848, when he was insulted by family members of his Maratha friend, a bridegroom for his participation in the marriage procession, an auspicious occasion. Jotiba was suddenly facing the divide created by the caste system. Influenced by Thomas Paine books *Rights of Man* (1791), Phule developed a keen sense of social justice, becoming passionately critical of the Indian caste system. He argued that education of women and the lower castes was a vital priority in addressing social inequalities.

Satyashodhak Samaj

On 24 September 1874, Jotirao formed 'Satya Shodhak Samaj' (Society of Seekers of Truth) with himself as its first president and treasurer. The main objectives of the organisation were to liberate the Shudras and Ati Shudras and to prevent their 'exploitation' by the upper caste like ruling caste Maraths. Through this Satya Shodhak Samaj, Jotirao refused to regard the Vedas as sacrosanct. He opposed idolatry and denounced the chaturvarnya system (the caste system). Satya Shodhak Samaj propounded the spread of rational thinking and rejected the need for a Brahman priestly class as educational and religious leaders.

Beliefs

When Phule established the Satya Shodhak Samaj, Savitribai became the head of the women's section which included ninety female members. Moreover, she worked tirelessly as a school teacher for girls. Deenbandhu publication, the mouthpiece of the Satya Shodhak Samaj, played an important role in Satya Shodhak Samaj's movement. After Jotiba's death in 1890 his spirited followers went on spreading the movement to the remotest parts of Maharashtra. Shahu Maharaj, the ruler of Kolhapur princely state, gave a lot of financial and moral support to Satya Shodhak Samaj. In its new incarnation party carried on the work of superstition removal vigorously.

Jotiba firmly believed that if you want to create a new social system based on freedom, equality, brotherhood, human dignity, economic justice and value devoid of exploitation, you will have to overthrow the old, unequal and exploitative social system and the values on which it is based. Knowing this well, Jotiba attacked blind faith and faith in what is given in religious books and the so-called god's words. He tore to pieces the misleading myths that were ruling over the minds of women, shudras and ati-shudras. Yielding to god or fate, astrology and other such rituals, sacredness, god-men, etc. was deemed irrational and absurd.

He also led campaigns to remove the economic and social handicaps that breed blind faith among women, shudras and ati-shudras. Jotiba subjected religious texts and religious behaviour to the tests of rationalism. He characterised this faith as outwardly religious but in essence politically motivated movements. He accused them of upholding the teachings of religion and refusing to rationally analyse religious teachings. He maintained that at the root of all calamities was the blind faith that religious books were created or inspired by god. Therefore, Phule wanted to abolish this blind faith in the first instance. All established religious and priestly classes find this blind faith useful for their purposes and they try their best to defend it. He questions " if there is only one God, who created the whole mankind, why did he write the Vedas only in Sanskrit language despite his anxiety for the welfare of the whole mankind? What about the welfare of those who do not understand this language?" Phule concludes that it is untenable to say that religious texts were God-created. To believe so is only ignorance and prejudice. All religions and their religious texts are man-made and they represent the selfish interest of the classes, which are trying to pursue and protect their selfish ends by constructing such books. Phule was the only sociologist and humanist in his time that could put forth such bold ideas. In his view, every religious book is a product of its time and the truths it contains have no permanent and universal validity. Again these texts can never be free from the prejudices and the selfishness of the authors of such books.

Phule believed in overthrowing the social system in which man has been deliberately made dependent on others, illiterate, ignorant and poor, with a view to exploiting him. To him blind faith eradication formed part of a broad socioeconomic transformation. This was his strategy for ending exploitation of human beings. Mere advice, education and alternative ways of living are not enough, unless the economic framework of exploitation comes to an end.

Religion

Attack on the Sanctity of Vedas

Jyotirao Phule's critique of the caste system began with his attack on the Vedas, the most fundamental texts of Hinduism. He considered Vedas as 'idle fantasies' as 'palpably absurd legends'. He considered Vedas a 'form of false consciousness'.

Alternate Religion: Closer to Deism

Though his *akhandas* were based on the *abhangs* of Hindu saint Tukaram, the attack on the Vedas precludes any connection with Bhakti movement which, despite questioning the Brahminical orthodoxy, still affirmed the sanctity of Vedas or other Hindu texts such as Bhagvad Gita, etc. as true revelations. In fact Phule went on to explicitly reject any connection with the poet-saints of Varkari which was very much a part of Bhakti movement.

Quite opposed to rekindling of devotional aspects of Hindu scriptures, as advocated by Bhakti poet-saints like Chaitanya Mahaprabhu, Ramanuja, Vedanta Desika, Ramananda, etc., Phule instead called for creation of an alternate theology. In this new parallel faith he coined a new name for God as 'Nirmik' rougly translating as 'Creator'. He rejected all names of God which had roots in the accepted Hindu scriptures.

Despite rejecting Hinduism and not accepting any of the other accepted faiths of his time, Phule essentially remained a deist and believed that the true inhabitants of Bharat believed in God. He also believed that the Brahmins were outsiders to Hinduism. This was also the view spoken by Keshavarao Jehde.

Merger into Congress Party

After Jotiba's death in 1890, there was a period of lull, when the flame lit by Jotiba waned. The Satya Shodhak Samaj movement was totally a social movement and nothing to do with the politics, but the members of Satya Shodhak Samaj dissolved Satya Shodhak Samaj and merged it with Congress party in 1930. Phule had a favourable opinion about the British Rule in India at least from the point of view of introducing modern notions of justice and equality in Indian society and taking India into the future.

Social Activism

He was assisted in his work by his wife, Savitribai Phule, and together they started the first school for girls in India in 1848, for which he was forced to leave his home. He initiated widow-remarriage and started a home for upper caste widows in 1854, as well as a home for new-born infants to prevent female infanticide. Phule tried to eliminate the stigma of social Untouchability surrounding the lower castes by opening his house and the use of his water-well to the members of the lower castes. He formed Satya Shodhak Samaj (Society of Seekers of Truth) on September 24, 1873, a group whose main aim was to liberate the social Shudra and Untouchables castes from exploitation and oppression. Phule was a member of Pune municipality from 1876 to 1882.

Connection with Women Activists

Some of India's first modern feminists were closely associated with Phule, including his wife Savitribai Phule; Pandita Ramabai, a Brahmin woman who made waves in the atmosphere of liberal reformism; Tarabai Shinde, the non-Brahman author of a fiery tract on gender inequality which was largely ignored at the time but has recently become well-known; and Muktabai, a fourteen-year-old pupil in Phule's school, whose essay on the social oppression of the Mang and Mahar castes is also now justly famous.

Legacy

- The Crawford Market in Mumbai is officially named after him.
- Mahatma Phule Krishi Vidyapeeth in Rahuri, Ahmednagar District, Maharastra.

Quotes

- Vidyevina mati geli; mativina neeti geli; neetivina gati geli; gativina vitta gele; vittavina shudra khachale; itke anartha eka avidyene kele.

(Lack of education leads to lack of wisdom, which leads to lack of morals, which leads to lack of progress, which leads to lack of money, which leads to the oppression of the lower classes.

Followers

Krantisurya Phule has many followers. Dr. Babasaheb Ambedkar, the first minister of law of Republic India and the architect of Indian Constitution was inspired by his noble work towards humanity.

One among those is Hon. Minister Of Maharashtra Chhagan Bhujbal founder of Mahatma Fule Samata Parishad, an organisation works for social upliftment of dalits and OBCs and Telugu actor Chiranjeevi, who started a political party and stated that he is very much inspired by the work done by Phule especially creating social harmony.

Published Works

His famous published works are;

- *Tritiya Ratna*, 1855
- *Brahmananche Kasab*,1869
- *Powada : Chatrapati Shivajiraje Bhosle Yancha*, [English: Life Of Shivaji, In Poetical Metre], June 1869
- *Powada: Vidyakhatyatil Brahman Pantoji*, June 1869
- *Manav Mahammand* (Muhammad) (Abhang)

- *Gulamgiri* [full name in English: Slavery: In The Civilized British Government Under The Clock Of Brahmanism], 1873
- *Shetkarayacha Aasud* (Cultivator's Whipcord), July 1883
- *Satsar* Ank 1, June 1885
- *Satsar* Ank 2, October 1885
- *Ishara*, October 1885
- *Gramjoshya sambhandi jahir kabhar*, (1886)
- *Satyashodhak Samajokt Mangalashtakasah Sarva Puja-vidhi*, 1887
- *Sarvajanik Satya Dharma Poostak*, April 1889
- *Sarvajanic Satya Dharmapustak*, 1891
- *Akhandadi Kavyarachana*
- *Asprashyanchi Kaifiyat.*

Vitthal Ramji Shinde

Maharshi V.R. Shinde was born at Jamkhandi a small princely State, now a part of the Karnataka. Though Shinde's family was basically Marathi speaking, it was a typical example of a confluence of both the linguistc cultures of Kannada and Marathi (April 23, 1873 – January 2, 1944) He was a prominent campaigner on behalf of the Dalit movement in India who established the *Depressed Classes Mission of India* to provide education to the Dalits.

Education and Life Work

In 1898 he obtained B.A. Degree from the Fergusson College at Pune, India. He had also studied and passed the first year law and moved to Mumbai (Bombay) for LLB examination, however gave up this course in order to attend to other compelling callings in his life. This same year he joined the Prarthana Samaj, Where he was further inspired and influenced by G.B. Kotkar, Shivrampant Gokhle, Justice Ranade, R.G. Bhandarkar and K.B. Marathe and became its missionary.

The Prarthana Samaj selected him, to go to England in 1901, to study comparative religion at the Manchester College, founded by the Unitarian Church, at Oxford University. Maharaja Sahyajirao Gaikwad, of Baroda (a progressive and reformist in his own rights) provided some financial help for his travels abroad.

After returning from England in 1903 he devoted his life to religious and social reforms. He continued his missionary work of the Prarthana Samaj. His efforts were devoted mainly to the removal of Untouchability in India.

In 1905 he established a night school for the children of untouchable in Pune.

In 1906 he established the Depressed Classes Mission in Mumbai (Bombay). In 1922 the mission's Ahalyashram building was completed at Pune.

In 1917 he succeeded in getting the Indian National Congress to pass a resolution condemning the practice of untouchability.

From 1918 to 1920, He went on to convening the all India untouchability removal conferences. Some of these conferences were convened under the president-ship of Mahatma Gandhi and Maharaja Sahyajirao Gaikwad. His written communications with the Mahatmaji is noteworthy.

In 1919 he gave evidence before the South borough Commission, asking for the special representation for the untouchable casts.

In 1923 he resigned as the executive of the Depressed Classes Mission since some of the members of the untouchable castes wanted its own leaders to manage the mission's affairs.

His work and association with the Mission continued even though disappointed by the Separatist attitude of the leaders of the untouchables, especially under the leadership of Dr. B.R. Ambedkar. Like the Mahatma Gandhi, He wanted unity amongst the Harijans (untouchables) and the caste Hindus and feared that the British rule will take advantage of such divisions within the Indian society.

In 1930 he participated in the Civil Disobedience Movement of Mahatma Gandhi and was imprisoned for 6 months of hard labour, in the Yerawda prison near Pune.

In 1933 his book "Bhartiya Asprushyatecha Prashna" (India's untouchability question) was published.

His thoughts and examination of the Hindu religion and social culture were similar to Raja Ram Mohan Roy and Dayananda Saraswati. He has written extensively about it where he rejects cast system, Idol worship, inequities against woman & depressed classes. He rejected meaningless rituals, rejected the dominance of hereditary priesthood and the need for a priest to mediate between God and his devotees. This article is Edited by Harshad Bhosale).

Depressed Class Mission

He laid the foundation of Depressed Class Mission in order to work against untouchability on national level.It was establisheb on October 18, 1906. Aims of this mission were:

1. To try to get rid of untouchability.
2. To provide educational facilities to the untouchables.
3. To start schools, hostels, and hospitals for them.
4. To solve their social problems.

Many schools and hostels were founded by this mission..

Self-Respect Movement

The Self-Respect Movement was founded in 1925 by Periyar E. V. Ramasamy (also known as Periyar) in Tamil Nadu, India. The movement has the aim of achieving a society where backward castes have equal human rights, and encouraging backward castes to have self-respect in the context of a caste based society that considered them to be a lower end of the hierarchy. The movement was extremely influential not just in Tamil Nadu, but also overseas in countries with large Tamil populations, such as Malaysia and Singapore.

Among Singapore Indians, groups like the Tamil Reform Association, and leaders like Thamizhavel G. Sarangapani were prominent in promoting the principals of the Self-Respect Movement among the local Tamil population through schools and publications.

A number of political parties in Tamil Nadu, such as Dravida Munnetra Kazhagam (DMK) and All India Anna Dravida Munnetra Kazhagam (AIADMK) owe their origins to the Self-respect movement, the latter a 1972 breakaway from the DMK. Both parties are populist with a generally social democratic orientation.

The movement has been in political power in Tamil Nadu since 1967, when the DMK under C. N. Annadurai defeated the ruling Congress Party. The incumbent (as of 2009) Chief Minister is M. Karunanidhi of the DMK.

The Tenets of Self-Respect

Periyar was convinced that if man developed *self respect*, he would automatically develop individuality and would refuse to be led by the nose by schemers. One of his most known quotes on Self-Respect was, "we are fit to think of 'self-respect' only when the notion of 'superior' and 'inferior' caste is banished from our land".

Periyar did not expect personal or material gain out of this movement. He used to recall in a very casual manner that as a human being, he also was obligated to this duty, as it was the right and freedom to choose this work. Thus, Periyar opted to engage himself in starting and promoting the movement.

Periyar declared that the *Self-Respect Movement* alone could be the genuine freedom movement, and political freedom would not be fruitful without individual self-respect. He remarked that the so called 'Indian freedom fighters' were showing disrespect of self-respect, and this was really an irrational philosophy.

Periyar observed that political freedom as conceived by nationalists not excluding even Gandhi and Jawaharlal Nehru did not cover individual self-respect. To him neither revival of the original spirit of Hindu religion and ancient traditions which formed part of Gandhi's conception of freedom, nor complete liberation from the British rule which was considered by Nehru to be the meaning of freedom or both of them together could ensure individual self-respect or remove the ills from Indian societies. In his opinion the task of fulfilling the need for self-respect would have to be faced whatever be the extent of political freedom gained. Pointing out that even the British monarch in a sovereign independent nation had no freedom to marry a person of his choice and had to abdicate his kingdom, Periyar raised a question whether Gandhi's vision of freedom or Nehru's concept of independence contained even an iota of individual self-respect.

Periyar believed that self-respect was as valuable as life itself and its protection is a birth right and not *swaraj* ('political freedom'). He described the movement as *Arivu Vidutalai Iyakkam*, that is, a movement to liberate the intellect.

The terms *tan-maanam* or *suya mariyadai* meaning 'self-respect' are traceable in ancient Tamil literature considered a virtue of high valor in Tamil society. Periyar once claimed that to describe the ideology of his movement, no dictionary in the entire world, implying that no other language, could provide a word better than or equal to *suya mariyadai.*

Started as a movement (*Iyakkam* in Tamil) to promote rational behaviour, the *Self-Respect Movement* acquired much wider connotation within a short period of time. Periyar speaking with M.K. Reddy at the *First Self-Respect Conference* held in 1929, explained the significance of self-respect and its principles. The main tenets of the *Self-Respect Movement* in society were to be: no kind of inequality among people; no difference as rich and poor in the economic life; men and women to be treated as equals in every respect without differences; attachments to caste, religion, *varna,* and country to be eradicated from society with a prevalent friendship and unity around the world; and every human being seeing to act according to reason, understanding, desire, and perspective, and shall not be subject to slavery of any kind or manner.

Equality with stress on economic and social equality formed the central theme of the *Self-Respect Movement* was due to Periyar's determination to fight the inequalities ingrained in the caste system and religious practices. Working on the theme of liberating the society from the baneful social practices perpetrated in the name of *dharma* and *karma,* Periyar developed the idea of establishing this movement as the instrument for achieving his objective.

Anti-Brahmanism

Tamil Brahmins (Iyers and Iyengars) were frequently held responsible by followers of Periyar for direct or indirect oppression of lower-caste people on the canard of "Brahmin oppression" and resulted in attacks on Brahmins and which among other reasons started a wave of mass-migration of the Brahmin population. Periyar in regards to a DK member's attempt to assassinate Rajagopalachari, "expressed his abhorrence of violence as a means of settling political differences". Eventually, the anti-Brahmanism subsided with the replacement of the DMK party by the AIADMK.

Self-Respect Marriages

One of the major sociological changes introduced through the self respect movement was the self-respect marriage system, where by marriages were conducted without being officiated by a Brahmin priest. Periyar had regarded the then conventional marriages were mere financial arrangements and often caused great debt through dowry. Self-Respect marriages encouraged inter-caste marriages and arranged marriages to be replaced by love marriages. It was argued by the proponents of self-respect marriage that the then conventional marriages were officiated by Brahmins, who has to be paid for and also the marriage ceremony was in Sanskrit which most people did not understand, and hence were ritual and practices based on blind adherence.

Periyar E. V. Ramasamy

Periyar Erode Venkata Ramasamy (September 17, 1879 – December 24, 1973), also known as Ramaswami, EVR, Thanthai Periyar, or Periyar, was a Dravidian social activist, who founded the Self-Respect Movement and Dravidar Kazhagam.

Periyar was born in the Town of Erode, Tamil Nadu to a wealthy Nayakar family. At a young age, he witnessed numerous incidents of racial, caste and gender discrimination. Periyar married when he was 19, and had a daughter who lived for only 5 months. His first wife, Nagammai, died in 1933. Periyar married for a second time in July 1948. His second wife, Maniammai (also called *Maniammai Ammaiyar*), continued Periyar's social work after his death in 1973, but still his thoughts and ideas were being spread by Dravidar Kazhagam.

Periyar joined the Indian National Congress in 1919, but resigned in 1925 when he felt that the party was only serving the interests of the Brahmins. In 1924, Periyar led a nonviolent agitation (satyagraha) in Vaikom, Kerala. From 1929 to 1932 toured Malaysia, Europe, and Russia, which had an influence on him. In 1939, Periyar became the head of the Justice Party, and in 1944, he changed its name to *Dravidar Kazhagam*. The party later split and one group led by C. N. Annadurai formed the Dravida Munnetra Kazhagam (DMK) in 1949. While continuing the *Self-Respect Movement*, he advocated for an independent Dravida Nadu (*Dravidistan*).

Periyar propagated the principles of rationalism, self-respect, women's rights and eradication of caste. He opposed the exploitation and marginalization of the non-Brahmin indigenous Dravidian peoples of South India and the imposition of, what he considered, Indo-Aryan India. His work has greatly revolutionized

Tamil society and has significantly removed caste-based discrimination. He is also responsible for bringing new changes to the Tamil alphabet. However, at the same time, Periyar is also held responsible for making controversial statements on the Tamil language, Dalits and Brahmins and for endorsing violence against Brahmins. The citation awarded by the UNESCO described Periyar as "the prophet of the new age, the Socrates of South East Asia, father of social reform movement and arch enemy of ignorance, superstitions, meaningless customs and base manners".

Biography

Early Years

Periyar was born as Erode Venkata Ramasami Naicker on September 17, 1879, in Erode, Tamil Nadu. The name Naicker denoted the caste he was born into. Periyar's father, a rich businessman, was Venkata (Naicker), and his mother was Chinna Thayammal, alias Muthammal. He had one elder brother named Krishnaswamy and two sisters named Kannamma and Ponnuthoy. He later came to be known as "Periyar" meaning 'respected one' or 'elder' in Tamil. In 1929, Periyar announced the deletion of his caste title *Naicker* from his name at the First Provincial Self-Respect Conference of Chenggalpattu. He could speak three Dravidian languages: Kannada, Tamil and Telugu. His mother tongue was Kannada. Periyar attended school for five years after which he joined his father's trade at the age of 12. He used to listen to Tamil Vaishnavite gurus who gave discourses in his house enjoying his father's hospitality. At a young age, he began questioning the apparent contradictions in the Hindu mythological stories which he opined to be lies spread by the Indo-Aryan race. As Periyar grew, he felt that people used religion only as a mask to deceive innocent people and therefore took it as one of his duties in life to warn people against superstitions and priests.

Periyar's father arranged for his wedding when he was nineteen. The bride, Nagammai was only thirteen. It was not, altogether, an arranged marriage because Periyar and Nagammai had known each other and were already in love with each other. Nagammai actively supported her husband in his later public activities and agitations. Two years after their marriage, a girl child was born to them. However, this child lived only for five months. The couple had no more children

Kasi Pilgrimage Incident

In 1904, Periyar went on a pilgrimage to Kasi to worship in the revered Siva temple of Kashi Vishwanath. Though regarded as one of the holiest sites of Hinduism, he witnessed immoral activities, begging, and floating dead bodies. His frustrations extended to functional Hinduism in general when he experience what he called Brahmanic exploitation.

However, one particular incident in Kasi had a profound impact on Periyar's ideology and future work. At worship site there were free meals offered to guests. To Periyar's shock, he was refused meals at choultries which exclusively fed Brahmins. Due to extreme hunger, Periyar felt compelled to enter one of the choultries disguised as a Brahmin with a sacred thread on his bare chest, but was betrayed by his moustache. The gatekeeper at the temple concluded that Periyar was not a Brahmin as Brahmins were not permitted by the Hindu *shastras* to have moustaches. He not only prevented Periyar's entry but also pushed him rudely to the street.

As his hunger became intolerable, Periyar was forced to feed on leftovers from the streets. Around this time, he realized that the choultry which had refused him entry was built by a wealthy non-Brahmin from South India. This discriminatory attitude dealt a blow to Periyar's regard for Hinduism, for the events he had witnessed at Kasi were completely different from the picture of Kasi he had in mind, as a holy place which welcomed all. Ramasami was a theist till his visit to Kasi, after which his views changed and he became an atheist.

Member of Congress Party (1919-1925)

Periyar Ramaswamy joined the Indian National Congress in 1919 after quitting his business and resigning from public posts. He held the chairmanship of Erode Municipality and wholeheartedly undertook constructive programs spreading the use of Khadi, picketing toddy shops, boycotting shops selling foreign cloth, and eradicating untouchability. In 1921, Periyar courted imprisonment for picketing toddy shops in Erode. When his wife as well as his sister joined the agitation, it gained momentum, and the administration was forced to come to a compromise. He was again arrested during the Non-Cooperation movement and the Temperance movement.. In 1922, Periyar was elected the President of the Madras Presidency Congress Committee during the Tirupur session where he advocated strongly for reservation in government jobs and education. His attempts were defeated in the Congress party due to a strong presence of discrimination and indifference. He later quit the party on those grounds in 1925.

Vaikom Satyagraha (1924-1925)

In Vaikom, a small town in Kerala state, then Travancore, there were strict laws of untouchability in and around the temple area. *Dalits,* also known as Harijans were not allowed into the close streets around and leading to the temple, let alone inside it. Anti-caste feelings were growing and in 1924 Vaikom was chosen as a suitable place for an organized *Satyagraha,* passive resistance campaign as practiced by Gandhi. Under his guidance a movement had already begun with the aim of giving all castes the right to enter the temples. Thus, agitations and demonstrations took place. On April 14, Periyar and his wife Nagamma arrived in Vaikom. They were met with arrest and imprisoned for participation. In spite of Gandhi's objection to non-Keralites and non-Hindus taking part, Periyar and his followers continued to give support to the movement till it was withdrawn. He received the title *Vikkom Veeran,* mostly given by his Tamil followers who participated in the Satyagraha. However, a considerable section of intellectuals feel that Periyar's participation in the Indian independence movement and his contribution in the Vaikom Satyagraha have been highly exaggerated.

The way in which the *Vaikom Satyagraha* events have been recorded provides a clue to the image of the respective oraganizers. In an article entitle *Gandhi and Ambedkar, A Study in Leadership,* Eleanor Zelliot relates the 'Vaikom Satyagraha' including Gandhi's negotiations with the temple authorities in relation to the event. Furthermore, the editor of Periyar's *Thoughts* states that Brahmins purposely suppressed news about Periyar's participation. A leading Congress magazine *Young India* in its extensive reports on Vaikom never mentions Periyar.

Self-Respect Movement

Periyar and his followers campaigned constantly to influence and pressurize the government to take measures for removing social inequality even while other nationalist forerunners focused on the struggle for political independence. The Self-Respect Movement was described from the beginning, as "dedicated to the goal of giving non-Brahmins a sense of pride based on their Dravidian past". In 1952, the Periyar *Self-Respect Movement Institution* was registered with a list of objectives of the institution from which may be quoted as

> for the diffusion of useful knowledge of political education; to allow people to live a life of freedom from slavery to anything against reason and self respect; to do away with needless customs, meaningless ceremonies, and blind superstitious beliefs in society; to put an end to the present social system in which caste, religion, community and traditional occupations based on the accident of birth, have chained the mass of the people and created "superior" and "inferior" classes... and to give people equal rights; to completely eradicate untouchability and to establish a united society based on brother/sisterhood; to give equal rights to women; to prevent child marriages and marriages based on law favourable to one sect, to conduct and encourage love marriages, widow marriages, inter caste and inter-religious marriages and to have the marriages registered under the Civil Law; and to establish and maintain homes for orphans and widows and to run educational institutions.

Propagation of the philosophy of *self respect* became the full-time activity of Periyar since 1925. A Tamil weekly *Kudi Arasu* started in 1925, while the English journal *Revolt* started in 1928 carried on the propaganda among the English educated people. The *Self-Respect Movement* began to grow fast and received the sympathy of the heads of the Justice Party from the beginning. In May 1929, a conference of Self-Respect Volunteers was held at Pattukkotai under the presidency of S. Guruswami. K.V. Alagiriswami took charge as the head of the volunteer band. Conferences followed in succession throughout the Tamil districts of the former Madras Presidency. A training school in Self-Respect was opened at Erode, the home town of Periyar. The object was not just to introduce social reform but to bring about a social revolution to foster a new spirit and build a new society.

International Travel (1929-1932)

Between 1929 and 1935, under the strain of World Depression, political thinking worldwide received a jolt from the spread of international communism. Indian political parties, movements and considerable sections of leadership were also affected by inter-continental ideologies. The Self-Respect Movement also came under the influence of the leftist philosophies and institutions. Periyar after establishing the *Self-Respect Movement* as an independent institution began to look for strengthening it politically and socially. And for this, he undertook a study of the history and politics of different countries combined with personal observation of the systems at work.

Periyar toured Malaysia for a month from December 1929 to January 1930 to propagate the *self-respect* philosophy. Embarking on his journey from Nagapattinam with his wife Nagammal and his followers, Periyar was received by 50,000 Tamil Malaysians in Penang. During the same month, he inaugurated the Tamils Conference convened by the Tamils Reformatory Sangam in Ipoh and then went to Singapore. In December 1931 he undertook a tour of Europe, accompanied by S. Ramanathan and Erode Ramu, to personally acquaint himself with their political systems, social movements, way of life, economic and social progress and administration of public bodies. He visited Egypt, Greece, Turkey, Russia, Germany], England, Spain, France and Portugal, staying in Russia for three months. On his return journey he halted at Ceylon and returned to India in November 1932.

The tour shaped the political ideology of Periyar to achieve the social concept of Self-Respect. The communist system obtained in Russia appealed to him as appropriately suited to deal with the social ills of the country. Thus, on socioeconomic issues Periyar was Marxist, but he did not advocate for abolishing private ownership. Immediately after his return, Periyar in alliance with the enthusiastic communist M. Singaravelu Chettiar, began to work out a socio-political scheme incorporating socialist and self-respect ideals. This marks a crucial stage of development in the *Self-Respect Movement* which got politicized and found its compatibility in Tamil Nadu.

Opposition to Hindi

In 1937, when Chakravarthi Rajagopalachari became the Chief Minister of Madras state, he introduced Hindi as a compulsory language of study in schools, igniting thereby a series of anti-Hindi agitations. Tamil nationalists, the Justice Party under Sir A.

T. Panneerselvam, and Periyar organized anti-Hindi protests in 1938 which ended with numerous arrests by the Rajaji government.

During the same year, the slogan "Tamil Nadu for Tamilians" was first raised by Periyar in protest against the introduction of Hindi in schools. He explained that the introduction of Hindi was a dangerous mechanism used to the infiltration of Aryans on Dravidian culture. He reasoned that the adoption of Hindi would make Tamils subordinate to Hindi-speaking North Indians. Periyar explained that Hindi would not only halt the progress of Tamilians but would completely destroy their culture and nullify the progressive ideas that had been successfully inculcated through Tamil in the recent decades.

Cutting across party lines, South Indian politicians rallied together in their opposition to Hindi There were recurrent anti-Hindi agitations in 1948, 1952 and 1965.

As President of the Justice Party (1938-1944)

A political party known as the *South Indian Libertarian Federation* was founded in 1916, principally to oppose the economic and political power of the Brahmin jati groups. The party was later named the *Justice Party*, and its stated goal was to render social justice to non-Brahmin groups. In order to gain the support of the masses, non-Brahmin politicians began propagating an ideology of equality among non-Brahmin *jati* groups. Brahmanical priesthood and Sanskritic social class-value hierarchy were blamed for the existence of inequalities among non-Brahmin *jati* groups.

In 1937, when the government required that Hindi be taught in the school system, Periyar organized opposition through the *Justice Party* to this policy. After 1937, the Dravidian movement derived considerable support from the student community. In later years, opposition to Hindi played a big role in the politics of Tamil Nadu.

The fear of the Hindi language had its origin in the conflict between Brahmins and non-Brahmins. To the Tamil, acceptance of Hindi in the school system was a form of bondage. When the *Justice Party* weakened in the absence of mass support, Periyar took over the leadership of the party after being jailed for opposing Hindi in 1939. Under his tutelage the party prospered, but the party's conservative members, most of whom were rich and educated, withdrew from active participation.

Dravidar Kazhagam (1944-onwards)

At a rally in 1944, Periyar, in his capacity as the leader of the Justice Party, declared that the party would henceforth be known as the Dravidar Kazhagam or "Dravidian Association". However, a few who disagreed with Periyar started a splinter group claiming to be the original Justice Party. This party was led by veteran Justice Party leader P. T. Rajan and survived till 1957.

The Dravidar Kazhagam came to be well known amongst the urban communities and students. Villages were influenced by its message. Hindi, and ceremonies that had become associated with Brahmanical priesthood, were identified as alien symbols that should be eliminated from Tamil culture. Brahmins, who were regarded as the guardians of such symbols, came under verbal attack. From 1949 onwards, the *Dravidar Kazhagam* intensified social reformist work and put forward the fact that the superstitions were the cause for the degeneration of Dravidians. The *Dravidar Kazhagam* vehemently fought for the abolition of untouchability amongst the Dalits. It also focused its attention on the liberation of women, women's education, willing marriage, widow marriage, orphanages and mercy homes.

Split with Annadurai

In 1949, Periyar's chief lieutenant, Conjeevaram Natarajan Annadurai established a separate association called the *Dravida Munnetra Kazhagam* (DMK), or (Dravidian Advancement Association). This was due to differences between the two where Periyar advocated a separate independent Dravidian or Tamil state, while Annadurai compromised with the Delhi government combined with claims of increased state independence. Periyar was convinced that individuals and movements that undertake the task of eradicating the social evils in the Indian sub-continent have to pursue the goal with devotion and dedication without deviating from the path and with uncompromising zeal. Thus, if they contest elections aiming to assume political power, they would lose vigor and sense of purpose. But amongst his followers, there were those who had a different view. They wanted to enter into politics and have a share in running the government. They were looking for an opportunity to part with Periyar. Thus, when Periyar got married to Maniammai on July 9, 1948, they quit the *Dravidar Kazhagam* stating that Periyar set a bad example by marrying a young woman in his old age-he was 70 and she 30. Those who parted company with Periyar also joined the DMK. Though the DMK split from the *Dravidar Kazhagam*, the organization made efforts to carry on Periyar's Self-Respect Movement to the villagers and the urban students. The DMK advocated the thesis that the Tamil language was much richer than Sanskrit and Hindi in content, and thus was a key which opened the door to subjects to be learned. The *Dravidar Kazhagam* continued to counter Brahminism, Indo-Aryan propaganda, and uphold the Dravidians' right of self-determination.

Last Years of Service

In 1956, despite warnings from P. Kakkan, the President of the Tamil Nadu Congress Committee, Periyar organized a procession to the Marina in order to burn pictures of the Hindu God Rama. Periyar was subsequently arrested and confined to prison.

The activities of Periyar continued when he went to Bangalore in 1958 to participate in the All India Official Language Conference. There he stressed the need to retain English as the Union Official Language instead of Hindi. In 1962, Periyar welcomed the present General Secretary of Dravidar Kazhagam, K.Veeramani who offered to become a full time volunteer of the movement. Five years later, Periyar travelled to North India to advocate on the eradication of the caste system. Nearing Periyar's last years, an award was given to him by the United Nations Educational Scientific and Cultural Organization (UNESCO), and it was presented to him by the Union Education Minister, Triguna Sen in Madras (Chennai) on June 27, 1970. In his last meeting at Thiagaraya Nagar, Chennai on December 19, 1973, Periyar declared a call for action to gain social equality and a dignified way of life. On December 24, 1973 Periyar died at the age of 94.

Principles and Legacy

Periyar spent over fifty years working towards educating the people through his speeches. He propagated the realization that everyone is an equal citizen and the differences on basis of caste and creeds were man-made to keep the innocent and ignorant as underdogs in the society. Although Periyar's speeches were targeted towards illiterate and more mundane mass, scores of educated people followed them. These educated elites earlier knew nothing about how a few were propagating blind beliefs and caste distinction for their own selfish ends. Periyar considered reasoning as a special tool. According to him, all were blessed with his tool but very few use it. Thus it was reasoning that was used in Periyar's material, with respect to related subjects of social interest, presented to his audiences.

Periyar was not only a social revolutionary but also a champion of the underprivileged. His sphere of activity was wide and when he took up an issue he went deep into it, understanding the aspects, and did not rest until he found a permanent solution. Communal differences in Tamil society were deep-rooted and appeared to be permanent features until Periyar came to the scene.

Cho Ramaswamy wrote an article on E. V. Ramasami Naicker and C. N. Annadurai in the English magazine India Today. Cho remarked:

"Periyar was accepted and acclaimed as the leader by a significant section of the Tamil population in spite of all his contempt for Tamil and disdain for Tamils only because he was perceived to be a genuine individual, a rarity among those in public life. There was no shade of hypocrisy in him and he never attempted sophistry while propounding his social philosophy. And what a philosophy it was!

Rationalism

The bedrock of Periyar's principles and the movements that he started was rationalism. What drew him to public service and made him dedicate his life to it was man's inhumanity to man. He found that an insignificant minority in society was exploiting the majority and trying to keep them in a subordinate position forever. To set matters right, he wanted the exploited to sit up and think about their position. Unless they exercised their reason, there wouldn't be a realization that they were being exploited by a handful of people. If they started thinking, they would realize that they were human beings like the rest, that birth did not and should not endow superiority over others, and that they must awaken themselves and do everything possible to improve their own lot.

It was not an easy task for Periyar to create this awakening among the people who had, for generations, got used to a subordinate position. Most of them did not know that their subordinate position had been brought about by the cunning schemes of self-seekers. Thus, Periyar spoke to the people on innumerable platforms, over the years to arouse their thinking power.

Likewise, Periyar explained that wisdom lies in thinking and that the spear-head of thinking is rationalism. On caste, he stated that no other living being harms or degrades its own class. But man, said to be a rational living being does these evils. The differences, hatred, enmity, degradation, poverty, and wickedness, now prevalent in the society are due to lack of wisdom and rationalism and not due to God or the cruelty of time.

Periyar also blamed the capitalists for their control of machineries, creating difficulties to the workers. Consequently rationalism, which has to lead the way for peaceful life to all, had resulted in causing poverty and worries to the people because of dominating forces. He went on to explain that there is no use of simply acquiring titles or amassing wealth if one has no self-respect and scientific knowledge. An example he showed was the West sending messages to the planets, while the Tamil society in India were sending rice and cereals to their dead fore-fathers through the Brahmins.

In a message to the Brahmin community, Periyar stated, "in the name of god, religion, and sastras you have duped us. We were the ruling people. Stop this life of cheating us from this year. Give room for rationalism and humanism". He further explained that "any opposition not based on rationalism, science, or experience will one day or another, reveal the fraud, selfishness, lies and conspiracies".

Self-Respect

Periyar's philosophy of *self-respect,* was based on his image of an ideal world and a universally accepted one. It is a philosophy preaching that human actions should be based on rational thinking. Further, it is an outcome of the natural instinct of human beings to examine every object and every action and even nature with a spirit of inquiry; and to refuse to submit to anything *irrational* as equivalent to slavery. Thus, the philosophy of *Self-Respect* taught that human actions should be guided by reason; right and wrong should follow from rational thinking, and; conclusions drawn from reason should be respected under circumstances. Freedom means respect to thoughts and actions considered 'right' by human beings on the basis of 'reason'. There is not much difference between 'freedom' and 'self-respect'. Periyar's foremost appeal to people was to develop self-respect. He preached that the Brahmins have monopolized and cheated other communities for decades and deprived them of self-respect. He continued to remind them that most Brahmins claimed to belong to a "superior" community with the reserved privilege of being in charge of temples and performing archanas. He felt that they were trying to reassert their control over religion by using their superior caste status to claim the exclusive privilege to touch idols or enter the sanctum sanctorum. He claimed that in certain places the scheduled caste people were not allowed to use the tanks, wells and at times even the streets used by Brahmins. Though sporadic caste-violence and atrocities continue to occur in Tamil Nadu, discrimination has largely been eliminated due to Periyar's agitations against these unjust restrictions.

Women's Rights

Periyar has explained that it is extremely cruel on the part of the Hindu brethren to witness the gradual destruction suffered by one half of their society, without taking any action. This apart, men and women are both human beings. The difference in physical features will not change the human quality. The difference in intellect and physical strength which we find among men can be found among women also. Practice improves the position equally in both men and women. Just as there are foolish people, weaklings and people with bad qualities among men, among women also there are likely to be people belonging to these categories.

Marriages

With regards to marriage, Periyar has stated that it is one of the worst customs in India. He claimed that the marriage principle, briefly, involves the enslavement of a woman by her husband and nothing else. This enslavement is concealed under the cover of marriage rites to deceive the women concerned by giving the wedding the false name of a divine function.

There have been numerous papers in South India reporting how husbands have killed their wives, suspecting immoral behaviour. The husband's suspicion of his wife's character has often led to murders. Those who believe in the divine dispensation, according to Periyar, do not have the knowledge to ask themselves why marriages conducted according to religious rites and the approval of God end in this fashion. Periyar further states that the very idea that the only proper thing for women to do is to be slaves of domesticity, bear children and bring them up, is a faulty one. As long as these restrictions are imposed on women, we can be sure that women have to be subservient to men and depend on men for help. If women have to live on terms of equality with men, they must have the liberty, like men, to have the kind of education they like and also to do unhampered, any work suitable to their knowledge, ability and taste. Furthermore, Periyar objected to terms like "giving of a maid" and "given in marriage". They are, "Sanskrit terms" and treat woman as a thing. He advocated the substitution of the word for marriage taken from the Tirukkual "Valkkati Tunni" or "helpmate in prosperity".

Expenses

With marriage comes the expenses. Periyar stated that in our country, and particularly in Hindu society, a marriage is a function causing a lot of difficulties and waste to all people concerned. But those who conduct the marriage function and those who are getting married do not appear to notice the attendant difficulties because they think that social life necessitates wasteful expense and many difficulties and therefore they must necessarily face those inconveniences and hardships.

Wedding feast, jewels, expensive clothes, procession, pandal, dance, music — money is spent on all these to satisfy the vanity of the organizers. Whatever may be the amount of money spent on the wedding and however pompous each of the items may be, the mirth and jollity associated with these are over in two or three days. In a week's time the prestige and honour connected with these are forgotten. But the wedding expenses leave many families crushed; for many poor families hese expenses leave an enormous burden and the debts remain uncleared for a number of years. However, if the money intended for the wedding expense is not borrowed and belongs to either of the marriage parties, then that amount could be used by her to bring up her children and to educate them. Such a procedure would be highly beneficial to her.

Arranged Marriages

In South Asia we mostly hear of arranged marriages as part of custom, heritage, and religions. Periyar thought that the Aryan wedding methods were barbarous because of the Aryan religion and art: Vedas, Sastras, Puranas, and Epics belong to the barbaric age. He further stated that is the reason why their wedding methods involve the parents giving the girl, prostituting the girl children and some stranger carrying the girl away by force or stealth.

Arranged marriages in general were meant to enable the couple to live together throughout life and derive happiness, satisfaction and a good reputation, even years after the sexual urge and sexual pleasure are forgotten.

But, with the selfish manipulation of this pact, Periyar claimed that women find 'pleasure' in slavish marriage because they have been brought up by their parents without education, independence and self-respect and because they have been made to believe that marriage means subordination to males. The inclusion of such slavish women in the group of 'chaste' women is another lure to them, leading them to find pleasure in such marriages.

Because a man is also married before he has understood the nature of life, its problems and its pleasures, he is satisfied with the slavish nature of the wife and the sexual pleasure she gives. If he finds any incompatibility, he adapts himself to his partner and the circumstances and puts up with his lot.

Love Marriages

Love marriages, claims Periyar, on the other hand will suit only those who have no ideals in life. Such a wedding gives primacy to sexual union along and it is doubtful if it indicates an agreement between the couple for good life. Sexual compatibility alone does not ensure happy married life; the couple should be able to live together cheerfully. Suitability for life or living together can be determined only if the man and woman get used to the company of each other, and are satisfied with each other. Only then, they can enter into an agreement to live together.

Periyar further states that love marriages can give pleasure only as long as there is lust and the ability to satisfy that lust. If there is no compatibility between the partners in other respects, such marriages end only in the enslavement of women. The lies of such women resemble the lives of bullocks which are tied to a cart, beaten up and made to labour endlessly until they die.

Therefore, there is a proverb stating, *"A deeply loving girl is unfit for family life; a suitable life partner is unfit for love." Periyar believed that the agreement between partners to live together will constitute a better marriage than a love marriage.*

Self-respect Marriages

In a leading article of *Viduthalai*, Periyar states that a self-respect wedding is based on rationalism. Rationalism is based on the individual's courage. Some may have the courage to conduct it during the time which almanacs indicate as the time of the planet Rahu and that, particularly in the evening. Some others may have just enough daring to avoid the Brahmin priest and his mother tongue-the Sanskrit language. Some may feel nervous about not keeping the traditional lamp burning in broad daylight. Some others may have the rotten thought that conducting a wedding without 'mangala sutra' is disgraceful.

Still, the self-respect weddings conducted during the past thirty years have some basic limits. They are: Brahmins and their *mantras* should be utterly avoided; meaningless rituals, piling mud pots, one on another, having the traditional lamp during day time, ritual smoke-all these should be avoided. Rationalism does not approve of these. Periyar then asks why can't the government pass an Act that legalizes weddings which avoid the above-mentioned superstitious practices. If all these details cannot be accommodated in the Act, the latter can legalize weddings which don't have Brahmin priests, the Sanskrit language and the so called holy fire.

Thus, marriages styled as Self-Respect marriages carried a threefold significance: a) replacing the Purohit, b) inter-caste equality, c) man-woman equality. Periyar claimed to have performed Self-Respect marriages unofficially since 1925 and officially since 1928. Self-Respect marriages were legalized in 1967 by the Dravida Munnetra Kazhagam (DMK) Government.

Widow-remarriage

On the remarriage of widows, Periyar states that among the atrocities perpetrated by the Hindu male population against women, here we have to consider the treatment meted out to widows alone. If a girl loses her husband, even before knowing anything of worldly pleasures, she is compelled to close her eyes to everything in the world and die broken-hearted. Even in Periyar's community at the time, there were widowed girls below the age of 13 years. Periyar stated how it is a touching sight to see the parents of those widowed children treating them like untouchables.

He goes on to say that whatever may be the reason for the present state of the Hindu society, my firm belief that the low position given permanently to widows may prove to be the reason for the utter ruin of the Hindu religion and the Hindu society.

If we try to find the reason for such conduct, we will have to conclude that they instinctively feel that women are slaves, subservient to men and that they must be kept under control. That is why these people treat women like animals. They seem to feel that giving freedom to women is equivalent to committing a very serious crime. The result of this attitude is that there is no independence or freedom to one half of the human race. This wicked enslavement of half of the human race is due to the fact that men are physically a little stronger than women. This principle applies to all spheres of life and the weaker are enslaved by the stronger.

If slavery has to be abolished in society, the male arrogance and wickedness which lead to the enslavement of women must be abolished first. Only when this is achieved, the tender sprouts of freedom and equality will register growth.

One of the reasons why Periayr hated Hinduism and the orthodoxy practiced in the name of Hinduism was the practice of child marriage. Many of the girl children who were married before they were ten or twelve years old became widows before they knew the meaning of the word. According to the 1921 All India Census the details of the child widows reported living in the country that time were as follows:

- 1 year baby widows-497
- 1 to 2 year child widows-494
- 2 to 3 year child widows-1,257
- 3 to 4 year child widows-2,837
- 4 to 5 year child widows-6,707
- Total number of widows-11,342
- 5 to 10 year young widows-85,037
- 10 to 15 year young widows-232,147
- 15 to 20 year young widows-396,172
- 20 to 25 year young widows-742,820

- 25 to 30 year young widows-1,163,720
- Total number of widows-2,631,238.

Periyar was deeply disturbed when he realized that among the widows in India, 11,892 were little children below 5 years and that young widows below 15 years numbering 232,147 were denied the pleasures of life.

With regards to the re-marriage of widows, Periyar stated that it is the practice of our people to refer to such a wedding as "a widow's marriage". Such an expression is used only with reference to women and in connection with men. Just as this lady is marrying another husband after the death of the first husband, many men marry again after the death of the first wife. But the second marriage of a man is not referred to as "a widower's marriage", though that is the proper thing to do.

Periyar himself was a widower. After becoming one, he took a second wife. He claimed that in the ancient days, both men and women in the country had this practice. There were numerous instances in sastras and puranas of women getting married again after the death of their first husband. Periyar further stated that this is not an unusual practice in the rest of the world though it might appear strange for us at the present time. Christian and Muslim women marry again after the death of the first husband. 90 percent of women in Muslim countries get married again soon after the death of the first husband. This may be unusual in certain sections of Indian societies. But it is a common practice in certain other sections of our society which are called very backward communities.

Further, inter-caste marriages and remarriage of widows are on the increase in India. Brahmins oppose these because they are afraid that they cannot exploit the people any more in the name of sastras. For the same reason they oppose the Sharada Act which is necessary for social well-being.

Child Marriage

In all the meetings of the non-Brahmins and the Self-Respectors, Periyar condemned child marriages and emphasized the need for educating all girl children and giving right to young widows to get married again. Periyar has been very much against child marriage and stated that it reflects the cruelty to which innocent girls were subjected by their well-meaning parents. Periyar asked that if these parents can be considered civilized in any sense of the term. There was no other leader other than Periyar who reacted against this practice of child marriage.

Those who supported child marriage were strongly against Periyar's condemnation of this act. Take for example, the Sharada Act. Those who opposed this Act say that it was against the Sastras to conduct the marriage of a girl after she has attained puberty. They further say that those who conduct such marriages are committing a sin and therefore will go to hell.

Chastity

Periyar claimed that "household duties" have risen out of the foolishness of people and were not natural duties. He went on to say that it was our selfish greed which has multiplied our household work. Nobody need worry that without household work, the women will lose their "chastity". On chastity, Periyar went on to say that it is something that belongs to women and is not a pledge to men. Whatever, chastity is, it was something that belonged to individuals.

In society, it was believed that if people lose their chastity, they will get divine punishment. Others are not going to get that punishment. Referring to the doctrines of institutionalized orthodox religions, he went on to say that men need not to worry themselves that women are committing a sin by not doing household work. Thus, let men realize that women are not slaves and that men are not their masters or guardians. Women should be allowed to develop the competence to protect themselves and their chastity and men need not be their watchdogs. He also believed that it was derogatory for men to play such a role.

It was said by the orthodox that women will develop diseases if they lose their chastity. The disease that a woman gets affects the husbands also. If we educate the women, they will develop the capability to keep themselves and their husbands pure. Thus, Periyar stated in the *Kudi Arasu* for the society to think deeply about taking a decision and do the right thing for their sisters and girl children.

Periyar kindled the thoughts of everybody by also ridiculing the use of the word chastity only with reference to women. (Periyar-Father of Tamil 32) He stated that character is essential for both men and women and that speaking of chastity only with reference to women degraded not merely women but men also. He extended this thought and said that in any sphere of activity, civilized society cannot think of one law for men and another for women. He also said that they way most men treated their women was far worse than the way the upper class people treated the lower class, the way in which rich men treated the poor and the way in which a master treated his slave.

Education

On education, Periyar stated that some foolish parents believe that if girls get educated, they will correspond with their secret lovers. That it is a very foolish and mischievous notion. No parent need be anxious about it. If a girl writes a letter, it will only be to a male. We can even now caution men not to read any love letter addressed to them by a woman and, even if they read it, not to reply to it. If men do not listen to this advice, they, as well as the girls who write them must be punished. It will be a hopelessly bad thing, if parents keep their girl children uneducated for this reason.

At a speeched delivered by Periyar at the Prize Distribution function in the Municipal School for Girls at Karungal Palayam, Erode, he stated that girl children should be taught active and energetic exercises like running, high jump, long jump, and wrestling so that they may acquire the strength and courage of men. Their time and energy should not be wasted in light pastimes like *Kummi* (groups going in a circle, clapping their hands rhythmically) and in *Kolatam* (striking with sticks rhythmically).

In ancient Tamil literature, poets have stressed the value of education for women. In a famous verse, a poet by the name of Naladiar stated that, *"What gives beauty to a woman is not the hair style or the patter of her dress or the saffron on her face but only education"*. In a verse of *Eladhi* it states, *"Beauty does not lie in the style of wailing or in the charm of a blush but only in the combination of numbers and letters (education).*

In a 1960 issue if *Viduthalai* Periyar stated that *"There should be a drastic revolution in the desires and ideals of Indian women. They should equip themselves to do all types of work that men are doing. They should have good domestic life without allowing nature's obstacles in their own lives. Therefore, there should be a welcome change in the minds of our women. The administrators also most pay special attention to the advancement of women".*

Armed Forces

Periyar even advocated for women to be given weapons to protect themselves in reply to a question put in the Central Legislature. He stated that we have no hope that the State Governments will do anything in this sphere because most of the State ministers hold the orthodox belief that women are slavish creatures. Though here and there we find women also as ministers, hey are old-fashioned traditionalists who will say, *"We don't want any kind of freedom. We are perfectly happy with slavery".*

In Periyar's time he explained that *""Indian" women had no self-determination in any sphere of life like education property and marriage. They thought that modern civilization meant dressing themselves like British and American women and adorning themselves. Even our educated women do not entertain any thought that they must enter the police and army departments and learn to pilot airplanes like the women of Russia and Turkey. Just as modern education has made men cowards an book-worms, it has made our women decoratie* [sic] *dolls and weaklings".*

In a leading article written by Periyar in *Viduthalai in 1946*, he claimed that unless there is a drastic, fundamental and revolutionary change in our administrative machinery, it is impossible to make our women independent beings.

Periyar goes on to explain that in our country also, there are thousands of women with the courage, competence and desire to work in the police department. Just as girls going to school was considered wonderful and cycle-riding by girls was considered funny, a few years ago, women on police duty may appear to be wonderful or strange for a few years. Then, in course of ime, this will be considered natural.

We need methods that will effect an astounding revolution in the world of women. Until we acquire those methods, we will be moving forward like a tortoise and writing and talking about Drowpath and Sita.

Periyar, in a 1932 article of *Kudi Arasu* explained that *"women should develop physical strength like men. They must take exercise and get training in the use of weapons. They must acquire the ability to protect themselves when any sex-mad person tries to molest them. They should get the necessary training to join the armey* [sic] *when need arises and fight the enemy. This is the view of all civilized people. Women also wholeheartedly support this view. When the general view in the world is like this, who can accept the statement of some people that there is no use in giving higher education to women?"*

Birth Control

- *"Others advocate birth-control, with a view of preserving the health of women and conserving family property; but we advocate it for the liberation of women."*

In the *Kudi Arasu* of 1932, Periyar explained the basic differences between the reasons given to us for contraception and the reasons given by others for this. We say that contraception is necessary for women to gain freedom. Others advocate contraception taking into consideration many problems like the health of women, the health and energy of the children, the poverty of the country and the maintenance of the family property. Many Westerners also support contraception for the same reasons. Our view is not based on these considerations. We recommend that women should stop delivering children altogether because conception stands in the way of women enjoying personal freedom. Further, begetting a number of children prevents men also from being free and independent. This truth will be clear if we listen to talk of men and women when their freedom is hampered.

He went on to say how birth control does not aim at preventing the birth of children altogether, but aims only at limiting births. A man and his wife may have two children, or at the most, three children. This birth control policy is against bringing forth an unlimited number of children.

While Periyar and the Self-Respect movement were advocating for birth control, Rajaji (C. Rajagopalachariar) very strongly opposed it. Others who opposed birth control was Thiru Adhithanar, the publisher of an extremely popular newspaper, *Dina Thandhi* at the time. In response to Rajaji's stand against birth control, Periyar explained that he was against this since he was of the Vedic Brahmin community that staunchly engrossed in the Manu Dharma. Thus, limiting births of overpopulation would limit diseases and death from many and therefore leave Brahmin priests without a job of doing ceremonies for the sick and funerals. In a 1959 article of *Viduthalai* he exclaimed that *"If people like Rajaji discover new islands, make the forests habitable, do propaganda for the birth of more and more children and have farms for the upbringing of children, we may be in a position to understand them."*

During the late 1950s, 80 percent of the men and 90 percent of the women in Tamil Nadu were illiterate. Periyar argued in a 1959 article in *Viduthalai* that *"in this situation, if birth control is not practiced and people are allowed to have any number of children, the result will be the multiplication of castes among the "Sudras", like washermen, barbers, pot-makers, kuravas or gypsies, hunters, fishermen, famers* [sic]*, toddy tappers, padayachies, pillars, cobblers, pariahs, and a thousand others and a limitless increase in population. The increase in population will foce the 'Sudras' to preserve themselves from starvation by standing with folded hands before lazy fellows and calling them 'swami', 'master' and 'landlord'. What good result can we expect if birth control is not adopted?"*

Previously in a 1933 article of the *Kudi Arasu*, Periyar, in his words, explained that *"even a High Court Judge in India does not know the amount of trouble that a mother takes to bring up a child. If a husband is kind to his wife and shows concern for her health and happiness, he must adopt the contraceptive method. Otherwise, he must be one who could manage to see that in delivery and in the brining* [sic] *up of children, she does not have much trouble. Therefore, the proper thing to do now is to drastically cut the expenses mentioned above and spend money on the proper upbringing of children with the help of nurses."*

Property Rights and Divorce

With regards to property rights for women, Periyar stated that there was no difference between men and women. He went on to say that like men, women should have the right to own property and enjoy its benefits. With regards to divorce or separations, he advocated that a woman can lie away from her husband if he is an undesirable person and if he has nay virulent disease. When a woman has to live apart from her husband in these circumstances, she is entitled to maintenance allowance and a claim on the husband's property. Even if a widow gets remarried, she must be given the right to claim a share of the first husband's property.

On February 4, 1946, the Central Legislature passed an Act giving the right the Hindu married woman to get from her husband in certain circumstances a separate place to live in and a maintenance allowance. Periyar explained how that it was a useless Act. since it seems that the members of the Hindu Mahasabha and Sanadahnis agitated against the grant of even this right.

Dowry

On the Dowry system practiced widely throughout the Indian sub-continent not only by Hindus but Christians too, Periyar calls it a *"serious disease that was spreading fast amongst Tamilians"*. He went on to state that the disease was also found in its virulent form among the Andhras and the Brahmins of Tamil Nadu. Periyar also argued that if a man with property worth one lakh has three daughters, he has to become a beggar by the time these daughters are married. In the name of dowry, the parents of the young men who marry the three daughters, squeeze the man's property out of him.

In the 1959 issue of Viduthalai, Periyar stated that, "according to a new legislation, women have the right to a share of the parents' property. Therefore every girl will definitely get her legitimate share from the parents' wealth-if the parents are wealth. It is inhuamane [sic] on the part of the parents of a boy to dump on him a girl whom he does not like and to plan to such as much as they can from the property of the girl's father. There is basically no difference between selling education and love for money and selling one's chastity for money. 'Prostitute' is a germ of contempt for a woman; a boy should not be reduced by his avaricous [sic] parents to get the name, 'a prostituted boy' or 'a boy that has been sold'. A father-in-law who has means, however miserly he may be by nature, will not be indifferent when his daughter suffers out of poverty. Therefore, it is very shameful on the part of the bridegroom's parents to demand from the bride's father that at the time of the marriage he should gie jewels worth so many thousands along with so many thousand rupees as dowry and that he should provide the bridegroom with a house and a care. The fact that another party makes such demands at the time of his daughter's marriage does not justify any parent's demands at the time of his son's wedding. All people must realize that both demanding and giving dowry are wrong and they must boldly declare this when occasion arises."

Periyar calls the dowry an evil and exploitative practice depriving tens of thousands of talented and beautiful young women with sound character remaining spinsters without any chance of getting married.

Devadasis

Among the atrocities the Tamil society committed against women was the practice of keeping some women attached to temples as *Devadasis*. Dr. Muthulakshmi proposed the resolution at the Madras Legislature that the *Devadasi* system should be abolished. The Government wanted comments on that from all important people. Periyar in his statement pointed out that the *Devadasi* system was a disgrace to Hindu religion. The fact that, in the name of a temple or a god, some women are kept as common property is an insult to all the women in the society. He also remarked that the prevalence of this system encouraged immorality among men and thus set the pattern for unprincipled life in many families. This was stoutly opposed in the Assembly by Satyamurthi Iyer, an orthodox Congress member, under the pretext of safeguarding the Hindu traditions. It should be said to the credit of Dr. Muthulakshmi and the leaders like Periyar that the proposal of the Doctor was accpeted and a law was enacted against the *Devadasi* system.

Periyar's example of the degradation of women in the *Devadasi* system is explained that *"if a man's physical passion is aroused when his wife is not with him, he immediately goes to a prostitute. Rough stones are planted where cows and bufaloes* [sic] *graze to facilitate the animals to rub against the stones when they feel like it. Likewise, Devadasis served in temples and in all villages rough stones planted on the borders and they say that these two (employing devadasis and the planting rough stones) are aamong* [sic] *the 32 dharmas mentioned in the sastras. When we consider why his kindness to the suffering and also the 32 dharmas are all bogus"*.

Resolutions Passed

As the Self-Respect conference held in Chengalpattu, Tamil Nadu in 1929, the following were among the many resolutions passed with regards for women's rights:

1. Women should be given equal right along with men for the family property.
2. There should be no objection to employing women to any job for which they are qualified.

3. Schools, particularly schools, should try to employ only women teachers.

At the conference held in Erode in 1930, the same resolutions were passed again reminding the delegates and others that the interest of women was still uppermost in Periyar's mind. M.R. Jayakar who presided over the Erode conference was greatly impressed by the progressive views of Periyar and other members. He was particularly happy that the movement included not merely non-Brahmin Hindus but Christians and Muslims too. He pointed out that the Self-Respect movement was more progressive than Congress. Furthermore, at the Virudhnagar conference the women members held a separate conference and passed some resolutions demanding that women should have the right to select their life partners without any consideration of religion or community and that weddings should not involve wasteful expenditure and elaborate ceremonies.

Social Reform and Eradication of Caste

Periyar's philosophy did not differentiate social and political service. According to him, the first duty of a government is to run the social organization efficiently, and that the philosophy of religion was to organize the social system. Conditions appeared to him such that the government was not for the people, but, in a "topsy-turvey" manner, the people were for the government. He attributed this situation to the state of the social system contrived for the advantage of a small group of people.

Therefore, Periyar was of the view that for the progress of the people in the country, great social changes were necessary and a good government could be formed only after making those changes. He thought that under the existing social system, there was and there could be no means of removing the hardships of the people even to a small extent, regardless of who came to power.

Rural Upliftment

One of the areas of focus was in the upliftment of villages. In a booklet called *Village Uplift*, Periyar plead for rural reform. It should be stressed in this context that rural India still forms the largest part of the Indian subcontinent in spite of the ongoing process of urbanization. Thus, the distinction between rural and urban has meant an economic and social degradation for the rural inhabitant. Periyar wanted to eradicate the concept of "village" as a discrimination word among places just as the concept outcast among social groups. Periyar advocated for a location where neither the name nor the situation or its conditions imply differences among people.

With the same aim in view, Periyar wanted farm labourers to be called "partakers in agriculture" and be paid 60 percent of the income, while 40 percent would go to the landowner. In his booklet on rural uplift of 1944, Periyar gave an action program for modernizing villages which mentioned: mechanization of agriculture, that is, ploughing, sowing, digging wells, and harvesting by machines; reformulation of agricultural land to facilitate mechanization and separation of land unsuitable for this for growing other crops; marketing of agricultural products, through farmers' cooperative so that the proceeds would go to the agriculturists; combining villages as a small town for provision of a school, hospital, park, cinema, drama, reading room, library, radio station, roads, bus transport, police station, an educated judge, and shops; organizing mobile exhibitions; establishing appeals courts and providing for field camp of officers for redressal of grievances; and establishing small industries.

Periyar and the *Self-Respect Movement* wanted to reduce Government salaries because they spoiled men's purity. He explained that they want industries producing things necessary for public welfare to be state-owned. Furthermore, cooperative societies should be introduced to remove the brokers and moneylenders that come between farmers and consumers. Farmers must be helped to get rid of their debts. Litigation and conflicts on account of rules should be reduced and death taxes fixed. Periyar also believed that local boards, municipalities, and cooperative managements must be given more power.

In his rural uplift, he puts every stress on education as the sure way to rational thinking and action which would lead to the abolishment of injustices in society, economic as well as social. Periyar came up with a fourteen point program which were as follows: "the landless agriculturists should be safeguarded from exploitation by landlords and money lenders, where the government should do everything to see that agricultural workers are not deprived of their scroll land holdings for defaulting payment of rent; cooperative societies and banks should be formed to save the farmers from the exorbitant rate of interest collected by pawnbrokers and money lenders; to reduce the number of cases arising out of the dispute of the ownership of land the Government should itself possess all clear land documents; the laws pertaining to agriculture should be so framed that the actual agricultural labourers get reasonable returns for their labour, and to prevent landlords and middle-men from cornering away the bulk of the agricultural products; like railways, post and telegraphs, waterways and electricity which are now under the control of Government, the other public utilities and services should be taken over by the Government; insurance schemes should be undertaken by the Government itself and to be extended to workers as in the case of other people; legislation should be so framed as to increase the income of public as well as the workers with a view to upgrade their standard of living under income ratio; children should be given facilities for education within the target period; considering the baneful influence of toddy and other kinds of drink, the government should work towards total prohibition before a specified period of time; the evils of untouchability, discrimination based on birth, superstition and blind belief should be done away with; State Government appointments should be apportioned according to the percentage of population of people and political aspirations; land tax should be levied progressively taxing the rich more and leaving the poor from the rigorous clutches of tax; opportunities to get revenue in the case of local bodies and cooperatives should be enlarged and the management should be vested with the Government servants; and the motto of the public administration should aim at efficiency and a good administration with reasonable expenditure.

Periyar sent a copy of these resolutions to the government and political parties, including the Congress. The Congress ignored these resolutions because they had come from Periyar and his party. But the *Just Party* accepted the resolutions and assured Periyar that it would implement those resolutions, when administrative power came into its hands. The acceptance of the resolutions by the *Just Party* was indeed a victory for Periyar's *Self-Respect Movement.*

Periyar felt that a small number of cunning people created caste distinctions in order to dominate over society. That was why he emphasized the view that we must first develop self-respect and learn to analyse propositions rationally. A self-respecting rationalist will readily realize that caste system has been stifling self-respect and therefore he will strive to get rid of this menace. One of Periyar's quotes on caste was, "a sizable population today remains as *Untouchables*, and another sizable population exists in the name of *Sudras* and as serfs, coolies and menials. Who wants an independence that cannot help change these things? Who wants religion, scriptures and gods, which cannot bring about a change in this sphere"?

Periyar explained that the caste system in south India is, due to Indo-Aryan influence, linked with the arrival of Brahmins from the north. Ancient Tamil Nadu (part of Tamilakkam) had a different stratification of society in four or five regions (*Tinai*), determined by natural surroundings and adequate means of living. Periyar also mentions that birds, animals, and worms, which are considered to be devoid of rationalism do not create castes, or differences of high and low in their own species. But man considered to be a rational being, is suffering from these because of religion. He further explains that amongst dogs you do not have a Brahmin dog, or a Pariah (untouchable) dog. Among donkeys and monkeys we also do not find such things. But, amongst men there is such discrimination.

Periyar argued on how a person with an iota of sense or rationalism in could do such things such as giving special treatment only to Brahmins. Some examples practiced were for lower castes to fall at their feet and to even, sometimes, wash their feet and drink that water. Periyar explains that if this is Hindu doctrine and philosophy, such a religion must go. He gives examples of rituals such as christening, house warming, marriage, and for puberty, that they are for the Brahmin's gain as the only ones to conduct these occasions. We do not respect our knowledge nor are we ashamed of our actions. Are we merely a mass of flesh and bones? Why should anybody get angry when I say all these to make you think over. Who is responsible of our degradation? Is it religion or government"?

Gandhi advocated for the caste system in its preservation. On the question of *Untouchables* being prevented from drawing water from wells and entering temples, Gandhi suggested having separate wells and temples made for them instead. Periyar argued against this by demanding the Vedas of Indo-Aryans to be burnt and their deities to be destroyed since it was their creation of the castes and *Untouchables*. He also went on to state that "it was absurd to quote religion, god, or religious doctrines to render people as lowest castes".

Periyar argued that the caste system has "perverted peoples ideas about human conduct. The principle of different codes of conduct for each caste based on birth and life, led in accordance with it for centuries, have spoiled the Hindu mentality almost beyond repair, and destroyed the idea of uniformity in conduct. Graded inequality has got so much into the Hindu blood that general intelligence is warped and refused to mend even after English education and higher standards of living".

Hereditary Education Policy

In 1952, Rajaji introduced a new education policy based on family vocation which its opponents dubbed *Kula Kalvi Thittam* (Hereditary Education Policy). As per this policy, schools will work in the morning and students had to compulsorily learn the family vocation of their caste in the afternoon. Thus, a carpenter's son would learn carpentry, a priest's son chanting hymns, and a barber's son would learn hair cutting and shaving after school. Periyar felt that this scheme was a clever device against Dalits and Other Backward Classes as their first generation was getting educated only then.

Periyar demanded its withdrawal and launched protests against the *Kula Kalvi Thittam* which he felt was caste-based and was aimed at maintaining caste hegemony. Rajaji quit in 1954, and his successor Kamaraj scrapped it after becoming chief minister.

Removal of Caste Names

Periyar realized that the domination of Brahmins was not restricted to the spheres of administration and worship. It was found that most of the hotels in Tamil Nadu indicated on the name boards that they were maintained by Brahmins and only served Brahmins. Periyar organized agitations throughout Tamil Nadu for the removal of the words "for the brahmins" and "by the Brahmins" from the name boards of hotels. He drew the attention of the common people and particularly the philanthropists to this practice in the chowltries of feeding the Brahmins and non-Brahmins separately. Today this practice is no longer in existence.

Inter-caste Marriages

Periyar encouraged inter-caste marriages in order to combat the superstitions of the caste system practiced in India. He pointed out that a marriage is a contract between a young woman and a young man and it is not a function for the parents to get involved in for a reason or another. Generally, orthodox elders arranged the marriages of their children and tried to perpetuate the dowry system. One of the projects of the *Self-Respect Movement* started by Periyar was to make young people realize that a marriage is the concern of a young man and a young woman and that other considerations brought in by the parents were utterly irrelevant. The Self-Respect Movement also pointed out that there were facilities for registering marriages and that the practice of employing Brahmin priests to conduct the marriages betrayed the superstition of the concerned people and encouraged exploitation by Brahmins. In the course of over the past fifty years, thousands of weddings between people of different communities and without the intervention of Brahmin priests have taken place as a result of the influence that the *Self-Respect Movement* has exerted on society. Arignar Anna in his capacity as Chief Minister of Tamil Nadu passed a law in 1967 by which marriages conducted without the intervention of priests became lawful marriages.

Service to the Backward Classes

As soon as Periyar entered the Congress, he realized that the Brahmins had many more government jobs than the non-Brahmins and that higher education was more or less their prerogative. He wanted the Congress to pass a resolution demanding communal representation in education and in employment. Though he tried hard for five years continuously, he could not persuade the Congress party to realize the need for such a resolution. Therefore he left the Congress, supported the Justice party, started the Self-Respect Movement and finally got the government of Madras to pass a law on communal representation in education and employment.

Kumarasami Kamaraj was thoroughly convinced that Periyar was only demanding justice for the non-Brahmins who had been neglected and exploited by certain sections of the people for hundreds of years. Therefore he readily accepted Periyar's suggestion that poor people should have free education. When

Kamaraj became Chief Minister of Madras he allowed all children to have free education up to standard ten. Through Periyar's spirit of social service, Kamaraj introduced the free midday meal scheme for school children and later granted free books and free clothes to school children. When Kalaignar Karunanidhi was Chief Minister in 1969, he extended free education up to the pre-university class. As a result of Periyar's devoted service for the cause of the under privileged, scheduled caste men and women occupy high positions in government offices and also serve as doctors and engineers.

Tamil Language and Writing

Periyar claimed that Tamil, Telugu, Malayalam, and Kannada came from the same tongue, or same mother language of Old Tamil. He explained that the Tamil language is called by four different names since it is spoken in four different Dravidian states,and thus she has four different names. With relation to writing, Periyar stated that using the Tamil script about the arts which are useful to the people in their life and which foster knowledge, talent and courage, and propagating them among the masses, thereby will enlighten the people. Further, he explained that it will enrich the language, and thus it can be regarded as a zeal for Tamil. Periyar also stated that if words of North Indian origin (Sanskrit) are removed from Telugu, Kannada, and Malayalam all that will be left will only be Tamil.

On the Brahmin usage of Tamil, he stated how the Tamil spoken by the Andrhas and the Malayalee peoples were far better than the Tamil spoken by the Brahmins. Periyar believed that Tamil language will make the Dravidian people unite under the banner of Tamil culture, and that it will make the Kannadigas, Andhras and the Malayalees be vigilant. With regards to a Dravidian alliance under a common unbrella language, Periyar stated that "a time will come for unity. This will go on till there is an end to the North Indian domination. We shall reclaim an independent sovereign state for us".

At the same time, Periyar was also known to have issued controversial remarks on Tamil language and Tamil people from time to time. On one occasion, he referred to Tamil people as "barbarians" and Tamil language as the "language of barbarians". However, Anita Diehl explains that Periyar made these remarks on Tamil because it had no respective feminine verbal forms.

Periyar's ideas on Tamil alphabet reforms and his reasons were for the following such as the vowel '^' (i), having a cursive and looped representation of the short form, '‡' (I). In stone inscriptions of 400 or 500 years ago, many Tamil letters are found in other shapes. As a matter of necessity and advantage to cope with the printing technology, Periyar thought that it was sensible to change a few letters, reduce the number of letters, and alter a few signs. He further explained that the older and the more divine a language and its letters were said to be, they need reform. Because of changes brought about by means of modern transport and international contact, and happenings that have attracted words and products from many countries, foreign words and their pronunciations have been assimilated into Tamil quite easily.

Thoughts on Thirukkural

Periyar hailed the *Thirukkural* as a valuable scripture which contained many scientific and philosophical truths. He also praised the secular nature of the work. Periyar praised Thiruvalluvar for his description of God as a formless entity with all positive attributes. He also suggested that one who reads the Thirukkural will became a Self-respecter absorbing knowledge in politics, society, and economics. Though certain items in this ancient book of ethics may not relate to today, Periyar explained that it permits such changes for today's society.

On caste, he showed that the Kural illustrates how Vedic laws of Manu was against the Sudras and other communities of the Dravidian race. On the other hand, Periyar opined that the ethics from the Kural was comparable to the Christian Bible. The Dravidar Kazhagam adopted the Thirukkural and advocated that Thiruvalluvar's Kural alone was enough to educate the people of the country. One of Periyar's quotes on the Thirukkural from Veeramani's *Collected Works of Periyar* was "when Dravida Nadu (Dravidistan) was a victim to Indo-Aryan deceit, Thirukkural was written by a great Dravidian Thiruvalluvar to free the Dravidians".

Self-Determination of Dravidistan

Dravidistan, Dravidasthan, or Dravida Nadu was the name of a proposed sovereign state for all non-Brahmin speakers of Dravidian languages in South Asia. Initially, the demand of Dravida Nadu proponents was limited to Tamil-speaking region, but later, it was expanded to include other states with Dravidian speakers in majority (Andhra Pradesh, Kerala, and Karnataka.) Some of the proponents also included parts of Ceylon (Sri Lanka), Orissa and Maharashtra. Other names for the proposed sovereign state included "South India", "Deccan Federation" and "Dakshinapath".

The movement for Dravidistan was at its height from 1940s to 1960s, but failed to find any support outside Tamil Nadu. Even in Tamil Nadu, where the anti-Hindi agitations attracted many supporters, there was no serious demand on the part of the common people for a sovereign Dravidian state.

The reorganization of the Indian states along linguistic lines through the States Reorganisation Act of 1956 weakened the separatist movement., and the prominent Tamil leader E. V. Ramaswamy Naicker gave up the demand for Dravidistan in 1956.. The movement was continued by the Dravida Munnetra Kazhagam, which formally gave up its demand for a separate sovereign state in 1963.

The concept of Dravidistan had its root in the anti-Brahmin movement in Tamil Nadu, whose aim was to end the alleged Brahmin dominance in the Tamil society and government. The early demands of this movement were social equality, and greater power and control. However, over the time, it came to include a separatist movement, demanding a sovereign state for the Tamil people. The major political party backing this movement was the Justice Party, which came to power in the Madras Presidency in 1921.

Since the late 19th century, the anti-Brahmin Tamil leaders had stated that the non-Brahmin Tamils were the original inhabitants of the Tamil-speaking region. The Brahmins, on the other hand, were described not only as oppressors, but even as a foreign power, on par with the British colonial rulers..

The prominent Tamil leader, E. V. Ramasami Naicker (popularly known as "Periyar") stated that the Tamil society was free of any societal divisions before the arrival of Brahmins, whom he described as Aryan invaders. Periyar was an atheist, and considered the Indian nationalism as "an atavistic desire to endow the Hindu past on a more durable and contemporary basis".

The proponents of Dravidistan constructed elaborate historical anthropologies to support their theory that the Dravidian-speaking areas once had a great non-Brahmin polity and civilization, which had been destroyed by the Aryan conquest and Brahmin hegemony. This led to an idealization of the ancient Tamil society before its contact with the "Aryan race", and led to a surge in the Tamil nationalism. Periyar expounded the Hindu epic *Ramayana* as a disguised historical account of how the Aryans subjugated the Tamils ruled by Ravana. Some of the separatists also posed Saivism as an indigenous, even non-Hindu religion.

The Indian National Congress, a majority of whose leaders were Brahmins, came to be identified as Brahmin party. Periyar, who had joined Congress in 1919, became disillusioned with what he considered as the Brahminic leadership of the party. The link between Brahmins and Congress became a target of the growing Tamil nationalism.

In 1925, Periyar launched the Self-respect movement, and by 1930, he was formulating the most radical "anti-Aryanism". The rapport between the Justice Party and the Self-Respect movement of Periyar (who joined the party in 1935) strengthen the anti-Brahmin and anti-North sentiment. In 1937-38, Hindi and Hindustani were introduced as new subjects in the schools, when C. Rajagopalachari of Congress became the Chief Minister of Madras Presidency. This led to widespread protests in the Tamil-speaking region, which had a strong independent linguistic identity. Periyar saw the Congress imposition of Hindi in government schools as further proof of an Aryan conspiracy.

Characteristics and Pre-cursors

At the 14th Confederation of the *Justice Party* held in Madras in 1938, rules and regulations, or precursors of a *Dravida Nadu* were adopted. The objectives were defined as: to attain *Purna Swaraj* and complete control for *Dravida Nadu* in social, economic and industrial, and commercial fields; to liberate *Dravida Nadu* and Dravidians from exploitation and domination by non-Dravidian foreigners; to acquire for the citizens of *Dravida Nadu* without discrimination on account of caste and class and inequalities arising there from, in law and society, equal rights and equal opportunities; to remove from the Dravidian people the sense of difference and superstitious beliefs existing in the name of religion, customs, and traditions and unite them as a society of people with a liberal outlook and intellectual development, and to get proportionate representation in all fields till the achievement of these objectives and until the people who have a sense of caste, religious and class differences cooperate with the party in full confidence and goodwill. Thus, Periyar also stated that "Self Respect should come before self-rule".

The characteristics of the separate *Dravida Nadu* was described by Periyar as: the area then comprising Madras Presidency; system of passport to enter the state; duty on goods from other provinces and entry with permit; demarcation of boundaries according to the needs and convenience of *Dravida Nadu*; and continuing an existing system of defence till grant of full independence. He also assured religious freedom to Muslims, Christians, Buddhists and others within this area. On the same accord, the separation of religion and politics was a part of this leaving religion as a matter of individual belief. It was made clear that the political movement should not be used for religious propaganda.

Recognition and Non-recognition

In December 1938, the Justice Party Convention passed a resolution stressing Tamil people's right to a separate sovereign state, under the direct control of the Secretary of State for India in London.

In 1939, Periyar organized the Dravida Nadu Conference for the advocacy of a separate, sovereign and federal republic of Dravida Nadu. In a speech on December 17, 1939, he raised the slogan "Dravida Nadu for Dravidians", which replaced the earlier slogan "Tamil Nadu for Tamils". In 1940, the South Indian Liberal Federation (Justice Party) passed a resolution demanding a sovereign state of Dravidistan.

Periyar was clear about the concept of a separate multi-linguistic nation, comprising of Tamil, Telugu, Malayalam and Kannada areas, that is roughly corresponding to the then existing Madras Presidency with adjoining areas into a federation guaranteeing protection of minorities, including religious, linguistic, and cultural freedom of the people. The proposition was made with a view to safeguarding the national self-respect of Dravidians threatened by Indo-Aryan culture, language, political leadership, and business interests. A separatist conference was held in June 1940 at Kanchipuram when Periyar released the map of the proposed *Dravida Nadu*. With the promised grant of full self-government after World War II, and posed another threat to the

Indian Freedom Movement However, it failed to get British approval. On the contrary, Periyar received sympathy and support from people such as Bhimrao Ramji Ambedkar and Muhammad Ali Jinnah for his views on the Congress, and for his opposition to Hindi. They then decided to convene a movement to resist the Congress. By the 1940s, Periyar supported Muslim League's claim for a separate Pakistan, and expected its support in return. In an interview with the Governor of Madras, Jinnah, the main leader of Muslim League, said that India should be divided into four regions: Dravidistan, Hindustan, Bengalistan and Pakistan; Dravidistan would approximately consist of the area under the Madras Presidency. Jinnah stated "I have every sympathy and shall do all to help, and you establish Dravidistan where the 7 per cent Muslim population will stretch its hands of friendship and live with you on lines of security, justice and fairplay."

In July 1940, a secession committee was formed at the Dravida Nadu Secession Conference held in Kanchipuram. On August 24, 1940, the Tiruvarur Provincial Conference resolved that Dravda Nadu should be an independent state (*thaninaadu*). The proponents of Dravidistan also sought to associate and amalgamate·Tamil Islam within a supposedly more ancient Dravidian religion, which threatened the Islamic identity of Tamil Muslims, some of whom had earlier supported the demand for a sovereign Dravidistan movement.

In August 1941, Periyar declared that the agitation for *Dravida Nadu* was being temporarily stopped. The reason cited was that it was necessary to help the government in its war efforts. The agitation would be renewed after the conclusion of the war. Even though the agitation for *Dravida Nadu* was being stopped, the demand was very much intact. When the Cripps Mission visited India, a delegation of the *Justice Party*, comprising Periyar, Soundrapandiya Nadar, Samiappa Mudaliar and Muthiah Chettiar, met the members of the *Cripps Mission* on March 30, 1942, and placed before them the demand for a separate Dravidian nation.

In August 1944, Periyar created a new party called Dravidar Kazhagam out of the Justice Party, at the Salem Provincial Conference. The creation of a separate non-Brahmin Dravidian nation was a central aim of the party. In 1944, when Periyar met the Dalit leader B. R. Ambedkar to discuss join initiatives, Ambedkar stated that the idea of Dravidistan was applicable to entire India, since "Brahminism" was "a problem for the entire subcontinent". At the Dravidar Kazhagam State Conference in Tiruchi in the 1940s, prominent Tamil leader C. N. Annadurai stated that it was necessary to divide India racially to prevent "violent revolutions" in future, that according to him, had been prevented due to the British occupation of India.

On July 1, 1947, the separatist Tamil leaders celebrated the "Dravida Nadu Secession Day". On July 13, 1947, they passed a resolution in Tiruchirapalli demanding an independent Dravidistan. On July 16, Mahatma Gandhi expressed his opposition to the demand. Also in 1947, Jinnah refused to help Periyar to help create a Dravidastan.

When India achieved Independence in August 1947, Periyar saw it as a sad event that marked the transfer of power to "Aryans", while Annadurai considered as a step towards an independent Dravida Nadu, and celebrated it. Over the time, disputes arose between the two leaders. They fell out after Periyar anointed his young wife to as his successor to lead the party, superseding senior party leaders.

Dravida Munnetra Kazhagam

In 1949, Annadurai and other leaders split up and established Dravida Munnetra Kazhagam. Annadurai was initially more radical than Periyar in his demand for a separate Dravidistan. In highlighting the demand for *Dravida Nadu,* the economics of exploitation by the Hindi-speaking, Aryan, Brahminical North was elaborated upon. It was contended that *Dravida Nadu* had been transformed into a virtual marketplace for north Indian products. And, thus, Annadurai explained that to change this situation, a separate *Dravida Nadu* must be demanded. Throughout the 1940s, Periyar spoke along the lines of a trifurcation of India, that is dividing the existing geographical region into *Dravida Nadu* (Dravidistan), *Muslim India* (Pakistan), and *Aryan Land* (Hindustan). In public meetings that he addressed between March and June 1940, he projected the three-nation doctrine as the only solution which could end the political impasse in the country.

In 1950, Periyar stated that Dravidistan, if it comes into being, will be a friendly and helpful state to India. When the political power in Tamil Nadu shifted to the non-Brahmin K. Kamaraj in the 1950s, Naicker's DK supported the Congress ministry. In late

1950s and early 1960s, the Dravida Nadu proponents changed their demand for an independent Dravida Nadu to an independent Tamil Nadu, as they didn't receive any support from the non-Tamil Dravidian-speaking states. Periyar changed the banner in his magazine *Viduthalai* from "Dravida Nadu for Dravidians" to "Tamil Nadu for Tamils".

The reorganization of the Indian states along linguistic lines through the States Reorganisation Act of 1956 weakened the separatist movement. In June-July 1956, the founder of Kazhagam, E. V. Ramaswamy Naicker, declared that he had given up the goal of Dravidistan.

However, by this time, DMK had taken over from DK as the main bearer of the separatist theme. Unlike Khalistan and other separatist movements in Republic of India, DMK never considered violence as a serious option to achieve a separate Dravidistan.

DMK's slogan of Dravidistan found no support in any state of India other than Tamil Nadu. The non-Tamil Dravidian speakers perceived the ambitions of the Tamil politicians as hegemonic, ultimately leading to the failure of the Dravidistan concept. Even in Tamil Nadu, the common people did not seriously support the idea of a separate Dravidian state. C. Rajagopalachari, the former Chief Minister of Madras State, stated that the DMK plea for Dravidistan should not be taken seriously.

Decline

The decline in support for the Dravida Nadu within the DMK can be traced back to as early as the Tiruchi party conference in 1956, when the party decided to compete in the Tamil Nadu state assembly elections of 1957. E.V.K. Sampath, who was leading a faction within DMK, argued that Dravida Nadu was "not feasible". However, the party did state Dravida Nadu a "long-range goal" during the elections. The political observers doubted the seriousness of their demand for a sovereign state, and stated that the demand for a separate Dravida Nadu was just a side issue, and a slogan to catch the imagination of an emotional public. In the 1957 elections, DMK managed to win only 15 of the 205 seats in the state assembly.

In 1958, V. P. Raman, a Brahmin leader, joined the party and became a strong opponent of the Dravida Nadu concept. In November 1960, the DMK leaders, including Raman, decided to delete the demand of Dravida Nadu from the party programme at a meeting held in absence of Annadurai. Political scientist Sten Widmalm writes, "It seems that the more the party distanced itself from the demand for Dravida Nadu, the more it was supported." In the 1962 election, DMK more than tripled its seats, winning 50 seats to the State Legislative Assembly, but still could not displace the Congress from power.

On September 17, 1960, a "Dravida Nadu Separation Day" was observed, which resulted in arrests of Annadurai and his associates. The demand for a sovereign Tamil state was considered as a threat of Balkanization to India, and also raised concerns among the Sinhalese politicians in Sri Lanka. In 1962, a Sinhalese M.P. stated in the Parliament: "The Sinhalese are the minority in Dravidistan. We are carrying on a struggle for our national existence against the Dravidistan majority."

Annadurai, who had been elected to the upper house of Indian parliament (Rajya Sabha) in 1962, reiterated DMK's demand for independence for Dravida Nadu in his maiden speech on May 1, 1962. However, at the time of Sino-Indian War of 1962, he proclaimed that his party would stand up for the integrity and unity of India. A faction of DMK contended that the party should publicly abandon the demand for Dravida Nadu.

In 1963, on the recommendation of the Committee on National Integration and Regionalism of the National Integration Council, the Indian parliament unanimously passed the Sixteenth Amendment to the Constitution, which sought to "prevent the fissiparous, secessionist tendency in the country engendered by regional and linguistic loyalties and to preserve the unity, sovereignty, and territorial integrity" of India. This was essentially in response to the separatist movement demanding a sovereign Dravidistan.

At a party conference in 1963, DMK formally dropped the secessionist demand, but also asserted that it will continue to address the issues that led it frame its demand for separation earlier. The Sino-Indian war doesn't seem to be a decisive factor in dropping the demand for Dravida Nadu; prominent DMK leaders Era Sezhiyan and Murasoli Maran have stated that the demand for Dravida Nadu had been dropped in practice before 1962. Maran explained that the there was not really enough support for Dravida Nadu in Tamil Nadu at the time, and it was concluded that there was no use pursuing the demand. He declared "I am Tamil first but I am also an Indian. Both can exist together provided there is space for cultural nationalism." Era Sezhiyan declared that it was impossible to continue to demand Dravida Nadu when the policy lacked support even in the Tamil-speaking areas, let alone Kannada, Telugu and Malayalam-speaking areas. Sezhiyan was a member of the committee that wrote the new party programme, which omitted the demand for Dravida Nadu. Sezhiyan stated that it was more practical to demand a higher degree of autonomy for Tamil Nadu instead.

After DMK decided to relinquish its demand for Dravida Nadu, it devoted more attention to the language issue (anti-Hindi agitations), and the 1962 election figures were almost exactly reversed in the subsequent 1967 elections. In 1962, the Congress had won the majority of seats, while DMK managed to win only 50 seats. In 1967, DMK won a clear majority of 138 seats, while Congress won only 50 seats. DMK came to power with Annadurai as the Chief Minister of Tamil Nadu.

Comparisons with Gandhi

In the Vaikom Satyagraha of 1924, Periyar and Gandhi both cooperated and confronted each other in socio-political action. Periyar and his followers emphasized the difference in point of view between Gandhi and himself on the social issues, such as fighting the Untouchability Laws and eradication of the caste system. According to the booklet *Gandhi and Periyar* Periyar wrote in his paper *Kudi Arasu*, in 1925, reporting on the fact that Gandhi was ousted from the Maha Sabha, because he opposed resolutions for the maintaining of caste and Untouchability Laws which would spoil his efforts to bring about Hindu-Muslim unity. From this Gandhi learned the need of pleasing the Brahmins if anything was to be achieved. Peiryar in his references to Gandhi used opportunities to present Gandhi as on principle serving the interests of the Brahmins in 1927, Periyar and Gandhi met at Bangalore to discuss this matter. The main difference between them came out when Periyar stood for the total eradication of Hinduism to which Gandhi objected saying that Hinduism is not fixed in doctrines but can be changed. In the *Kudi Arasu*, Periyar explained that:

"With all his good qualities, Gandhi did not bring the people forward from foolish and evil ways. His murderer was an educated man. Therefore nobody can say this is a time of high culture. If you eat poison you will die. If electricity hits the body you will die. If you oppose the Brahmin you will die. Gandhi did not advocate the eradication of Varnasrama *Dharma* structure but sees in it a task for the humanization of society and social change possible within its structure. The consequence of this would be continued high-caste leadership. Gandhi adapted Brahmins to social change without depriving them of their leadership".

Thus, Gandhi did not advocate the eradication of the Varnasrama Dharma structure but saw in it a task for the humanization of society and social change possible within its structure. The consequence of this would be continued high-caste leadership. Gandhi accepted *karma* in the sense that "the *Untouchables* reap the reward of their *karma,* but was against discrimination against them using the revaluing term *Harijans*. As shown in the negotiations at Vaikom his methods of abolishing discrimination were: to stress on the orthodox inhumane treatment of *Untouchables*; to secure voluntary lifting of the ban by changing the hearts of caste Hindus; and to work within a Hindu framework of ideas. On the Temple Entry issue Gandhi never advocated the opening of *Garbha Griha* to *Harijans* in consequence of his Hindu belief. These sources which can be labelled "pro-Periyar" with the exception of M. Mahar and D.S. Sharma, clearly show that Periyar and his followers emphasized that Periyar was the real fighter for the removal of Untouchability and the true uplift of Hairjans, whereas Gandhi was not. This did not prevent Periyar from having faith in Gandhi on certain matters.

Religion and Atheism

He has been a harsh critic of the Aryan influenced Hinduism in Tamil Nadu, more than the faiths of Islam, Buddhism and Christianity. He has spoken appreciatively of these other faiths in India finding in their ethics principles of equality and justice, thus advocating them if they can prove an alternative to Brahamanic Hinduism. With regards to institutionalized religion being used for personal gain, Periyar stated that *"religion goes hand in hand with superstition and fear. Religion prevents progress and suppresses man. Religion exploits the suppressed classes."* As religions, however, they are prone to be hit by accusation of superstition, exploitation and irrationalism.

Hinduism

In Periyar's school of thought, there was no religion by name Vedic Hinduism derived from the name of a place. With no distinct doctrines and no particular sacred book, it was said to be an imaginary religion preaching the superiority of the Brahmin the inferiority of the Shudra, and the untouchability of the Panchama.

"His contemptuous attitude to the baleful influence of Hinduism in Indian public life is strikingly akin to the anti-Catholic diatribes of the enlightenment philosophes."

Through the Self-Respect Movement, Periyar preached that compared to other religions, Hinduism placed many restrictions on men by prohibiting all except a small minority of Brahmins from reading the religious texts or discusing religious matters and by evolving a caste system in the name of divine law, and by creating several gods and festivals to provide an assured income and prosperity to the small Brahmin group at the expense of all others.

Periyar Ramasamy and Mahatma Gandhi – the former on a mission to destroy the essential practices perpetuated under Hinduism and the latter on a mission to protect, safeguard and rejuvenate the essence of Hindu religion – agreed on the basic point of the need to remove many evils practiced in the form of religion. Gandhiji aspired to 'reform' the religion by rejecting its formalities and moving out of it. Both believed that the Hindus should realize that Hinduism was not a religion and whatever they practiced in the name of Hindu religion had no religious basis or sanction. Both were of the opinion that religious faith was used to perpetuate inequalities on the basis of birth and ideas of purity and pollution.

When the ideal of Dravidian nationalism was projected in the 1940s, Periyar's religious philosophy also underwent a modification to assert that Hinduism was not the religion of the Dravidians. There was no Dravidian *Veda* and the Aryan *Vedas* prevalent among Dravidians were said to be the sacred books which prescribed how Dravidians should be treated but put a bar on Dravidians from acquiring a knowledge of these texts. In his Presidential Address at the Justice Confederation in 1940 EVR said:

"We have to bring about certain reforms in our religion. Many of our countrymen think that they are Hindus. When you call yourself a Hindu you admit Aryan principles. The words Hindu and Hinduism were not used by our forefathers in any of their works. Historians of world religions say that the sacred books of the Hindus are the Vedas, the Upanishads, the Agamas, the Puranas and the Itihasas. You will notice that none of the ancient religious works of the Dravidians have been included among those religious books. A careful study of the Vedas, etc., proves beyond doubt that they were written with a view to disgrace, enslave and exploit the Dravidians. It is this Hinduism which says that we are Sudras and Rakshasas. Again it is this Hinduism which is responsible for the introduction of caste distinction and growth of feud among the sons of the soil. All our superstitions and meaningless and absurd rituals and ceremonies are the result of following the tenets of Hinduism. In addition to our social subjugation and enslavement it paved the way for our political enslavement also by Aryans. If we think calmly we shall see that it is as necessary to be free from Hinduism in the field of religion as it is to be separated from Aryavarta in the field of politics."

Periyar, even while upholding rationalism, executed his duties of a 'dharmakartha' of a temple at Erode, to everybody's appreciation.."

Marai Malai Adigal is an eminent Tamil Saivite scholar who founded Shaiva Siddhantha Association. He lived as a Shaiva saint. This orthodox Shaiva scholar was once invited by Periyar to stay in his place or ashram. Maraimalai Adigal agreed to stay with Periyar for a month. In that one month, Periyar respected the orthodoxy of Adigal and ordered not to cook non-vegetarian food in the ashram and instructed his aides not to do anything that would offend the shaiva practices of Adigal. Periyar respected true believers.

Islam

In the early days of the Self-Respect Movement when Periyar was vociferous that Hindu religion, Manudharma and the Congress should be destroyed, he was inclined to play a political game by expressing an opinion that Islam alone was the religion that carried political weight and those depressed in the Hindu order could consider conversion to Islam.

For eradicating the evil of 'shudrahood', the threat of conversion was occasionally exercised. The Dravidian movement repeatedly complained about the imposition of Aryan religion on Dravidians. *"Unless we become either the Panchama, i.e., Adi Dravida or Muslims, we will not get respect, justice and progress,"* said EVR. He clarified that the idea was not to place the Dravidian people under the authority of Muslim religious leaders abroad but to practice the tenets of equality, righteous conduct and mutual respect. He emphasized that he was not an advocate of Islam but was only trying to find a remedy to the sufferings under Aryan, brahminical system and to find a rightful place for Dravidians in the independent country.

In one of Periyar's booklets titled *"Islam is good for abolishing the disgrace in human relationship"* based on his speech to railway employees in Tiruchirapalli on March 18, 1947, Periyar in the year of partition recommended conversion to Islam to non-Brahmins. He stated that *"re-commendable facts in Islam were: confession of one invisible and formless God; proclamation of equal rights for men and women; and advocating of social unity. Furthermore, Islam is not an Aryan religion. It attacks the very root of Vedic Hinduism. There are no caste distinctions in Islam. On the other hand Periyar declares that if you can find another way better than Islam so much the better".*

According to Periyar, "If people leave Hinduism they should follow some other religion. What religion should be recommended to people? Christianity was more like the Brahmin religion, so I recommended Islam to people. Because, in Christianity there are untouchable Christians, Nadar Christians, Vellala Christians and so on. So even in Christianity there is differences followed based on Varnashrama Dharma; so, in India, it is Hindu Christianity! If the Depressed Classes embraced Islam they would get social equality in a very short period"..

Periyar was an atheist. He never believed in any of the religious texts. He said "Bane of tamils is Brahmins, muslims and christians consider themselves to Tamilans". In his book "Vedangalin Vandavalangal", he had separate chapters where he critcized Kuran and Bible.

Buddhism

Buddhism was highly praised by Periyar. The fact that Buddha denied the classical Hindu concepts of Brahman, "god" and Atman soul, appealed to Periyar and so also the fact that Buddha-Bodhi could be interpreted as wisdom, sense and that early Buddhism thus advocated reason or enlightenment. Periyar linked this interpretation with his rationalist concepts.

Periyar found in Buddism a basis for his philosophy though he did not accept that religion as self-respect movement. The search for basis began in the course of the movement and was intensified soon after independence. It was again an experiment in the search for self-respect and the object was to get liberation from the shudrahood of Hinduism. A conference to propagate Buddhism was convened in Erode on January 31, 1954. Later that year, he and his wife went to Burma to attend the celebration of the 2500th anniversary of Buddha.

Periyar stated that what he was propagating could be found in the teachings of Buddha given 2000 years ago and wanted to revive them as the independent government had accepted the wheel of the Buddha and Hindus have regarded Buddha as an *avatar*. Brahmins were accused of covering Buddha within the Aryan religion as they had been hiding Tiruvalluvar within the Aryan fold. EBR pointed out that Buddha also laid stress on rationalism, on intellect as the precept, and on thought process for accepting anything. The persecution of Buddha by Brahmins, the burning of Buddhist institutions and teachings and the 'export' of Buddhism to China, Japan and Ceylon were recalled at the conference and Periyar observed that Buddha Vihars at Srirangam, Kanchi, Palani and Tirupati were converted as Hindu temples.

Christianity

Christianity was viewed by Periyar similar to monotheistic faith of Islam. He stated that, "So far as god is concerned we find the Christians and Muslims, somewhat reformed from the olden days of barbarians. They say that there can be only one god. They say that it is beyond human comprehension. They say that god does good to those who are good and punishes those who are bad. They say that god has no name or shape. They talk of good qualities". He took an interest in Rev. Martin Luther, where both he and his followers wanted to liken him and his role to that of the European reformer. A superficial comparison could be made between Luther's attack on established, institutionalized religion, meaning the Roman Catholic Church and Periyar's anti-Brahminism. Some scholars see a possibility of comparing contemporary rationalist movements in Tamil Nadu, of which the

D.K. forms an integral part, with the Reformation in Europe in the 16th century.

In the context of influence on Periyar the question of Christianity is relevant. Christian thinking and values have to a much greater extent influenced South Indian society than its statistically measured presence. Examples of this are the concept of the dignity of man and social ethics. The classical example is *The Precepts of Jesus* by Ram Mohan Roy, the Hindu reformer of the beginning of the last century. It can be argued that the whole process of secularization which has been taking place also in Tamil Nadu, and of which Periyar himself services as an example, is a product of Christianity. Thus Christian views have had at least an indirect influence on Periyar.

Periyar was an atheist. He never believed in any of the religious texts. He said "Bane of tamils is Brahmins, muslims and christians consider themselves to Tamilans". In his book "Vedangalin Vandavalangal", he had separate chapters where he critcized Kuran and Bible.

He was against evangelical movement of DGS Dinakaran and fought with him on this issue. In Periyar's publication, Naathigan, he used to vehemently oppose and criticize Dinakaran calling him fraud.

Alleged Controversies

However, Dalit intellectual Ravikumar claims that Periyar was not much of a supporter of the minorities. He cites Periyar's sayings from the book "Periyar E V R Sinthanaigal" by Anaimuthu in support of this claim

We feared the Brahmin, and yielded extra space to Muslims. We are facing the consequences today. It's like that proverb: Fearing the dung, we have stepped on shit. If sahibs (meaning Muslims) get proportionate representation and the Scheduled Castes get representation in jobs and education and if the rest of the slots are monopolised by Brahmins, O Shudra, what will be your future

These comments, along with other controversial comments allegedly made by Periyar, were also perceived as anti-Dalit by a section of the intelligensia and were the subject of a book "'E V Ramasamy Naickarin Marupakkam" or "The other side of E V Ramasamy Naicker" written by M. Venkatesan. However, Dalit leader and founder of Puthiya Tamizhagam Krishnasamy praises Periyar and credits him for administering justice to Dalits during the 1957 Ramnad riots. His views are echoed by Punitha Pandian of *Dalit Murasu*.

In 1954, Periyar controversially referred to Tamil Nadu's Christians and Muslims as non-Tamils.

Violence by Periyar's Followers

In response to Hindu processions during Ganesha Chathurthi and Ram Navami, Periyar led processions which slippered and broke idols of Rama, Lakshmana and Pillaiyar. Though Periyar claimed to follow peaceful means of protest, nevertheless, these processions often caused violent clashes between Periyar's followers and theists, represented in modern times by right-wing organisations as Hindu Munnani and Hindu Makkal Katchi. From time to time, activists of the Dravidar Kazhagam have also launched physical attacks on Brahmins. Tempers reached a boiling point when a member of the Dravidar Kazhagam tried to assassinate Rajagopalachari. The attack was, however, unsuccessful and was severely condemned by Periyar who prohibited the usage of violence.

On December 7, 2006, a statue of Periyar opposite the Ranganathaswamy temple at Srirangam was defaced by activists of the Hindu Makkal Katchi. Supporters of Periyar retaliated with violence against Hindu mutts and temples. Petrol bombs were allegedly hurled and devotees attacked at Ayodhya Mandapam, a Hindu religious congregational centre in West Mambalam, by members of Thanthai Periyar Dravidar Kazhagam, a splinter group of the Dravidar Kazhagam.

God Believer?

On July 22, 2009, Deccan Chronicle published an article saying Periyar may not have been an atheist at all. Information available with the newspaper has indicated that he is said to have prayed to God to help the Kovai Sarvajna school flourish during his visit here in 1925.

Followers and Influence

After the death of Periyar in 1973, conferences were held throughout Tamil Nadu for a week in January 1974. Members were assured that their whole-hearted support and previous activities which the *Dravidar Kazhagam* was engaged in under the direct guidance of Periyar would continue with the same vigor. During the same year, at Periyar Thidal, Madras Tmt., Periyar's wife, Maniyammai, the new head of the *Dravidar Kazhagam,* set fire to the effigies of 'Rama', 'Sita' and 'Lakshmana' as a retaliation to the *Ramaleela* celebrations where effigies of 'Ravana', 'Kumbakarna' and 'Indrajit' were burnt in New Delhi. For this act she was imprisoned. During the 1974 May Day meetings held at different places in Tamil Nadu, a resolution urging the Government to preserve 80 percent of jobs for Tamils was passed. Soon after this, a camp was held at Periyar Mansion in Tiruchirapalli to train young men and women to spread the ideals of the *Dravidar Kazhagam* in rural areas.

On Periyar's Birthday of September 17, 1974, Periyar's *Rationalist Library* and *Research Library* and *Research Institute* was opened by Tamil Nadu Chief Minister M. Karunanidhi. This library contained Periyar's rationalist works, the manuscripts of Periyar and his recorded speeches. Also during the same year Periyar's ancestral home in Erode, was dedicated as a commemoration building. On February 20, 1977, the opening function of *Periyar Building* in Madras was held. At the meeting which the Managing Committee of the *Dravidar Kazhagam* held, there on that day, it was decided to support the candidates belonging to the *Najata Party,* the *Dravida Munnetra Kazhagam* (DMK), and the *Marxist Party* during the General Elections.

On March 16, 1978, Annaiyar Maniyammai died. The *Managing Committee of the Dravidar Kazhagam* resolved on the day that in memory of Thanthai Periyar and Annaiyar Maniyammai they would carry on the activities of the *Dravidar Kazhagam* as vigorously as ever. Thiru Krishnasamy Veeramani was elected as General Secretary of the *Dravidar Kazhagam* on March 17, 1978. From then on, the *Periyar-Maniyammai Educational and Charitable Society* started the *Periyar Centenary Women's Polytechnic* at Thanjavur on September 21, 1980. On May 8, 1982, the *College for Correspondence Education* was started under the auspices of the *Periyar Rationalist Propganda Organization.*

Over the years, Periyar's influence had an impact on Tamil Nadus political party heads such as former Chief Minister C.N. Annadurai and present Chief Minister M. Karunanidhi of the

Dravida Munnetra Kazhagam' (DMK), V. Gopalswamy founder of the Marumalarchi Dravida Munnetra Kazhagam (MDMK), S. Ramadoss founder of the Pattali Makkal Katchi (PMK), Thol. Thirumavalavan, founder of the Dalit Panthers of India (DPI), and *Dravidar Kazhagam's* K. Veeramani. Other political figures influenced by Periyar were former Congress minister K. Kamaraj, former Chief Minister of Uttar Pradesh Mayawati, and former Municipal Chairman of Kumbakonam S. Kumarasamy. Periyar's life and teachings have also influenced writers and poets such as Kavignar Inkulab, and Bharathidasan, including actors such as Kamal Hassan and Sathyaraj.

Justice Party (India)

The Justice Party, officially known as South Indian Liberal Federation (S. I. L. F.), was the political wing of Then Nala Urimai Sangam (literal translation: The South Indian Welfare Association). The Justice Party derived its name from an English-language daily of that time, named *Justice*.

The Justice Party was established in 1917 as the South Indian Liberal federation by Sir P. Theagaroya Chetty and Dr. T. M. Nair as a result of a series of non-Brahmin conferences and meetings in the Madras Presidency. The formation of the SILF or the Justice Party marked the culmination of a series of failed efforts to establish an organisation representing the non-Brahmins of the Presidency. The early political work of the party involved petitioning the imperial administrative bodies and British politicians demanding more representation for non-Brahmins in administration and in the government.

In 1920, elections were held in the Madras Presidency as per the Montagu-Chelmsford reforms. The Justice party contested the elections and was elected to power. The party ruled the province for six years before giving way to the independent ministry of P. Subbarayan in 1926. The Justice Party, however, recaptured power in the Presidency in the 1930 elections and ruled till 1937 when it lost to the Indian National Congress. During this time, Justice Party leader L. Sriramulu Naidu served as the First Mayor of Madras. It never recovered from the defeat and was eventually withdrawn from politics in 1944 by its then President E. V. Ramaswamy Naicker. A rebel faction called itself the Justice Party and survived till 1957 when it was eventually disbanded due to poor performance. The Justice Party's period in power is remembered for the introduction of caste-based affirmative action and also for the educational and religious reforms it introduced. The Justice Party under E. V. Ramasami spearheaded the anti-Hindi agitations of 1937 and allied with Mohammad Ali Jinnah in its demand for separation from the Indian union.

Origin

Brahman and Non-Brahman Devide

The Brahmans in Tamil and Malabar areas enjoyed a higher position in social hierarchy compared to North Indian Brahmans. By 1850s, Telugu and Tamil Brahmans comprising only 3.2% of the population began to increase their political power by filling in most of the jobs which were open to Indian men at that time. The higher literacy and English proficiency among Brahamans were instrumental in this ascendancy. The political, social, and economical divide between Brahmans and non-Brahmans became more apparent in the beginning of the 20th century. This breach was further exaggerated by Annie Besant and her Homer Rule for India movement. The following table shows the distribution of selected jobs among different caste groups in 1912 in Madras presidency.

Caste group	*Deputy collectors*	*Sub judges*	*District Munsifs*	*% of total male population*
Brahmans	77	15	93	3.2
non-Brahman Hindus	30	3	25	85.6
Muslims	15	nil	2	6.6
Indian Christians	7	nil	5	2.7
Europeans and Euraseans	11	nil	3	.1

British Policies-seeds of Communal Division

The development of the non-Brahman movement is often attributed to the practices and policies of the provincial British Government. The statistics used by the non-Brahman leaders during their 1916 manifesto was prepared by senior Indian Civil Service officers for submission to the 1913 public services commission. During the early 20th century a group of Brahmans from Mylapore (often referred to as Mylaporeans) had emerged powerful in political circles. British, while aware of the usefulness of these men were also wary of their growth and resorted to support non-Brahmans for several Government posts. They sought to weaken the Mylaporean Brahmans by incorporating non-Brahman men in several Government posts. An early example of British patronage to non-Brahmans involved a High court bench job to C. Sankara Nair in 1903 by Lord Ampthill solely because he was a non-Brahman. The job fell vacant after Bashyam Iyengar left and V. Krishnaswami Iyer was widely believed to be the successor. Sir Alexander Cardew was vocal opponent of Mylapore Brahmins and advocated for the induction of non-Brahman members in Government. In 1912, under his influence the Secretariat for the first time used Brahman and non-Brahman as a category for job appointments and by 1918 and it had maintained a list of Brahman and non-Brahmans and directed preference to the latter.

D. A. Washbrook in his book, *The Emergence of Provincial Politics: The Madras Presidency 1870-1920* goes as far as to say,

Non-brahmanism became for a time synonymous with anti-nationalism-a fact which surely indicates its origins as a product of government policy.

Foundation of South Indian Liberal Federation

In 1909 two lawyers, P. Subrahmanyam and M. Purushotham Naidu, expressed their plans to establish an organization named "The Madras Non-Brahmin Association", an organization that never saw the light of the day.

Later in 1912 *Madras United League* was established with C. Natesa Mudaliar as Secretary. However, the League restricted itself to social activities and distanced itself from contemporary politics. The Madras United League was a predecessor of the Justice Party and the establishment of a hostel for non-Brahmin students in Madras was considered to be its main achievement. The League was subsequently renamed as the Madras Dravidian Association.

On 20 November 1916, about 30 prominent non-Brahmin leaders met in Victoria Public Hall in Madras under the leadership of Theagaroya Chetty and Dr. T. M. Nair to establish the South Indian People's Association for the purpose of publishing English, Tamil and Telugu newspapers esposuing the non-Brahman grievances. It later renamed the South Indian Liberal Federation but was more popularly known as the Justice Party after the English daily *Justice* which the party published.

At a meeting organized in October 1917, the leaders described the objectives of the organization thus:

- to create and promote the education, social, economic, political, material and moral progress of all communities in Southern India other than Brahmins,
- to discuss public questions and make a true and timely representation to Government of the views and interests of the people of Southern India with the object of safeguarding and promoting the interests of all communities other than Brahmins and
- to disseminate by public lectures, by distribution of literature and by other means sound and liberal views in regard to public opinion".

The South Indian Liberal Federation wholeheartedly supported British rule in India and launched virulent attacks on the Indian National Congress and the Home Rule League. At the same time, it also campaigned for the adequate representation of non-Brahmins in the Madras Legislative Council. In 1919, Dr. T. M. Nair was sent to London to argue in front of parliamentarians on behalf of the Justice Party for more representation of non-Brahmins of the Madras Presidency in the Legislative Council.

Their efforts bore fruit when in 1920 a dyarchy was established in Madras Presidency as per the Montagu-Chelmsford Reforms and elections were held to a designated number of seats in the Madras Legislative Council. The Justice Party won a landslide victory in the elections and formed the first elected government in Madras Presidency with A. Subbarayalu Reddiar as the Chief Minister.

In Office

A dyarchy was created in Madras Presidency in the year 1920 as per the Montagu-Chelmsford reforms and provisions were made for elections in the Presidency. In the first elections held in November 1920, the Justice Party was elected to power. A. Subbarayalu Reddiar became the first Chief Minister of Madras Presidency. However, he resigned soon after a short period due to declining health and was replaced with Sir P. Ramarayaningar, the Minister of Local Self-Government and Public Health. The party split in late 1923 when C. R. Reddy resigned from primary membership and formed a splinter group which allied with Swarajists who were in opposition. A no-confidence motion was passed against Ramarayaningar's government on November 27, 1923, which was however defeated 65-44. Ramarayaningar, popularly known as the Raja of Panagal, remained in power till November 1926. The passing of the First communal Government Order (G.O. No.613) which introduced reservations to government jobs, in August 1921, remains one of the highpoints of his rule. In the next elections held in 1926, the Justice Party lost to the Swarajya Party. However, as the Swarajya Party refused to form the Government, the Governor set up an independent government under the leadership of P. Subbarayan and nominated members to support it.

Soon after the demise of the Raja of Panagal, the Justice Party broke into two factions: the Constitutionalists and the Ministerialists. The Ministerialists were led by N. G. Ranga and were in favour of allowing Brahmins to join the Party. In the 1930 elections, the Justice Party was victorious and B. Munuswamy Naidu became the Chief Minister. However, the exclusion of *Zamindars* from the Ministry split the Justice Party once again. Fearing a no-confidence motion against him, Munuswamy Naidu resigned in November 1932 and the Raja of Bobbili was appointed Chief Minister. During this time, Justice Party Leader L. Sriramulu Naidu served as Mayor of Madras. The Justice Party eventually lost in the 1937 elections to the Indian National Congress and Chakravarti Rajagopalachari became Chief Minister of Madras Presidency.

During the 1920s and 1930s, the Anti-Brahmin movement evolved in the Madras Presidency. This movement was launched by a Congressman E. V. Ramaswamy Naicker, who, unhappy with the principles and policies of the Brahmin leadership of the provincial Congress, left the Congress in 1925. E. V. R., or Periyar, as he was called, launched venomous attacks on Brahmins, Hinduism and Hindu superstitions in periodicals and newspapers such as *Viduthalai* and *Justice*. He also participated in the Vaikom Satyagraha which campaigned for the rights of untouchables in Travancore to enter temples.

In Opposition

The Indian National Congress won the 1937 elections in the Madras Presidency, the first held as per the Government of India Act 1935 by capturing 159 seats out of 215 in the Province and formed the government in the Presidency. The results were especially disappointing for the Justice Party as most of its leaders including its President, the Raja of Bobbili, the Kumara Raja of Venkatagiri and A. P. Patro were defeated.

As part of a national policy, Hindi was introduced as a compulsory subject in schools. Non-Hindi speakers in southern India rebelled. Periyar, and the Self-Respect Movement wanted to put a stop to this turmoil.

When the Justice Party was defeated in the 1937 general elections after being in power for a very long spell from 1921, most of its leaders were disheartened and became inactive. It was at this moment of crisis, Periyar accepted the leadership of the party because he always felt the need for the existence of a vigorous political party essentially oriented to work for the upliftment of the socially deprived sections of the people.

Tamils opposed Hindi imposition immediately and the Justice Party under A. T. Panneerselvam and Periyar organized anti-Hindi imposition protests in 1938. More than 1200 people, including women and children, were imprisoned in 1938, of which two, Thalamuthu Nadar belonging to Kumbakonam and Natarasan, lost their lives. Paneerselvam and Periyar started Anti-Hindi agitations and was arrested and jailed by the Rajaji government. When the protests gained momentum Periyar was sentenced to imprisonment for two years, although he was released in six months. While in prison, the Justice Party elected him as its president on 29 December, 1938. In 1939 the Rajaji government quit and it was withdrawn in 1940.

During World War II

Periyar was offered the power and the support to rule Madras by Rajaji and the Congress Party as they have to resign from the Government. British government declared war on Germany and the Axis partners and involved India without consulting the Indian government. Some of the Congress leaders like Netaji were indeed in alliance with Germany and Japan and wanted to drive the British out of India with an armed struggle.

Periyar and Justice Party supported the British and opposed the Nazis and the Fascists as they were found to be obnoxious and racist. Furthermore, Periyar wanted the social reform more than the political power and he refused to take over the Madras government even though the Congress Party offered to support him from outside.

Change of Name and Transformation

In 1944, Periyar, the President of the Justice Party at that time, announced the party's withdrawal from politics and converted it into a social organisation, renaming it as Dravidar Kazhagam. Most of the members of the now defunct Justice Party joined this organisation. However, a few dissidents led by B. Ramachandra Reddi and later, P. T. Rajan, floated a new party claiming to be the original Justice Party. This party contested nine seats in the 1952 Assembly elections winning one, its leader being the sole candidate elected to the Madras Legislative Assembly. Eventually, this new Justice Party was dissolved after the 1952 elections.

In 1949, a few rebels in the Dravidar Kazhagam led by C. N. Annadurai formed a political party called the Dravida Munnetra Kazhagam (DMK). This political party opposed the unification of Tamil Nadu with India and did not, initially, participate in the political process. However, in 1957, the party changed its stand and participated in the elections winning 15 assembly seats. The party did better in the 1962 with 50 seats and in 1967 capturing power in the state after the 1967 elections. In 1972, the DMK split and M.G. Ramachandran formed the Anna Dravida Munnetra Kazhagam. Since then, Tamil Nadu has been ruled by either of these two Dravidian parties both of which claim the legacy of the Justice Party.

Issues

Attitude Towards Brahmins

At the First Non-Brahmin Confederation, Theagaroya Chetty, as the President of the Reception Committee spoke:

Towards the Brahmins, we cherish no feelings of bitterness. If we have to fight them we do so in the interests of truth and justice, and we shall be prepared to extend to them too the right hand of fellowship, when they shall see the wrongs inflicted upon us and repent. Ours is essentially a movement of love and not of hate, or love based upon a sense of what is due to the various classes which constitute the population of this vast and ancient land

At a tripartite conference between the Justice Party, Ministerialists and Constitutionalists in Madras in 1929 a resolution was adopted recommending the removal of restrictions on Brahmins joining the organization. The Executive Committee of the party drafted a resolution to this effect and placed it before the Eleventh Confederation of the party at Nellore, for approval. At this Confederation, P. Munuswamy Naidu, the President of the Justice Party, spoke:

So long as we exclude one community, we cannot as a political speak on behalf of or claim to represent all the people of our presidency. If, as we hope, provincial autonomy is given to the provinces as a result of the reforms that may be granted, it should be essential that our Federation should be in a position to claim to be a truly representative body of all communities. What objection can there be to admit such Brahmins as are willing to subscribe to the aims and objects of our Federation? It may be that the Brahmins may not join even if the ban is removed. But surely our Federation will not thereafter be open to objection on the ground that it is an exclusive organization

Senior Justice Party leader and former Education Minister A. P. Patro supported Naidu's viewpoint and brought the following amendment to the resolution:

That every person, who is willing to subscribe to the creed and aims and objects of the South Indian Liberal Federation and is willing to abide by the rules framed by the Executive Committee, is eligible to become a member of the Federation

However, this resolution was vehemently opposed by E. V. Ramasami and R. K. Shanmukham Chetty. E. V. Ramasami reasoned thus:

At a time when non-Brahmins in other parties were gradually coming over to the Justice Party, being fed up with the Brahmin's methods and ways of dealing with political questions, it was nothing short of folly to think of admitting him into the ranks of the Justice Party

The resolution was passed for vote and was eventually rejected. However, the suggestion that Brahmins be admitted into the Justice

Party were continued to be made as late as 1934. Even though Brahmins were not allowed to join the Justice Party, Brahmins and Europeans were, however, permitted to attend Justice Party meetings as "observers".

Indian Independence Movement

The Constitution of the Justice Party in 1930 stated its object as:

.. to obtain *Swaraj* for India as a component of the British Empire at as early a date as possible by all peaceful and legitimate and constitutional means

The inclusion of this clause had been influenced by the appointment of C. R. Reddy as the President of the Madras branch of the South Indian Liberal Federation who was in favour of self-rule. However, the Justicites definition of *Swaraj* varied from that of the Indian National Congress. To the Justice Party, *Swaraj* meant partial self-government under British rule and not complete independence.

P. Ramamurthi once said that the Justice Party was the only organization in India which did not condemn the Jallianwala Bagh massacre. However, this claim of Ramamurthi had been disputed by political historians.

Presidents

The following is the list of Presidents of the Justice Party and their terms:

	Term start	*Term End*
Sir P. Theagaroya Chetty	1917	1925
Raja of Panagal	1925	1928
P. Munuswamy Naidu	1928	1932
Raja of Bobbili	1932	1938
E. V. Ramaswami	1938	1944
B. Ramachandra Reddi	1944	1945
P. T. Rajan	1945	1957

Theagaroya Chetty

Sir Pitti Theagaroya Chetty KCSI (b.April 27, 1852-d.June 23, 1925) was an eminent lawyer, industrialist and a prominent political leader from the erstwhile Madras province. He was one of the founders of the Justice Party in 1916 along with Dr. T. M. Nair. T.Nagar is a locality in Chennai which is named after him.

Theagaroya Chetty was born in a Telugu Chetty family of Madras Presidency. After graduating from Presidency College, Madras he served as a corporator and legislator. He had an avid interest in politics and served as a member of the Indian National Congress before founding the South Indian Liberal Federation in 1917. He served as the President of the federation from 1917 till his death in 1925.

Theagaroya Chetty is regarded as one of the founders of the non-Brahmin movement in Tamil Nadu and the first to lead the movement.

Early Life

Theagaroya Chetty was born in Egathur, Madras Presidency in a Telugu Devanga Chetty family on April 27, 1852. He did his schooling in Chennai and graduated in law from Presidency College, Madras. On graduation, he entered public life and served as a member of the Corporation of Madras from 1882 to 1922. He also served terms as the President of the Corporation of Madras, and then as a Councillor till 1922. He was the first non-official President of the Madras Corporation.

Theagaroya Chetty was one of the founder-members of the South Indian Chamber of Commerce and served as its President from 1910 to 1921. When the Industrial Conference came to Madras, Theagaroya Chetty was the Chairman of the Reception Committee. Theagaroya Chetty fought on behalf of the *Indian Patriot* newspaper and its editor Karunakara Menon against Dr. T. M. Nair who later became his close associate.

The Dravidian Movement

The Madras Non-Brahmin Association was formed in 1909 by two lawyers from Madras city, P. Subramanyam and M. Purushotham Naidu. Sir Theagaroya Chetty did not involve himself in the movement until 1912, when the Madras United League (Later renamed as Madras Dravidian Association) was formed.

At a meeting held in Madras in November 1916 by a group of about thirty people, including Theagaroya Chetti and Dr. T. M. Nair, it was resolved to start a company for publishing newspapers advocating the cause of the non-Brahmin community. The newspaper was named *Justice* and started publishing from February 26, 1917 onwards. Dr. T. M. Nair was its first Editor.

The South Indian People's Association was later formed as the mouthpiece of non-Brahmins with organizing the media arm of the non-Brahmin Movement as its main objective. A political party was organised by the South Indian People's Association under the leadership of Sir P.Theagaroya Chetty and Dr. T. M. Nair and was named the South Indian Liberal Federation. It later came to be popularly known as the Justice Party after the English daily Justice which the party published. The Federation was organised in October 1917 and its objectives wore defined as :

- to create and promote the education, social, economic, political, material and moral progress of all communities in Southern India other than Brahmins,
- to discuss public questions and make a true and timely representation to Government of the views and interests of the people of Southern India with the object of safeguarding and promoting the interests of all communities other than Brahmins and
- to disseminate by public lectures, by distribution of literature and by other means sound and liberal views in regard to public opinion ".

Early Years of the Justice Party

Theagaroya Chetty was elected the first President of the Justice Party and served as President until his death in 1925. A constitution was drawn on October 17, 1917. District and city boards were established all over the Presidency.

In the initial stages, the Justice Party concentrated its energies on work of a social character than political. During this period, the Justice Party held all-India non-Brahmin conferences to unit non-Brahmins all over the country.

The Justice Party argued for separate electorates and reservations in government jobs and civil service for non-Brahmins, at the British Parliament in London. In 1919, Dr. T. M. Nair, the President of the Justice Party and leader of the delegation died in London at the age of fifty-one and was succeeded as President by Theagaroya Chetty.

1920 Elections

When elections were held in December 1920 in the Madras Presidency as per the Montagu-Chelmsford reforms, the Justice Party obtained a comfortable majority by winning 63 seats out of 98. The Governor of Madras invitied Theagaroya Chetty to form the Government. However, Theagaroya Chetty refused on account of his old age and failing health. As a result, A. Subbarayalu Reddiar was appointed Chief Minister. He served for a few months before being succeeded by the Raja of Panagal.

Attitude Towards Brahmins

In his speech as the President of the Reception Committee of the First Non-Brahmin Confederation, Theagaroya Chetty spoke:

Towards the Brahmins, we cherish no feelings of bitterness. If we have to fight them we do so in the interests of truth and justice, and we shall be prepared to extend to them too the right hand of fellowship, when they shall see the wrongs inflicted upon us and repent. Ours is essentially a movement of love and not of hate, or love based upon a sense of what is due to the various classes which constitute the population of this vast and ancient land

Death and Legacy

Theagaroya Chetty died on April 28, 1925 and was succeeded by the Raja of Panagal as the President of the Justice Party. He is usually credited for the victories of the Justice Party in the 1920 and 1923 elections and for turning the Justice Party into a formidable force in the Presidency.

T. M. Nair

Taravath Madhavan Nair (b. January 15, 1868-d.July 17, 1919) was an Indian politician and political activist of the Self-Respect Movement from the Madras Presidency. He founded the Justice Party along with Theagaroya Chetty.

Early Life

Nair was born near Tirur on January 15, 1868 in the Taravath family of Palghat, Madras Presidency. His father Chingicham Veetil Sankaran Nair was a District Munsiff in the Judicial service at Tirur. Madhavan Nair's elder brother Sankaran Nair studied law and served as Deputy Collector while his sister Taravath Ammalu Ammal was a Sanskrit and Malayalam scholar who wrote a book in Malayalam on the lives of the 63 Nayanmars.

Nair did his schooling at Government High School, Palghat. He was known for his academic proficiency and he passed his matriculation exam one year in advance. He did his graduation from Presidency College, Madras and joined Madras Medical College. However, he did not complete his course in medicine. Instead, he discontinued his course and moved to Edinburgh. He graduated in M.B., Ch.B. at Edinburgh and obtained his M. D. in 1896, with Sanskrit as the compulsory classical subject. He researched in E. N. T. diseases at Paris and returned to India in 1897. During his stay in the United Kingdom, he was a member of the Edinburgh Student's Representative Council, Secretary and later, President of the Edinburgh Indian Association, member of the Edinburgh University Liberal Association and University Union and one of the editors of Edinburgh University Liberal's magazine "The Student". Prior to his return to India, Nair spent some time in London where he served as Secretary and later Vice-President of London Indian Society which was led by Dadabhai Naoroji. He also served as a member of the British Medical Association, the Royal Asiatic Society, the National Liberal Club and the Royal Society.

Public Offices

Nair represented Triplicane in the Madras Corporation from 1904 to 1916. During his term, he frequently attacked the Corporation and its President Mr. Molony over the quality of water supplied. In 1910, he agitated for the revival of the Palghat Municipal Council.

In 1908, Nair was appointed member of the Labour Commission by the Government of India. He submitted a report condemning the situation of workers in factories and recommended the reduction of hours of work. He personally submitted his condemnation and recommendations before the Secretary of State for India at London.

In 1912, Dr. Nair was elected to the Madras Legislative Council. When the First World War broke out, Dr. Nair served as one of the surgeons in the hospital ship, S. S. Madras and was commissioned as a Lieutenant. At the end of the War, he was awarded the Kaiser-i-Hind medal and the War Service medal posthumously.

In the Indian National Congress

Nair was associated with the Indian National Congress right from the time of his return to India in 1897. In the Congress sessions in 1898 and 1899, he strongly condemned the present status of Indian officers in the Medical services and campaigned for equal treatment to be meted out to them. He presided over the District Congress at Chittoor, North Arcot in 1907.

Formation of the South Indian Liberal Federation

When Dr. Nair lost the elections to the Imperial Legislature of India held in 1916, he blamed caste-based prejudices in the Indian National Congress for his loss. Nair felt that the Brahmins Tamil Brahmins were dominating the Indian National Congress. He protested the Home Rule Movement launched by Annie Besant.

In 1917, Dr. Nair left the Indian National Congress. At a meeting on August 1917, Dr. T. M. Nair spoke:

Non-Brahmins were looking to the British Government for protection, to hold scales evenly and to mete out Justice, but when they saw a movement progressing whose object was to undermine British influence and power in this country, they thought it their duty to rally round the British Government and to support them

In October 1917, Dr. T. M. Nair launched the South Indian Liberal Federation, also known as the Justice Party in collaboration with Sir Pitti Theagaroya Chetty.

Editorship of the Justice

In November 1916, a meeting was held at Madras in which Sir P. Theagaroya Chetty and Dr. T. M. Nair participated. The meeting brought out a resolution mandating the establishment of a newspaper for voicing the aspirations of non-Brahmins.

Accordingly, from February 26, 1917 onwards, the *Justice* began to be published. Dr. Nair was the Chief Editor until his death in 1919. In his newspaper, Dr. Nair attacked his opponents in the Indian National Movement and supporters of the Home Rule Movement. Once when the Indian National Congress carried out agitations in Ernad Tirur and Valluvanad, he prophesized that "the Congress was smoking in a gunpowder magazine". His words proved to be true when the Moplah Rebellion broke out in the region in the year 1921.

Mission to England and Death

In 1918-19, despite warnings from fellow doctors not to travel abroad considering that his health was deteriorating, he led a mission to England to speak in support of communal representations before a Joint Parliamentary Committee. He remains one of the few Indians to have addressed a meeting of the members of the British Parliament. However, he was prohibited from speaking to the public on the orders of Edwin Samuel Montagu, the Secretary of State for India. Dr. Nair died on July 17, 1919 at the age of fifty-one due to heart seizure following diabetic gangrene and Bright's disease. His body was brought to India and cremated at Golders Green.

Inclination

Nair always wore Western clothes and followed Western manners and customs. Due to this reason, he was frequently criticized as an Anglophile. However, at the same time, he displayed his love for his mother tongue Malayalam by speaking and writing in chaste Malayalam.

Vaikom Satyagraha

Vaikom Satyagraha (1924-25) was a satyagraha (movement) in Travancore, India (now part of Kerala) against untouchability in Hindu society. The movement was centred at the Shiva temple at Vaikom, near Kottayam. The Satyagraha aimed at securing freedom of movement for all sections of society through the public roads leading to the Sri Mahadevar Temple at Vaikom.

Introduction

The *Vaikom Satyagraha* was the first systematically organized agitation in Kerala against orthodoxy to secure the rights of the depressed classes. For the first time in history, the agitation brought forward the question of civil rights of the low caste people into the forefront of Indian politics. No mass agitation in Kerala acquired so much all-India attention and significance in the twentieth century as the *Vaikom Satyagraha*. Vaikom is a small temple town in Central Travancore on the eastern banks of the backwaters of vembanad Lake. The town is famous for its Shiva temple, which in the early twentieth century was the citadel of orthodoxy and casteism. As was the custom prevalent in those days, the Avarnas were not allowed to enter the temples. But at Vaikom, they were not permitted even to use the public roads around the temple. Notice boards were put up at different spots prohibiting the entry of Avarnas reminding them of their social inferiority. All the more unbearable to them were the fact that a Christian or a Muslim was freely allowed on these roads. An Avarna had to walk through a circuitous route, two to three miles longer to avoid the road beside the temple. It seems that when Ayyankali, a Dalit leader and member of Pulaya caste, had to travel through this road, he was asked to get down from his bullock cart, and walk through the circuitous route and his bullock cart without him was allowed to pass through the road.

Why Vaikom was Selected for the Agitation?

Historical Background

During 1865 the Government of Travancore had published a notification that all public roads in the state were open to all castes of people alike. In July 1884, the Government by a fresh notification reaffirmed the policy laid down in the previous order and enjoined that any violation of these orders would be visited with the severest displeasure of the Government. This notification came up for a judicial review before the High Court. The High Court then considered it expedient to draw a distinction between *Raja Veedhis* (King's Highways) and *grama veedhis* (village roads). The court decided that the public roads mentioned in the notification of the Government were intended to mean only the *Raja veedhis* and not *grama veedhis*. The roads around Vaikom Temple were considered ' *grama veedhis* and consequently even after 65 years of Government proclamation, they were barred to the Avarnas and a unit of police (consisting of Savarnas) was stationed in the vicinity to enforce the custom.

Other Probable Reasons

About two hundred years ago at Vaikom, there was an attempt at temple entry and a gruesome end to it. Balarama Varma was the king of Travancore and *Kunchukutti Pillai* was the Diwan (Dalawa). About two hundred Ezhava young men, in and around Vaikom decided to enter the temple and worship. A date was fixed. Those who were in charge of the temple carried the news to the king and the authorities and the king promised to take necessary action. On the day of the proposed temple entry one messenger from the king came to Vaikom, and met the temple authorities. They wondered how this single man would stop 200 able-bodied young men. The young men organized themselves in to a procession from Iruvelikkunnu on Kottayam Road. Their plan was to enter the temple from the eastern road. As they were nearing the temple the King's messenger along with a large number of armed personnels started attacking the unarmed civilians. The dead bodies were collected and buried in the pond at the northeastern side of the temple. It seems *Dalawa Kunchukutti Pillai* had ordered the massacre; hence the pond came to be known as *Dalawa Kulam*. The pond is no longer there. It is filled in and the present private bus stand is constructed there.

There was another crucial incident, which triggered the action. Sree Narayana Guru himself was prohibited from passing through the roads around the temple. *Sri Bhargavan Vaidyar* mentions this in the golden Jubilee Souvenir of Neyyattinkara S N D P Union. The editorial of the Malayala Manorama on 29 March 1924 (the day before the starting of the Satyagraha) mentions, *If a venerable sage like Sree Narayana Guru and his disciple Mahakavi Kumaran Asan were driven away from the road around the temple by a drunken upper caste buffoon in the name of caste, can their people take it lying down? If they rise up in revolt can any authority stop them by force?*

Long ago on the streets of Vaikom in a rickshaw, The great sage Sree Narayana was going, An idiot born as god on earth, Came up and ordered the rickshaw to withdraw.

If this is the truth, T. K. Madhavan, the favourite disciple of Sree Narayana Guru, must have taken an inner pledge to annihilate the tradition, which insulted his Guru, and the result was the *Satyagraha at Vaikom.*

Protests by Ezhavas

The Ezhavas first took up issue in 1905. The Ezhava representatives in the Travancore Legislature (Kochu Kunjan Channar, Kunju Panicker and Kumaran Asan) raised the question of use of the public roads around the temples by avarnas. The authorities remained adamant and refused to take up the matter even for discussion as it was considered a religious question. In

1920-21, representative Asan also raised the question and it was decided to shift the notice boards a little, so that some parts of the roads would be accessible to the avarnas.

T. K. Madhavan, the organizing secretary of the SNDP, became a member of the Travancore Legislature, and felt that Asan and the others has accepted a humiliating compromise. Madhavan wanted to demand outright temple entry, but he was denied permission to even introduce the resolution in the Legislature. Madhavan met the then Divan Raghaviah at his residence and requested him to reconsider his decision. The Divan refused; Madhavan then requested for permission to make a representation to the Maharaja himself which was denied. Frustrated and enraged, Madhavan raised his voice of protest before the Divan, proclaiming *We are denied the right to present our problems to the legislatures, and we are denied permission to represent to the Maharaja. How are we to resolve our problems? Are we to leave Travancore?* The Divan retorted, *You may leave Travancore to solve your problems.*

While Madhavan's main objective was to achieve unconditional temple entry, he understood that the right to use the public roads around the temples was the first step. He already had the idea of launching an agitation at Vaikom against the forbidding of roads around the temple, as an activity of the SNDP Yogam. He discussed the matter in detail with Sardar K.M.Panikkar. Panikkar told that the Ezhavas, under the leadership of Sree Narayana Guru, "had united and uplifted themselves, and have become a formidable force in the socio-economic-political atmosphere of Kerala." Although the SNDP has become a mouthpiece for all downtrodden people and the standard bearer of social revolution, the issue at Vaikom needs handling at a higher and wider level. Instead of being just a fight for gaining access to road, Panikkar suggested making it a symbolic battle against atrocities in the name of caste, giving it a national and cosmopolitan look to gain the attention of the entire world. To do that, it was necessary to include it as an activity of the Indian National Congress, and get Mahatma Gandhi to approve it.

Involvement of the Indian National Congress

T. K. Madhavan met Mahatma Gandhi at Tirunelveli on 23rd September 1921, and apprised him of the conditions of the Ezhavas and their achievements through the SNDP. Because they had already achieved admission to school, Mahatmaji agreed that the time was ripe for temple entry. Mahatmaji promised to write to the State Congress Committee to take up the issue.

Madhavan attended the Kakinada AICC meet (1923) in the company of Sardar Panikkar and K. P. Kesava Menon. Madhavan got a pamphlet printed *A request to the Indian National Congress on behalf of the untouchables of India.* Madhavan tried with all his might to convince the members, of the need to eradicate untouchability. The Congress agreed to include the eradication of untouchability in their constructive programs and resolved to lend full support to the Vaikom Movement, and authorized the Kerala Provincial Congress Committee (KPCC) to undertake the task.

In accordance with the Kakinada Congress resolution, the KPCC met at Ernakulam on 24 January 1924, and formed an Untouchability Abolition Committee (UAC) consisting of T. K. Madhavan, Kurur Nilakantan Namboothiri, T.R. Krishna Swami Iyer, K. Velayudha Menon and K. Velappan (convener). A publicity Committee of five members including T. K. Madhavan was also formed.

The KPCC, the UAC and the Publicity Committee reached Vaikom on 28 February 1924. There was a huge public meeting. T. K. Madhavan made a public request to the UAC to get the prohibitory notice boards removed from the roads around the temple. The Committee resolved to take procession of Avarnas through the roads on the very next day of the Pulaya Mahasabha meeting.

The news of the decision reached far and wide. It evoked mixed reactions. The caste Hindus who tolerated the speeches at the meeting could not digest the idea of a procession as proposed by the KPCC and the UAC. They along with the local Magistrate, the Police Inspector, and the Tahsildar, met the congress leaders at their camp, and suggested a postponement. They promised that they would try to prevent communal tensions, and make the procession a success, if they were given time. The congress also realized the situation. They could also make use of the time to plan and prepare properly for launching the agitation. The date was fixed as 30 March 1924, and the idea was to take out a procession. Meanwhile, the local Magistrate fearing communal tensions issued prohibitory orders against the procession. Hence the UAC changed its tactics. It was decided to send only three volunteers every day instead of a procession. Volunteers were selected from all castes.

A Satyagraha Ashram was set up about one furlong south of the temple. The Ashram was packed with volunteers who came from different parts of the country. The venue of Satyagraha was decided to be on the western road where a prohibitory board announced:

Ezhavas and other low castes are prohibited through this road.

Hundred of policemen armed with lethal weapons, ready to meet any eventuality, were on the vigil round the clock at the spot where the Satyagraha was to begin.

On the morning of 30 March a bugle call for action was sounded. The first batch of volunteers selected to offer Satyagraha were Kunjappy (Pulayan), Bahuleyan (Ezhava) and Venniyil Govinda Panicker (Nair). Before leaving the Ashram, they were strictly instructed not to offer any resistance and remain calm against all provocations. The Satyagrahis, wearing khadi and Gandhi caps and garlands, marched forward with the Congress flag fluttering before them. All the volunteers followed them shouting *Satyagraha ki jai, Mahatma Gandhi ki jai.* All of them would stop at a distance of fifty feet from the notice board, and only the selected three would walk to the point where the prohibition board hung. The police would stop them and ask them their caste. The police would pronounce that the low caste men would not be allowed to pass; only the Savarnas could. The upper-caste men would insist that their companions should go with them. The police would prevent them. The Satyagrahis would wait there patiently until they were arrested just before noon. When they were produced before the court, invariably they were convicted and sentenced to jail and fined. They refused to pay the fine, and courted extra imprisonment. In the evening there would be a procession and public meeting, protesting against the arrest. The meetings were given wide publicity and people thronged in from all directions. They returned, rejuvenated by the inspiring speeches of the leaders to come back again next morning to start the routine.

The Satyagraha was temporarily stopped for two days on 5 and 6 April to try for a compromise between caste Hindu leaders and the Congress. All talks failed and Satyagraha was resumed. T. K. Madhavan and K. P. Kesava Menon (KPCC President) volunteered on 7 April and courted arrest. They were later released. All those who were arrested at Vaikom were released when the Maharaja of Travancore, Sree Moolam Thirunal, died.

The struggle continued like this up to 10 April, when the police adopted the new tactics of barricading the roads and thus tried to prevent the Satyagrahis from reaching the disputed roads. The police also decided not to arrest the Satyagrahis, and they responded with fasting. But Gandhiji disapproved of fasting as it went against his theory of Satyagraha.

The police who were watching the progress of the agitation were convinced that their policy of not arresting the Satyagrahis was not very effective. So they wanted to use strong-arm tactics to crush the agitation.

The conservatives joined the police, and in due course, the conservatives took over and the police became silent witnesses to the atrocities committed on the volunteers by the conservatives. When the Satyagraha started the ruling Maharja of Travancore was Sree Moolam Thirunal. He and his minister *Divan Bahadur T. Raghavaiah* were golden props of extreme orthodoxy. They wanted to keep old customs in Toto. Divan Raghvaiah made a speech in the Travancore legislature strongly defending the Savarnas and denouncing the Satyagraha.

Meanwhile hundreds of letters were sent to Gandhiji to suspend the agitation. Two advocate brothers from Kerala, '*Sivarama Iyer and Vancheeswara Iyer* met Mahatmaji and argued that the roads around Vaikom temple are private property and hence the Satyagraha was irrelevant.

All newspapers in India flashed headlines about the Satyagraha. Money flowed from different states to Vaikom. The Akalis of Punjab came to Vaikom to open a free kitchen for the Satyagrahis. Non-Hindus like Barrister George Joseph, Bhajematharam Mathunni and Abdul Rahman (the Editor-in-Chief of The Young India) came forward to offer Satyagraha. But Gandhiji did not accept any of these. Gandhiji wrote in the Young India on April 24 1924, and May 1, 1924 against accepting outside aid.

As for accepting assistance from Hindus from outside, such acceptance would betray un readiness on the part of the local Hindus for the reform. If the Satyagrahis have the sympathy of the local Hindus, they must get locally all the money they need.

Gandhiji wrote to Mr. George Joseph on April 6, 1924, As to Vaikom, I think you shall let the Hindus do the work. It is they who have to purify themselves. You can help by your sympathy and your pen, but not by organizing the Movement and certainly not by offering Satyagraha. If you refer to the Congress resolution of Nagpur, it calls upon the Hindu Members to remove the curse of untouchability. Untouchability is the sin of the Hindus. They must suffer for it; they must pay the debt they owe to their suppressed brothers and sisters. Theirs is the shame and theirs must be the glory when they have purged themselves of the black sin. The silent loving suffering of one pure Hindu as such will be enough to melt the hearts of millions of Hindus, but the sufferings of thousands of non-Hindus on behalf of the untouchables will leave the Hindus unmoved. Their blind eyes will not be opened by outside interference, however well intentioned and generous it may be, for it will not bring home to them their sense of guilt. On the contrary, they would probably hug the sin, all the more, for such interference. All reforms to be sincere and lasting must come from within. Anyway before George Joseph received this letter, he offered Satyagraha and was arrested. The Akalis also withdrew on Gandhiji's word.

There were more than 200 volunteers in the camp. After some time, it became difficult to maintain the camp. It was brought to the notice of Gandhiji at the Belgaum Congress and the Congress records show that an amount of Rs, 1000.00 per month was sanctioned from the Congress funds for Vaikom Movement. Important people like Vinoba Bhave and Swami Shraddhananda visited the spot and gave mental support for the Movement.

Involvement of Periyar

E. V. Ramasami Naicker (affectionately called Periyar by the Tamilians) came with his wife Nagamma and a group of followers and offered Satyagraha on April 14. As the head of the *Satyagraha,* Periyar was imprisoned twice. Gandhi, who was also present on the Vaikom scene, was disturbed about the whole affair but seemingly unable to stop it. His concern grew when other religious groups became involved. Thus the Sikh community offered to meet expenses. Money was also said to have come in from Burma, Singapore, and Malaysia, from non-Brahmin immigrants, Muslims and Christians. Gandhi tried under the circumstances to keep the whole thing an inter-Hindu affair. However, in the end a compromise was reached. The streets in the temple area were opened to *Harijans* or *Untouchables*. In 1936, they were allowed to enter the temple. The *Satyagraha* paved the way for subsequent Temple Entry Act.

Vaikom had been chosen as a place for *Satyagraha* organized by the heads of the Congress Party. Periyar who was touring Madurai district received "a private letter" asking him to join in the *Satyagraha*. He immediately proceeded to Vaikom where he violated the order not to address public meetings and was imprisoned for one month a light punishment on order of the Raja. Gandhi became more and more troubled as the *Satyagraha* took a turn of communal riot because of conversions to Islam taking place. Vain efforts were made to return Periyar to Madras state. After his first release from prison Periyar was advised to stay away from Vaikom which he did not do. His second imprisonment was more severe, six months in the Central Jail Trivandrum. Meanwhile Nakammai, Periyar's first wife, organized women's campaigning.

Nagamma with Mrs. Joseph, Mrs. T. K. Madhavan and Mrs. Govindan Channar, among others formed a Women's committee to persuade the women of the villages and get them ready to participate in the Satyagraha. They went around villages explaining to the women, the meaning and purpose of this Satyagraha and collecting from them, handfuls of rice and small changes to maintain the volunteers' needs. The women started to offer Satyagraha on May 20, 1924. Nagamma was arrested along with Mrs. T.K. Madhavan and later released. Nagamma's leadership induced courage and solidarity in the women.

When the Raja unexpectedly died Periyar was released from the Trivandrum prison because additional trouble was feared, since the death of the Raja somehow connected with Preiyar's imprisonment as a bad omen. Later, on the order of the Government, Periyar was, for breaking public laws sent to prison again in Madras to be kept out of the way. The compromise to open the streets in the temple areas was the outcome of the negotiations between Gandhi and the two Ranis. Gandhi had unsuccessfully done everything to keep Periyar out of Vaikom. Periyar on his side had to accept that the *Vaikom Satyagraha* ended in a compromise. In 1925, the Madras Presidency (Tamil Nadu) Congress passed a resolution unanimously praising Periyar's contribution to the

Vaikom Satyagraha and hailing him as the *Vaikom Veerar* (Vaikom Hero) in the Kanchipuram Session.

The Role of Sree Narayana Guru in Vaikom Satyagraha

Sree Narayana Guru, who had never shown any interest in the activities of the Indian National Congress, involved himself with the Vaikom Satyagraha and extended much cooperation. The reason is quiet evident. The Vaikom Satyagraha was not an agitation for political freedom, it was a movement to purify the Hindu society of its blemishes, and this was what Guru also attempted through his actions and messages.

But some how, a small misunderstanding arose between Mahatma Gandhi and Sree Narayana Guru, regarding the modus operandi of the Satyagraha. One of Guru's dialogues with the General Secretary of the SNDP was misinterpreted in such a way that it led to believe that the ideals of Gandhiji and Guru clashed. There was a stage when someone suggested to Gandhiji to withdraw the support for the Satyagraha because the spiritual leader of the Thiyyas was urging his followers to use violence, which is against the principles of Satyagraha.

The Guru had thorough discussions with his favourite disciple T. K. Madhavan, about the Vaikom Movement, even beforeT. K. Madhavan met Gandhiji about the issue. The Guru had another discussion with K. M. Kesavan, the then General Secretary of the SNDP when the Satyagraha was launched.

Kesavan: Gandhiji wants to win over the other side and the Government by sympathy, by self inflicted suffering. That is how they gain their end.

Guru: The will to suffer and sacrifice should be there. But there is no need to get drenched or starved. Enter where entry is banned and face the consequences, Take blows without giving them. If a fence is raised in your path, don't turn back, jump over it. Don't stop with walking through the road, enter the temple, every temple, every day, everybody. If the offering of pudding is ready, take it. Go to the place where free food is served in the temple; and sit along with others. Let the Government be informed of what you intend to do. One should not fight shy of laying down one's life. Those who think another's touch pollutes him should not be left unmolested in their so called cleanliness. That is my view.... Give publicity to all these in the papers. Let people know that I subscribe to their views. But let there be no violence or show of force. Don't be perturbed by coercion.

Kesavan: Temple entry is the ultimate goal of Satyagraha. That is postponed to the next year.

Guru: Why? Isn't it too late even now?

This view was given wide publicity and the newspaper cutting containing it reached Mahatma Gandhi. Gandhiji wrote in the *Young India* on June 19, 1924.

His Holiness Sree Narayana Guru, the spiritual leader of the Thiyyas is reported to have disapproved of the present methods of Satyagraha at Vaikom. He suggests that volunteers should advance along barricaded roads and scale the barricades. They should enter temples and sit with others to dine. Now the action proposed is not Satyagraha. For scaling barricades is open violence. If you may scale barricades, why not break open temple doors and even pierce temple walls? How are the volunteers pierce through a row of policemen except by using force?. If the Thiyyas are strong and willing to die in sufficient numbers, they can gain their point. All I submit is that they will have gained it by some thing the reverse of Satyagraha. And then too, they would not have converted the orthodox to their views, but would have imposed it on them by force.

He wrote: A friend who has sent me the press cutting suggests that by reason of the violent advice of the guru, I should ask the local Congress Committee to call off the Satyagraha. I feel that would mean want of faith in one's means and surrender to violence. If Congressmen connected with the Vaikom movement entertain the suggestions said to be favoured by the Thiyyas' spiritual leader, there would be case for penance, and therefore suspension, but not otherwise. I would therefore urge the organizers at Vaikom to make redoubled effort and at the same time, keep stricter watch on the conduct of those who take part in the movement. Whether it takes a long or short time to reach the goal, the way is the way of peaceful conversion of the orthodox, by self-suffering and self purification and none other'

Careful analyses of both the statements reveal that there was no essential difference. The major objectives of both Gandhi and Sree Narayana Guru were the same, the eradication of untouchability, and the acceptance of human equality. And the immediate objective of the *Vaikom Satyagraha* was the establishment of a simple primary human right to make use of the public road around the temple. Both Gandhiji and the Guru agreed in this matter. What Gandhiji suggested is gain access to the road, and then try for temple entry. What Guru proposed is to go ahead without stopping until temple entry was achieved. *Don't stop with walking through the roads, but enter the temple*

At one point Gandhiji thought that Sree Narayana Guru had suggested to the volunteers to adopt open violence. *He suggested that the volunteers should advance along barricaded roads and scale the barricades...For scaling barricades is open violence.* Let a humble question be raised. What happened at Vaikom ? The volunteers were made to stand in the hot sun, drenched in the rain till midday, and then arrested. If they had followed what the Guru has suggested, tried to cross the fence, probably they would have received more blows, but would have arrested early, for defying orders. What Narayana Guru suggested was only to intensify the struggle or speed up the process in the Gandhian way. If the Guru's suggestion to the volunteers to scale the barricades was *open violence*, then Gandhiji's exhortation to the people to prepare salt at Dandi defying government orders is also equivalent to open violence. Attempt to scale the barricades is only open defiance, not open violence.

Sree Narayana Guru's exhortations were in unison with Gandhiji's idealism and practical wisdom. The Guru's words are clear indicators –

The will to suffer and sacrifice should be there.

Take blows without giving them

Let the government be informed of what you intend to do

Let there be no violence or show of force

Why did Gandhiji miss or ignore these words and interpret the guru's suggestion as an exhortation to violence and made blatant statements that the spiritual leader of the Thiyyas is reported to have disapproved of the present methods of Satyagraha at Vaikom ? It is for posterity to decide.

Any way, the Guru did not issue any statement to counter Gandhiji's writings in Young India. *It was never the Guru's technique to argue and win.* He expressed through actions what he had to say.

He offered his Vellore Mutt near Vaikom for the use of the Satyagrahis and Head Office was set up there. He made a personal contribution of Rs.1000.00 (a very big amount in those days) to the struggle fund, and set up a special collection box at Sivagiri. Two of his favourite disciples, Swami Sathyavrathan and Kottukoikal Velayudhan were deputed to work for the Satyagraha.

When the Satyagraha was at its peak, on September 27, 1924, the Guru visited the venue. He reached Vaikom by boat. Thousands were waiting at the jetty to receive him. He was welcomed with a multicolored garland of khadi yarn. He was also presented with the second khadi towel woven at the Satyagraha Ashram, the first one was sent to Mahatma Gandhi. The Guru jokingly offered to wear khadi garland and volunteer Satyagraha.

On the next day, he presided over a public meeting convened to pray for the good health and wellbeing of Mahatma Gandhi. Swami Satyavrathan remarked that it was a good fortune to have the Guru along with them. Suddenly, the Guru got up and said, *I am here not just to participate, I am here to pray.* He stood in meditation for a few minutes while the whole crowd waited. This was the single occasion when Guru had ever prayed in public.

The Guru stayed in the Ashram for two days, went around and saw all arrangements and joined the community meal. The volunteers felt, not the presence of a formal visitor, but the presence of an intimate advisor and an elderly leader. His presence and appreciation gave them renewed spirit and sense of commitment. The Guru was extremely happy to see a Pulaya boy in the kitchen to help the cooks. He was glad the seeds sown by him were proliferating and bearing fruit. The SNDP had most willingly taken over the task of supplying manpower for the endeavour, and continued to support until the Satyagraha was withdrawn.

During March 1925, when Gandhiji came to the Satyagraha site, he visited the Guru at Sivagiri. A part of their conversation is relevant here.

Gandhiji: Is there any difference of opinion for Swamiji about the Satyagraha started at Vaikom ? Does Swamiji think of adding or altering anything to the Movement?

Guru: My knowledge is that it is going smoothly and I am not of any opinion of making any alterations.

Gandhiji: Some are of the opinion that nonviolent Satyagraha is of no use, and to establish right, violence is necessary. What is Swamiji's opinion?

Guru: I do not think that violence is good.

The Savarna Processeion

In the meanwhile, Mahatmaji felt that the support of the Savarnas was essential for the success of the *Vaikom Movement*. So he suggested to the leaders at Vaikom, that a procession consisting of only Savarnas should march to Trivandrum, the capital, to register their solidarity with the Avarnas and lend their full support to the cause. The Savarna procession of about 500 men set out from Vaikom on November 1, 1924 under the leadership of Mannathu Padmanabhan, the unquestioned leader of the Nair Service Society. There was spontaneous welcome to the procession at every place they passed. On their way, the procession swelled as people joined. They halted at Sivagiri, paid homage to Sree Narayana Guru, and received his blessings. When the procession reached Trivandrum on November 12, 1924, with the jubilation of a conquering army, it had gathered nearly 5000 men. A similar procession of about a thousand men from Suchindram under the leadership of Perumal Naidu also reached Trivandrum on the same day. A mammoth public meeting was held.

Final Actions

On November 13, 1924, a delegation headed by *Changanasseri Parameswaran Pillai* waited on the Regent Maharani Sethu Lakshmi Bayi and submitted a memorandum signed by more than 25,000 Savarnas, *We the undersigned members of the deputation, loyally and respectfully beg leave to approach your Gracious Highness with the humble prayer that the roads around the Vaikom temple walls, and all other roads similarly situated in other parts of the State may be thrown open to all classes of Your Gracious Highness' subjects, without distinction of caste or creed*

Though the memorandum was submitted with much optimism, reaction was not that favourable. The Maharani expressed that the issue had to be decided in the legislature. The resolution was moved in the legislature on February 7, 1925, by the then SNDP Secretary N. Kumaran (Later he became High Court Judge). The text of the resolution was *All roads around the temple at Vaikom, and similar roads all over the state of Travancore must be open for travelling for people of all castes and creeds. The resolution was defeated by 22 votes against 21. (It is understood that Dr. Palpu's brother who was expecting favours from the Government voted against the resolution. He was a close associate of the Narayana Guru at Aruvippuram, but he turned Judas. He was haunted by the community and he fled from places to place to save his life. He became a social out caste and met with an ignoble death.)*

The defeat of the resolution severely affected the morale of the Satyagrahis and boosted the high-handedness of the Orthodox Hindus. While Gandhiji tried to lift the sinking morale through exhortations to remain patient and peaceful, Indanthuruthil Namboothiri, the leader of orthodoxy, arranged for hirelings to beat up the Satyagrahis. They were thrown into neck deep waters. Lime mixed with other strong irritants was poured in to their eyes. The police stood silently watching as they were secretly instructed not to interfere. Gandhiji wrote in Young India, *The Travancore authorities may, however, be respectfully told that the Congress cannot watch barbarity with indifference. The letting loose of the goondas on the devoted heads of the Satyagrahis, is bound to gather the Satyagrahis, the full weight of all-India public opinion.*

As a protest against atrocities, statewide agitation began. Big Savarna temples were boycotted, bringing down their revenue. The *Savarna Mahajana Sabha* organized meetings at their strongholds, against the Satyagraha. Tension was mounting, and it was time that something was to be done. There were even reactions among the volunteers that the slow passive method of Satyagraha was ineffective in the face of violence and goondaism.

It became imminent for Gandhiji to visit the place where his principle of Satyagraha was being tested. So he came down to Vaikom on March 10, 1925. His secretary Mahadev Desai, his son Ramdas Gandhi, Alladi Krishnaswamy Iyer, and C. Rajagopalachari came with him.

Gandhiji stayed in the Ashram and spoke to the volunteers. He tried to boost up their morale, by explaining to them the principle of Satyagraha and the role of scarifies and suffering in it, and the need for extreme patience. He tried to reach a compromise with the orthodoxy and for this; he had to meet the Savarna leaders. His secretary sent a note of invitation to the Savarna leader Idanthuruthil Devan Neelakandan Namboothiri to come over to the camp. The haughty Namboothiri not only refused to accept the invitation, but also said that those who wanted to see him must go over to his house. So it was that Gandhiji and his party reached the Indanthuruthil Mana (a Namboothiri household) on the next day noon. They were made to sit in the portico of the house, while the Namboothiri and his Savarna comrades occupied the inner room. The Namboothiri believed that Gandhi and his followers were polluted by the touch of untouchables, and could not be admitted in to the pure interior of an orthodox Mana.

Their dialogue continued for nearly three hours. Gandhiji made three practical proposals:

- The unapproachability that is practiced at Vaikom is not found in any Hindu scriptures. The orthodoxy contended that Adi Sankaracharya laid down the custom. In that case, Gandhiji proposed that an impartial Hindu Pundit must scrutinize Adi Shankara's Smirithis, and if this custom is not mentioned then it has to be withdrawn.
- The second proposal was that a referendum was to be taken from Savarnas. If the majority of Savarnas were willing to allow the roads to be opened to the Avarnas, it should be accepted.

Third proposal was that of arbitration. The orthodoxy appoints a Pandit, Gandhiji would appoint a Pandit on behalf of the Satyagrahis. The Divan of Travancore would act as an umpire. All must accept the winner's decision.

None of these was acceptable to the orthodoxy, who believed that the Avarnas are suffering because of their Karma (result of actions in their previous births). So Gandhiji left without a compromise and the Satyagraha continued, and the atrocities on them multiplied beyond words.

Final Settlement

Gandhiji had to do something about it. He wrote to *W. H. Pitt,* the then Police Commissioner of Travancore to put an end to goondaism. Pit being a European, was in a better position to intervene and bring an honourable settlement between Government and Gandhiji. Pitt agreed to influence the Government to remove all barricades and withdraw the prohibitory orders, on condition that Gandhiji instructed the Satyagrahis not to cross the point where the prohibitory board was. However the police would remain at the spot until all the terms of the agreement were implemented. An agreement was reached through correspondence.

Government agreed to withdraw the prohibitory orders passed in February 1924, and Gandhiji agreed to withdraw the Satyagraha. Government let the roads on three sides of the temple (north, south and west) open for public but the eastern approach road, and the two roads leading to it from the north and south remained reserved to the Savarnas only.

Gates were to be put up at three places: • At a short distance from the eastern gopuram on the eastern approach road. • At the north and south ends of the eastern road. These three gates were to be open only at the time of worship to admit those who had the right to enter the temple. It was also declared the portion of the road enclosed by the three gates would remain closed to Christians and Muslims as well as Avarna Hindus who have no right to enter the temple. A new road was to be constructed joining the eastern approach road to the northern road, for the convenience of the public. C. Rajagopalachari conveyed the details to Gandhiji through a letter and Gandhiji issued orders on October 8, 1925 to the Secretary of the *Satyagraha Ashram* to withdraw the Satyagraha. But action continued till November 1925 until all the conditions were implemented in Toto.

One view is that it was only a partial success for non-caste Hindus (Avarnas) as they gained access only to the roads on three sides of the temple. The fourth and most important eastern road remained inaccessible to them. It was really a blow to the Christians and Muslims as they lost their previously enjoyed freedom to have complete access on all the roads around the temple. Now the eastern road was blocked to them. Because of the gates, which remained closed the members of the Devaswam Board and the inmates of the temple who used the eastern road as thoroughfare were denied the opportunity. Anyway it was a great opportunity for the Indian National Congress party to grow in Kerala. Before this agitation, the Congress in Kerala was only a limited number of Upper Caste and Upper class people of Malabar (which was under British Rule). The Avarnas did not bother about the Congress, as the Congress leaders did not show any enthusiasm for the eradication of social inequalities. But when the party undertook to lead the agitation at Vaikom, the Avarnas underwent a sea of changes. At the exhortation of T. K. Madhavan, they joined the Congress en masse. *The Congress swelled from being a class party to a mass party.*

Another achievement of Vaikom agitation is certainly communal harmony. Progressive minded Savarnas and Avarnas came together with Christians, Muslims and even Sikhs. It is to be remembered that many Savarnas played the role of active leaders, till the withdrawal of the Satyagraha, and this has demonstrated the basic unity of the people.

Above all, the Vaikom Satyagraha was a testing ground for the Gandhian principles of Satyagraha. It was tested and proved as the most effective means for the first time.

Narayana Guru

Sri Narayana Guru (1855–1928), also known as Sree Narayana Guru Swami, was a Hindu saint, sage, prophet and social reformer of India. The Guru was born into an *Ezhava* family, in an era when people from backward communities like the Ezhavas faced much social injustices in the caste-ridden Kerala society. *Gurudevan*, as he was fondly known to his followers, revolted against casteism and worked on propagating new values of freedom in spirituality and of social equality, thereby transforming the Kerala society and as such he is adored as a prophet.

Narayana Guru is revered for his *Vedic* knowledge, poetic proficiency, openness to the views of others, nonviolent philosophy and his unrelenting resolve to set aright social wrongs. Narayana Guru was instrumental in setting the spiritual foundations for social reform in today's Kerala and was one of the most successful social reformers who tackled caste in India. He demonstrated a path to social emancipation without invoking the dualism of the oppressed and the oppressor.

Guru stressed the need for the spiritual and social upliftment of the downtrodden by their own efforts through the establishment of temples and educational institutions. In the process he brushed aside the Hindu religious conventions based upon *Chaturvarna*.

Biography

Narayana Guru was born in August 20, 1856, in the village of *Chempazhanthi* near Thiruvananthapuram, the son of Madan Asan, a farmer, and Kutti Amma. The boy was dotingly called

Nanu. Madan was also a teacher ("Asan") who was learned in Sanskrit and proficient in Astrology and Ayurveda.He had three sisters. As a boy, Nanu would listen to his father with keen interest when he narrated stories from the Ramayana and the Mahabharata to the simple folks of his village. Nanu was initiated into the traditional formal education *Ezhuthinirithal* by Chempazhanthi Pillai, a local schoolmaster and a village officer. Besides schooling, young Nanu continued to be educated at home, under the guidance of both his father and uncle Krishnan Vaidyan who was a reputed Ayurvedic physician and a Sanskrit scholar, where he was taught the basics of the Tamil and Sanskrit languages and traditional subjects such as *Siddharupam, Balaprobhodhanam* and *Amarakoœam.*

As a child, Nanu was very reticent and was intensely drawn to worship at the local temple. He would criticise his own relatives for social discrimination and the apartheid-like practice of segregating children from, supposedly, lower castes. He preferred solitude and would be found immersed in meditation for hours on end. He showed strong affinity for poetics and reasoning, composing hymns and singing them in praise of God. He lost his mother when he was 15. Nanu spent the most part of his early youth assisting his father in tutoring, and his uncle in the practice of Ayurveda, while devoting the rest of his time for devotional practices at the temples nearby.

Transformation as Master, Yogi and Seeker of Truth

The young Nanu had a keen mind and was sent to a famous scholar, Kummampilli Raman Pillai Asan at Karunagapalli, a village fifty miles away from his home, at the age of 21. Living as a guest in a prominent family house *Varanapally* near Kayamkulam, Nanu, along with other students, was taught Sanskrit language and poetry, drama and literary criticism, and logical rhetoric. He studied the Vedas and the Upanishads. He also began teaching in a near-by school. His knowledge earned him the respect of many and he came to be known as "Nanu Asan".

Nanu returned home to spend some time with his father, who was on the death bed. For a short period he ran a village school for the children of his neighbourhood. While continuing his quest for "the ultimate truth", Nanu would often spend time in the confines of temples, writing poems and hymns and lecturing to villagers on philosophy and moral values.

Married Life

Under pressure from his family, Nanu married *Kaliamma*, the daughter of a traditional village doctor. The marriage was a simple affair with the groom's sisters themselves investing the bride with the 'Thaali' (wedding knot) on his behalf. The bride remained with her parents, since Nanu Asan became a wanderer not long after.

'Parivrajaka' (A Spiritual Wanderer)

After the demise of his father and wife, Nanu Asan continued his life of a wandering Sanyasin. He became a 'Parivrajaka' (one who wanders from place to place in quest of Truth). It was during one of these days that Nanu met Kunjan Pillai, who later came to be known as Chattampi Swamikal. Kunjan Pillai, who discovered and appreciated Nanu Asan's philosophical genius and passion for Yoga, introduced him to *Thycaud Ayyavu*, a Hatha yogi. Under the Yogi, Nanu Asan mastered various Yogic practices including Hatha Yoga. The exposure gained from this scholastic experiences had a lasting impact on the later life and philosophy of Narayana Guru.

Enlightenment and its Poetic Expression

Nanu moved to his hermitage deep inside the hilly forests of Maruthwâmala, where he led an austere life immersed in meditative thought and yoga and subjected himself to extreme sustenance rituals.

This phase of solitude lasted for 8 long years. After an unpretentious life of over thirty years abounding in knowledge and harsh experiences, this epoch is considered the culmination of the meditative recluse; the point at which Narayana Guru is believed to have attained a state of Enlightenment.

Narayana Guru's later literary and philosophical masterpiece *Atmopadesa Satakam* (*one hundred verses of self-instruction*, written in Malayalam circa 1897) is considered a fertile poetic expression, encapsulating the Guru's philosophy of egalitarianism, emanating from the author's attainment of an experienced state of primordial knowledge and quintessence of the Universe; and his ensuing ability to view the human race, from a dignified and elevated perspective, as nothing but one of a genus, in unqualified equality and without any racial, religious, caste or other discriminations whatsoever.

Consecration of Siva Lingam *at Aruvippuram*

Learning from the sacred books and the practice of Yoga did not quench the thirst of Nanu. He continued his wanderings in quest of Truth. By and by, he came to a beautiful place called Aruvippuram. It was a forest area. There were hills around. A gurgling rivulet (of river Neyyar) also flowed there. As more people sought him out for healing or advice, he and his disciples felt the need for a regular temple for worshipping Shiva. At a beautiful spot near the river, he had his followers build a small canopy of coconut leaves and mango leaves over an altar on a rock jutting out in the water. The year was 1888. *They improvised lamps with shells and arranged them in rows. They were lighted at dusk and a piper began to play devotional tunes. The whole place was soon filled with pious village folk.* Gurudevan, who had been sitting apart and meditating all night, stood at midnight and walked into the river. As thousands watched silently (*If silence had music, the atmosphere was filled with it,* wrote one correspondent) he descended into the river and then reemerged, holding an idol of Shiva. He stood beneath the canopy with it in his arms for three hours, totally lost in meditation, tears flowing down his cheeks. Finally, at three in the morning, he installed the idol on the pedestal. His action was equivalent of overturning the tables of the money changers, or refusing to give up a seat on the bus. From the beginning of time, so far as anyone knew, only Brahmins had ever installed an idol. *Yet when Gurudevan performed the sacred rite it appeared so natural for him to pick up a small rock and install it. To those who questioned the timing of the consecration saying it was not an astrologically auspicious time, he replied:* Horoscope is to be cast after the birth of a child, not before. *He instructed to place a plaque containing a motto on the temple wall which read as:*

Devoid of dividing walls of Caste
Or hatred of rival faith,
We all live here
In Brotherhood,
Such, know this place to be!
This Model Foundation!

A new phase began in the Guru's life in 1904. He decided to give up his wandering life and settle down in a place to continue his Sadhana (spiritual practice). He chose Sivagiri, twenty miles north of Thiruvananthapuram. Goddess 'Amba' became his deity of worship.

Next, he started a Sanskrit school in Varkala. Poor boys and orphans were taken under his care. They were given education regardless of caste distinctions. Temples were built at different places-Thrissur, Kannur, Anjuthengu, Tellicherry, Calicut, Mangalore. A temple was built for Sharada Devi in 1912, at Sivagiri. Worship at such temples helped reduce to a large extent superstitious beliefs and practices.

One of the temples built in Thrissur is the Sri Narayana Temple at Koorkenchery. The temple has a school in its compound named Sri Narayana School. The School encourages students' talents by organising talent competitions. These competitions, regularly held every year, have been a platform for youngsters to stand up and recognise their talents.

In 1913, he founded the *Advaita Ashram* at Aluva. This was an important event in his spiritual quest. This Ashram was dedicated to a great principle-*Om Sahodaryam Sarvatra* (all men are equal in the eyes of God). This became the motto of the new Ashram.

When Narayana Guru attained the age of sixty, his birth day was observed throughout the west-coast from Mangalore to Sri Lanka. Between 1918 and 1923 he visited Sri Lanka many times. In 1921, a Conference of Universal Brotherhood was held at Aluva. Again in 1924, a conference of all religions was held there. Guru stressed the need for a *Brahma Vidyalaya* for a comparative study of different religious faiths.

Sree Narayana Guru had many followers and disciples. Nataraja Guru, a notable disciple of Sree Narayana Guru, introduced Guru's visions and ideals to the western world. He established Narayana Gurukulam in 1923 in the Nilgiri Hills with the blessings of Narayana Guru.

Om Sahodaryam Sarvatra (The Brotherhood of All)

In 1913, the Guru founded an Ashram at Aluva. It was called the *Advaita Ashram*. This was an important event in the life of the Guru. The Ashram was dedicated to a great principle-*Om Sahodaryam Sarvatra* (all human beings are equal in the eyes of God). In 1921, a Conference of Universal Brotherhood was held at Alwaye. Again in 1924, a conference of all religions was held there. The Guru stressed the need for a *Brahma Vidyalayam* for the comparative study of various religious faiths. An institution called *Narayana Gurukulam* was established in the Nilgiri Hills, Tamil Nadu by Bodhananda Swamikal and later handed over to Nataraja Guru.

Final Ceylon Journey

Gurudevan visited Ceylon again in 1926. He had some moving experiences while travelling in Tamil Nadu in connection with his journey to Ceylon. While he was in Sree Ganapathi temple in heavy rain he said, "If there is anyone writing my biography, these experiences should not be missed, they should be recorded." After that journey to Ceylon, Gurudevan did not want to return. He went back only after repeated requests of his disciples and devotees.

Message to Sree Narayana Dharma Paripalana (SNDP) Yogam

In a message to the SNDP Yogam in 1926 Gurudevan declared, *No community can make progress except through organization.* He further said in that message, *The name Ezhava does not denote a caste or a religion and he made temple rights to everyone. Therefore people can be admitted to this organization without paying heed to differences of caste.*

On June 14, 1927 Sree Narayana Guru consecrated a mirror-with the message "Om shanti" written on the surface-in a temple in Kalavankode. The prathishta of the mirror is symbolic in that Advaita philosophers interpret the mirror as the visible symbol of the unity of the Finite and the Infinite. That was the last prathishta that the Guru would do. Schools rather than temples are to be preferred, he exhorted in a dramatic shift of focus. Gurudevan participated in the anniversary of the SNDP Yogam held at Palluruthi in 1927. It was a splendid meeting which demonstrated the sincere, devout faith of the people in Gurudevan. T. K. Madhavan was one of the chief architects of this meeting. In 1928 Gurudevan took part in the special meeting of the SNDP Yogam at Kottayam and gave away registration certificates to the branch organizations.

Even though Guru started SNDP as a forum to lead the activities for social equality and caste less society, eventually SNDP turned out to be a forum of Ezhava caste, which is a contradiction to

Guru's vision. Various factions in the SNDP Yogam accuse others of financial irregularities and corruption. There are allegations that liquor barons are controlling the SNDP Yogam. It is an irony that today SNDP Yogam represents exactly those things/ideas which Guru opposed.

Sivagiri Pilgrimage

Sivagiri pilgrimage was conceived by Vallabhasseri Govindan Vaidyar and T K Kittan Writer. It was duly approved by Gurudevan on January, 1928. The setting was SNDP's Nagambadam Shiva temple. It was 3 pm and Gurudevan was resting under a mango tree when the two presented the concept of Sivagiri pilgrimage. Before giving its his blessings he set out the goals of such a pilgrimage. He said: "Let the pilgrims congregate at the beginning of the European New Year. It should be Dhanu 16-17 in Malayalam calendar. Let the pilgrims observe 10 days' self-purification according to Sri Buddha's principles of five purities (pancha dharma)-body, food, mind, word, deed. He ruled that pilgrims could wear yellow clothes-the colour of the garments Sri Buddha wore. *Let no one purchase yellow silk because we have recommended yellow garments. Not even new clothes are required on the pilgrimage. A pilgrim can dip a white garment in turmeric water and wear after drying. The pilgrimage should be conducted with simplicity and preferably be accompanied by the chanting of hymns. There should be no shouting and pilgrims should scrupulously avoid trappings of ostentation.*

To Govindan Vaidyar and Kitten Writer, Gurudevan counted on his fingers the goals of the pilgrimage, explaining how to achieve them. The goals were the promotion of;

- Education
- Cleanliness
- Devotion to God
- Organisation
- Agriculture
- Trade
- Handicrafts
- Technical training.

He advised them to organise a series of lectures on the themes with experts conducting them. The lectures should be listened to attentively. More important, the principles should be put into practice. Success must accompany efforts. Only then will the country and the people benefit this must be the core purpose of Sivagiri pilgrimage.

The Palluruthi event in 1927 was the last anniversary of the Yogam which Gurudevan attended. It was also the last public function Gurudevan attended.

Gurudevan went to Vellur Mutt at Vaikom to rest. There he was taken ill. He went to Alwaye and later to Trichur for treatment. Dr. Krishnan took Gurudevan to Palghat. From there Gurudevan travelled to Madras for treatment.

Death

Guru became seriously ill in September 1928. He remained bedridden for some time. Devotees came in large numbers to have a glimpse. The same year, Gurudevan's birthday was celebrated in many places, mostly in Kerala, Madras, Mangalore, Srilanka and Europe. On 20 September, Guru died.

Narayana Guru's Philosophy

Hailing from the land of Adi Shankara, Sree Narayana Guru was a great proponent and re-evaluator of Advaita Vedanta. Guru's philosophy, which is fundamentally of Advaitic and non-dual wisdom in principles, further extended Advaitic concepts into practical modes of self-realisation through spiritual education, compassion and peaceful coexistence of humanity, whilst promoting social equality and universal brotherhood. His philosophy strongly denounced discrimination in the name of caste or religion, and emphasised focusing on education and private enterprise for the ongoing upliftment of the quality of life. Guru's philosophy emphasised the consistency between true existence of the "common reality" on Earth and one Divine behind the creation and sustenance of the Universe.

Guru's philosophy is exemplified in his mystical writings that are truly interchanging warps and wefts of ethics, logic, aesthetics and metaphysics woven into masterpieces of silken rich poetry. Guru's literary works in Malayalam, Sanskrit and Tamil are of a conceptual and aesthetic quality at par with the Upanishads.

At the time of its conception, Narayana Guru's philosophy was in many respects ahead of its time and focused on a futuristic world order that could be shaped from his philosophical connotations that are underlain with transcendental aesthetics and logic embodied in knowledge and pure reason. Most of the serious scholars of Narayana Guru's philosophy have been from generations beyond his lifetime; and this list keeps growing.

Tolerance Toward Others

Guru had followers from all walks of life. Some of these were atheists. An Advaithin to the core, he did not differentiate people on the basis of their relegion, caste, colour or beliefs. He was tolerant toward all philosophies that stood for the progress of mankind.

To avoid the attempts made by a section of his followers to identify him with the community he was born into, Narayana Guru was forced to state explicitly that he did not belong to any particular caste or religion. Through a message he sent in the year 1916, he proclaimed : *It is years since I left castes and religions. Yet some people think that I belong to their caste. That is not correct. I do not belong to any particular caste or religion.*

The Guru's Influence on other Social Thinkers

Concerning the caste system, Gandhi said the following to Narayana Guru: "*The caste-Hindus and the low caste-Hindus are both the sons of Hinduism. The caste-Hindu is the elder brother who shoulders responsibility, and he therefore exercises certain privileges. The low caste-Hindu is his younger brother who is to be cared for. If the elder brother turns out to be somewhat rough and aggressive that should not make the younger brother a runaway from his mother Hinduism.*" Narayana Guru, however, disagreed, and voiced his tolerance for those who converted to other religions, with the argument that one should follow what one truly believes in. He also questioned the logic of Gandhi's argument, arguing that caste in India was a socioeconomic issue.

Guru's Famous Teachings

- One Jati (Caste) One Religion, One God for Man
- All are of one Self-fraternity Such being the dictum to avow, In such a light how can we take life And devoid of least pity go on to eat
- Whichever the religion It suffices If it makes a better man.
- Ask not, Say not Think not caste

- Acts that one performs For one's own sake Should also aim for the good Of other men
- Love of others is my happiness, Love that is mine is happiness for others. And so, truly, deeds that benefit a man Must be a cause for other's happiness too.
- Grace, Love, Mercy-all the three-Stand for one same reality-Life's Star. He who loves is who really lives.
- Whatever may be the difference in men's creed, dress, language etc. because they all belong to the same kind of creation, there is no harm at all in their dining together or having marital relation withone another.
- Liquor is poison Make it not Sell it not Drink it not.
- Devoid of dividing walls Of caste or race Or hatred of rival faith We all live here In Brotherhood
- Progress through education. Strengthen through organisation.

Public Acceptance, Honours and Veneration

Since his lifetime Narayana Guru has been conferred formal recognitions and honours by the State, intelligentsia and society. In 1901 the State Census Manual of Travancore recorded Sree Narayana as a revered "Guru" and an erudite Sanskrit scholar. A sharp drop in the statistics of the commission of crime was also attributed to the correcting and moralizing influence of Narayana Guru on the society. In 1904 the then Maharajah of Travancore exempted Narayana Guru from personal appearances in court, an honour recognizing the Guru as a distinguished living personality.

The first statue of the Guru was conceived by Moorkoth Kumaran and sculpted by an Italian sculptor Prof. Tavaroli whilst the Guru was still alive. The bronze statue, which took 14 months to complete, was installed at the Jaggannaatha temple at Thalassery and unveiled on 13 March 1927, after the consecration of the statue by Bodhananda Swamikal, the disciple and then spiritual successor-designate to Narayana Guru.

On the Guru's *Mahasamadhi* (passing away), the famed Jnanapith award winner poet Mahakavi G. Sankara Kurup paid tribute to Narayana Guru by writing a Malayalam verse venerating the Guru as The Second Buddha. Sree Narayana Guru's legacy continues to be revered at esteemed levels within social, intellectual and spiritually organised communities worldwide. All across the State of Kerala, and outside of the State, hundreds of small chapel-like *Guru Mandirams* are devoted to the reverence and worship of Sree Narayana Guru. Most recently, a distinctively styled iconographic statue of Narayana Guru named the Jnana Vigraham was conceived and created by a team of artists, as a suggestive model for the future, to improve the aesthetic quality of statues of Narayana Guru kept in homes and placed in *Guru Mandirams* worldwide.

At the turn of the 21st Century, Sree Narayana Guru was named as The Malayalee of the Century by Kerala's leading daily Malayala Manorama. The full cover-page spread of the newspaper was dedicated to Narayana Guru in its last issue of the Century on 31 December 1999. So also Narayana Guru was featured first among the "100 great lives" nominated by Malayala Manorama on the occasion of Malayala Manorama's centenary celebrations in the year 1988.

Saint Disciples of Guru

- Sree Bodhananda Swamikal
- Sad Guru Shivalingadasa Swamikal
- Satyavrata Swamikal
- Chaitanya Swamikal
- Nataraja Guru
- Swamy Ananda Theerthan
- Swamy Dharma Theerthan
- Swamy Ernest Kerk
- Govindhananda Swami
- Dharma Thirthar Swami
- Atmananda swami
- Sankarananda Swami
- Sreenarayana Theerthar.

In Malayalam

1. Swanubavageethi
2. Atmopadesa Satakam
3. Advaitha Deepika
4. Arivu

5. Daiva Dasakam Play Now
6. Jeevakarunya Panchakam
7. Anukamba Dasakam
8. Jathi Nirnayam
9. Jathi Lakshanam
10. Chijanda Chinthakam
11. Daiva Chintanam-1 & 2
12. Athma Vilasam
13. Shiva Satakam.

In Tamil

1. Thevarappathinkangal

Translations

1. Thirukural
2. Isavasyo Upanishad
3. Ozhivil Odukkam.

His knowledge earned him the respect of many and he came to be Known as "Nanu ashan".

Sree Narayana Dharma Paripalana

Sree Narayana Dharma Paripalana Yogam is an organisation formed to propagate and promote the moral teaching and Dharma of Shree Narayana Guru. Dr. P. Palpu, a devotee of Sree Narayana, was one of the founders. According to the biography of Narayana Guru written by Moorkoth Kumaran, the organization was registered on 15 May, 1903 under Travancore Regulation 1 of 1063 (Indian Company Act IV 1882).

Sree Narayana Guru was the Patron and life time President of the Yogam. Mahakavi Sri. Kumaranasan was the first General Secretary. Kumaran Asan was the peerless pioneer among modern Malayalam poets. He was one of the dedicated disciples of Sree Narayana Guru. In fact the spiritual philosophy and the battle against caste that illumine Kumaran Asan's poetry were inspired mainly by association with and inspiration from the great Guru.

History of SNDP Yogam

The history of Sree Narayana Dharma Paripalana Yogam is the rise of the socially backward, depressed classes in Kerala. It is the social development of Ezhava from (according to the 824 Royal Order) mere 'owner of thalappu and ladder" to the present state. It is also the shining story of the change of an almost food-gathering society into a cosmopolitan world order. Yogam is the first organisation which envizaged Kerala as a whole. Earlier organisations represented only part of Kerala, say, Malabar.

Caste System in Kerala

To know the history of Yogam, one has to learn the social set up of Kerala during that period. It was a Renaissance from the darkness brooded over Kerala society. In 1897, Swami Vivekananda said in Madras: "All Malabaries are lunatics. Their houses, lunatic asylums...." This was the reaction of his towards the caste system and the unique untouchability system that prevailed in Adi Sankaran's Kerala at that time. The worst form of untouchability in India existed in Kerala.Pulaya should not reach more than 96 feet near to a Brahmin. It was Nair's dharma to kill a Pulaya or Parayah who violated untouchavbility rule. Thiyya (Ezhava) kept 12 feet from Nair and a Nair would get salvation if he killed an Ezhava immediately when he (Ezhava) violated the 36 feet barrier to Nambudiri. Whenever the caste Hindus went through public roads, they would shout, "Go, go". The untouchables or backward classes had to run away from the road immediately after they heard the voice.

Besides, they were not permitted to cover their upper part of the body. Footwear, umbrella, special dressing ornaments etc. were not permitted to them. In public places, it was the sole right of Brahmins to wear umbrellas even it was raining. It was by bearing their breasts that the lower caste women showed their respect to upper caste people.

The first event which questioned this caste system was the order issued by Tippu Sultan, the then ruler of Mysore Empire. At that period, the Mysore Empire spread even in the Malabar region of Kerala. Besides, the works of Christian Missionaries also helped the untouchables a lot to free themselves from the social incapabilities.

It was Dr. Palpu who started works towards getting the rights of Ezhava community. With the 1891 Malayali Memorial Revolt, he came forward by taking the leadership of the community. He tried to make an organization called 'Ezhava Sabha'. In 1896, he created the bye-law of it and published the same in Malayali, a newspaper published from Thankussery. Eventhough he organised some meetings at Paravur and Mayyanad, that movement failed.

The Guru and SNDP Yogam

Before these, a noble, great power had been working towards the spiritual and social awakening of the community. It was none other than the great Sree Narayana Guru Devan. By installing a rock from the Neyyar River as Sivalinga at Aruvippuram on the Sivaratri day of Kumbha month in 1888 (1063 Aandu), he started a silent revolution in the history of Kerala. It caused a social revolution, which uprooted the old social system of Kerala.

Gradually, Aruvippuram became a pilgrim centre. On Vavu (Full moon) day, people began to come there to offer sacrifice. The deciples of the Guru which included the famous poet Kumaran Asan, decided to give food to the pilgrims which led to the creation of 'Vavoottu Yogam' (serving food to the people who come as pilgrims).

In 1889, Vavoottu Yogam had been expanded. Thus an organization, 'Aruvippuram Kshetra Yogam' had formed.

On Malayalam Era 1078 Dhanu 23, (1903), a special meeting of Aruvippuram Kshetra Yogam was conducted. They decided to change that into a big Yogam for the progress of Ezhavas both in religious and material ways. Thus, on 1078 Edavam 2, (1903, May 15), with Narayana Guru as its President, 'Aruvippuram Kshetra Yogam' has been registered as' Aruvippuram Sree Narayana Dharma Paripalana Yogam' according to the Indian Companies Act, No.6, 1882.

The permanent chairman of Yogam was Sree Narayana Guru Devan. N. Kumaranasan was elected as the General Secretary. Upto 1919, July 20, he was on the post, except in 1904 (1079 Vrischika 10). Difference of opinion exits about the role of the Guru in its establishment. On verifying the original records of registering the SNDP Yogam with the Government as a limited company, the following facts can be derived. The Government file (No 8338) regarding the registration has two parts. Pat I contain the bye-laws and proceedings, having sixteen clauses. Non of the clauses speaks of any caste. The sixteenth clause clearly states of the 'casteless' nature of the organization. Below the bye-laws, eleven persons have put their signature. The first signatory witnesses to the document were resident of the Siva Temple, P. Narayana Pillai. Narayana Pillai was the most trusted deciple of the Guru. He installed the first idol of the Guru at Thellicherry together with Moorkoth Kumaran.

Part II of the file (No 8338) gives a different picture. It is an application to the Dewan of Travancore to register the SNDP Yogam as a limited company. The applicants are P.Parameswaran and Marthandan Krishnan. Here the caste provision of the organization is clearly stated: " promoting and encouraging religious and secular education and industrious habits among the Ezhava community". The license of the Yogam was issued to the applicants P. Parameswaran and M. Krishnan.

Guru's View

The Guru wanted the Yogam to function as the vanguard of his 'Liberation Movement'. But the leadership of the Yogam could not rise Upto the expectation of the Guru. It could function only in a caste organisation. Hence, in 1916, the Guru sent his resignation letter to Dr. P. Palpu. The Guru attributed 'caste pride' to the leaders of the Yagam and declared that he belonged to no caste non-religious.

Early Stage of SNDP Yogam

From 1078 Dhanu 28, (1903), issuing of memberships was started. One member had to give Rs.100/-as share. On Makara 5th, Guru himself started a journey towards the northern areas as part of the membership campaign. By Makaram 28, Yogam had 90 members. In the same year on 14th Kumbha, the first public meeting of the Yogam held in the Sivaratri festival day at Aruvippuram. The first annual public meeting started on 1079 Makaram 30 and Kumbham 1, at the Northern Matt of Aruvippuram Kshetra. Matancheri

First Managing Committee

The first Managing Committee consisted of Sree Narayana Guru (Permanent chairman), Dr. Palpu (Vice Chairman), N. Kumaranasan (General Secretary), Mattancheri Govindan Vaidyar, B. Kochujutti Muthalai (Muttathara), Mangalasseri Govindan Channar, Perinad Govindanasan, P. Madhavan Vaidyar, Thiruvananthapuram, Paravur Kesavanasan, Kottaikkal Kumaran, Madan Neyyattinkara, S. Krishnan, Korothuparambu,

Peringottukara, Koyikkara Kochayyyan Channar and Kuttiyappi Asan, Kurichithottatha, Karichal.

After 15 months of the registration of the SNDP Yogam, on Malayalam year 1080 Kanni 21 (1904), under the leadership of Paravoor V. Kesavanasan, an Ezhava Mahasammelanam was convened at Paravur, Kollam. It was in that meeting that the decision to stop the ill practices of talikettu, thirandukuli, Pulikudi etc. which were leading Ezhava Community into social and economic decline, had taken. Further, the decision to start practicing new marriage ceremony was also taken according to the order of Gurudeva.

The second annual of Yogam was conducted in Kollam on 1080 Dhanu 24 and 25 (1905). A public exhibition (10 days) conducted as part of the Annual caused the rise of self-pride and confidence in Ezhavas. The desire of upper castes to suppress them led to the Nair-Ezhava riot. The riot spread strongly towards northern parts like Paravur and Kollam. The rioters set fire to Kerala Bhushanam Publishing Company and Sujananandini Newspaper Office, both owned by Paravur Kesavanasan.

By the time of 3 years of its establishment, SNDP Yogam was able to get the attention of both the Government and the public. In Travancore, it was not just a Communal organization; rather, it was a political organization. The relentless attempts of Kumaranasan, the General Secretary, were behind it. When he retired after his 15 years service as General Secretary, SNDP Yogam had 1783 members (Rs.25) and 2472 shares. At that time, Yogam was not a common people's organization. Because one had to pay Rs.25/-to get a share of the organisation. Due to his 15 years of restless works, all schools were open to backward classes and, even though on condition of nomination, they were permitted to enter into the Sabha.

The First Labour Conference

As part of the SNDP Yogam annual, a labour conference was held at Kollam in 1917. It was the first labour conference in Kerala of this kind. Provision was also made for the representation of the labour in the 'Director Board' of the SNDP Yogam

If we search at the 44 years history of legislature between 1888 to 1932, no Ezhava was elected to membership of Legislature. Due to the continuous effort of SNDP, in 1911 February, Ezhava representatives could participate in Sreemoolam Praja Sabha. It was during this time that Yogam raised voice for population wise representation in Govt. services and legislative Assembly and for establishing abolition of caste, temple entry and teetotalism.

The 16th annual meeting at Kayamkulam relieved Sri. Kumaranasan of the post of General Secretary according to his request and elected Sri N. Kumaran BA.BL. as new General Secretary.

Penitence of T.K Madhavan: Organisation of the Downtrodden

When T.K Madhavan became the Organisation General Secretary of the SNDP Yogam, he noticed that the Yogam had been alienated from the common people. His attempt to strengthen the Yogam through massive membership campaign failed due to lack of popular cooperation. The only way to make the campaign a success was to gain the confidence of the Guru and make him to give a call to the people to join the Yogam. Accordingly, Madhavan went to the Guru, an assurance was given to the Guru that he would enlist as members of the Yogam, people of all castes and communities and that the Yogam work for the uplift of the downtrodden. Throughout Kerala, the followers of Narayana Guru took initiative to organize the workers. In Travancore, the SNDP Yogam under T.K. Madhavan took initiative to organize the labourers. In Kochi, the 'Aadi Thozhilali Sangham' was organized by Sahodaran Ayyappan. In Malabar, Moorkothu Kumaran, the prominent 'non-sanyasi' disciple of the Guru mobilised the workers.

Boycott of Temple

On 17 Dhanu (2 January) 1924 at Sivagiri, the leaders of the SNDP Yogam took the decision to boycott temples. To make it a success, a committee consisting of T.K. Madhavan, Nl Mumaran and C.V. Kayyalakkal was constituted. They formulated a ten-fold programme of the boycott of temples and it was effectively propagated throughout Kerala through newspapers- Deshabhimani, Sahodaran, Kerala Kaumudi, Vivekodayam, Navajeevan, Thozhilali, Mithavadi etc. The propaganda works undertaken by the 'Karappuram Sevasangham of Sherthallai, made the message of 'Civil Liberty and Temple Entry' to reach at the grassroots level.

In the 18th meeting of SNDP Yogam, according to Guru's wish, Yogam envisaged activities not just for the prosperity of Ezhavas but for the whole depressed classes. Temple entry revolt was introduced as a live issue in this meeting. The forerunner of this was T.K. Madhavan. It was also decided that the branches of SNDP Yogam were being started in Taluk and Kara level. The responsibility was given to T.K. Madhavan, Assistant Secretary on 1102 Dhanu 17, (1927) Sri. T.K. Madhavan was appointed as Secretary.

Membership Campaign

He started membership works from Kuttanadu. Even though there were only 3878 members when he became the Secretary of the Organization, at the time of his retirement, there were 63674 members which included 2000 women. Besides these, there were 300 branches, 10 unions and more than 60 cooperatives to the credit of the Yogam.

When the SNDP Yogam started, the share of it cost Rs.100/- which, without much delay, was reduced to Rs.25/-per head. Even in this state, the number of members were not increased so that on 1922, the share value was reduced to Rs.5 and membership was divided into two as permanent and temporary. Now the membership fee is Rs.10/-.

The Agro-labour Strike in Kuttanad

Though serfdom existed in Kuttanad even during 1920s, due to the Sree Narayana Movement, the attitude of the landlords started to change. In 1927, the Yogam workers of Kuttanad requested through a resolution to T.K. Madhavan that the Yogam must interfere in the labour problem of Kuttanad. In 1929, Madhavan led the first agro-labour strike in Kuttanad. The incident occurred in Kainakari when female workers numbering forty were beaten by one landlord named 'Chirayil Kochuthomman'.

There existed the practice of the landlord kidnapping any female worker as a matter of right. This time, when the female workers were beaten up, the 'Kunnumel Jnanodayam Sabha', the local SNDP unit took up the issue and informed T.K. Madhavan. Madhavan directed them to strike work collectively. All farming works were completely stopped. Finally the landlord appologised before the workers. In 1103 (1928), General Secretary S.N. Kumaran vacated his position to Assi. Secretary V.K. Kunjuraman to become District Judge.

After the Guru

In 1104 Kanni 5, (1929), Guru passed away. In 1928 May 26, General Secretary G.V. Kunhiraman has submitted a memorandum to the authorities describing the disabilities of Ezhavas and stressing the need to give communal representation. The annual meeting of Yoga in 1932 June 29 demanded maturity voting right. In the meeting n 1932, December 17, at LMS Hall, Thiruvananthapuram where about one hundred people representing Christians, Muslims and Ezhavas created 'Akhila Thiruvithamcore Samyukta Rashtriya Mahasabha' and submitted a memorandum to Diwanji, demanding reservation for population wise representation in legislation and election through public areas. SNDP Yogam had a great représentation in the revolt. The LMS meeting saved the seeds of a great turning point in Travancore history.

On August 27, 1933, Sri. C. Kesavan had unanimously been elected as the Yogam General Secretary. At that time, according to his annual report, the total government jobs were 20,278 out of which only 787 were represented by Ezhavas who consisted a population of 8,72,174 while Nairs who had a population of 8,68,411 possessed 10,585 jobs. In 1935, Sri C. Kesavan was arrested and imprisoned charging traitorousness on the basis of Kozhancheri oratory. In 1936 October 8, Sri C.P. Ramaswami Iyer had taken charge of Diwan and on November 12, he published a decree permitting all Hindus to enter in the temples.

It was on Changanasseri Conference in which Yogam decided to participate in State Congress agitation. At that time both as an organisation and as a community SNDP Yogam and Ezhavas were the only participants in State Congress agitation. Later, Yogam decided to stop the relationship with State Congress only for the sake of the community. Accordingly, General Secretary, V.K. Velayudhan and Board Member R. Sankar resigned their posts in Yogam and entered in live politics.

In 1944 December 20, at Changanassery meeting, R. Sankar was elected as Yogam General Secretary. At that time, he was the Acting General Secretary of State Congress. Yogam had 933 branches, 24 unions, 4 union buildings, 214 branch buildings, 5 UP schools and more than 4000 permanent members. Ten years after when he retired, Yogam had 1224 branches, 662 branch buildings, 13 union buildings, 18 UP schools and 12 high schools. Temporary membership had been rised from 2 lakh to 3 lakhs.

In 1220 Makara (1945), Sree Narayana Guru Smaraka Committee has been formed as N. Kumaran, President and E.C. Govindanasan Treasurer. They met the Diwan and discussed about starting an A Grade College for Ezhavas.

Diwan agreed on the condition that the committee had to rise Rs.5 lakh, and the same amount will be given by the government. Due to the dullness in the field of cashewnut industry, the Committee was unable to rise the amount. At that time, a news about the starting of a college at Kollam by NSS came in the newspapers.

The Committee met again and informed the Yogam that they would give Rs. 2 lakh and the Yogam should rise the Rs. 3 lakh and start the college under its control.

The Yogam's annual meeting in 1945, November 24 and 25 at Kollam decided to start a first grade college at Kollam. In 1947, stone had laid for the college. In 1948, pre-university classes started. In 1951, Women's College was also started working at Kollam. Behind all these was the yeoman service of Yogam General Secretary R. Sankar and team. According to the decision of the Yogam, in 1952, Sree Narayana Trust was formed and the control and working of the colleges were taken under the custody of the trust.

In 1953, the 50th anniversary of Yogam was celebrated pompously with All India Exhibition, Art Exhibition etc. for 5 weeks under the leadership of R. Sankar at Kollam. It was the greatest in the history of the social organisations of Kerala.

After R. Sankar, Sri. Karthikeyan was the Yogam General Secretary for 2 years. Then again, R. Sankar became General Secretary for one year. After that, for three years Sri. K.R. Narayanan became the General Secretary.

From, 1961 to 1970, Sri. M.K. Raghavan was the General Secretary. In 1971, Sri Mangoozhi Madhavan became the General Secretary. In 1973, Sri. N. Srinivasan became President and Prof.. P.S. Velayudhan was the General Secretary. It was during that period that SNDP Yogam had conducted a great procession in Thiruvananthapuram. In 1973, SNDP Youth Movement & Vanitha Samajam started working.

Objectives of the Organisation

The main objectives of the organisation are:

- Introduce Shri Narayana devotees to each other and spread teachings of Shri Narayana Guru
- Help socially and economically weak in education
- Work in cooperation with other organizations for the betterment of all.
- Educate members about all religions.
- Establish a Temple and a School.
- Provide financial help to victims of disasters.

Organizational Contributions

The Yogam engaged itself in the laudable efforts of eradicating untouchability and voicing the fundamental human rights of the working class. These efforts actually paved the way for many of Guru's followers to accept later the Marxist interpretation of socialism as their most acceptable ideal. Under the aegis of Dr. Palpu, Kumaran Asan, T. K. Madhavan, C.V. Kunjuraman, Moolur Padmanabha Panickar and others, several drastic changes were brought about in the social structure and texture of the Kerala community The role that Narayana Guru played was only of a catalyst and not as a fighter in the front lines. To others he set an example by his own personal life. His high dignity and sense of oneness with mankind did not allow him to give vent to anger or protestation against any particular person or community. He believed that there was only one caste for man and that was humanity. In this attitude he was uncompromising. This organisation has done invaluable service in the epic struggle against caste system in Kerala.

Motivation

SNDP's follows Guru's social activities and its work is based the famous Quote of Guru:

"Without differences of caste, Nor enmities of creed', *Here it is, the model of an abode, Where all live like brothers at heart"*.

Organizational Structure

SNDP Yogam has been divided into 3 formation and they are;

- Yogam (Top Level Body)

- Union (Middle Level)
- Sakhas (Lower level).

It is head-quartered in Kollam, Kerala. Vellapally Natesan is the current general secretary of SNDP Yogam.

Schools and Colleges

SNDP founded schools and colleges in the independent India. Previously the only private colleges were those managed by the Church. The movement started with SN College, Kollam and continued to late 70s. Great leaders like R. Sankar had the vision for future. According to M.A.John (idealist Congress leader), R. Sankar was the best Chief Minister kerala had and R. Sankar ministry laid the foundation for long term progress in Kerala-in the form of educational institutions and industries.

A Multicaste Organization

Though SNDP Yogam is mainly managed by Ezhava community, there is nothing in the bye-laws stopping other castes or religions into the body. As had been the case, many social reformers of other 'castes' were close friends or associates of SNDP Yogam. This include notable names like Mannathu Padmanabhan (founder of Nair Service Society), V.T.Bhattathiripad, M.C.Joseph (Rationalist) and in recent times Singer Yesudas and P.A.Backer who produced the movie on Sree Narayana Guru. Both Mannam and Marxist leader A.K.Gopalan were influenced by Guru and shed their caste endings from their names.

Controversies

Even though Guru started SNDP as a forum to lead the activities for social equality and caste less society, eventually SNDP turned out to be a forum of Ezhava caste, which is a contradiction to Guru's vision. Various factions in the SNDP Yogam accuse others of financial irregularities and corruption. There are allegations that liquor barons are controlling the SNDP Yogam. It is an irony that today SNDP Yogam represents exactly those things/ideas which Guru opposed.

Mannathu Padmanabhan Nair

Mannathu Padmanabhan (January 1, 1877-February 25, 1970) was a social reformer and a freedom fighter from the State of

Kerala, India. He is recognised as the founder of the organisation called the Nair Service Society. This organisation represents the Nair community which constitutes almost 14.5% of the population of the state. Padmanabhan is considered as a visionary reformer who organised a 5 million Nair community under the NSS.

Early Life

He was born on New Years' Day in 1877 to Eswaran Namboothiri of Nilavana Illam and Mannathu Parvathy Amma of a respectable Nair family near Changanassery, in North Travancore. Padmanabhan started his career as a teacher in 1893 in a Government Primary School. After a few years he changed his profession and took up legal practice from 1905 onwards. He started practising law in the Magistrates' Courts and soon became an established member of the Bar.

NSS

In 1914, he with the help of a few others, established the Nair Service Society, his main ambition was to uplift the Nairs and to regain the lost power of this former ruling sect. From 1915 onwards, he gave up a lucrative practice and became full-time secretary of the Nair Service Society.

In 1924 he took part in the Vaikom and Guruvayoor temple-entry and anti-untouchability agitation. He even opened his family temple for everyone irrespective of any caste distinction. He became a member of the Indian National Congress in 1947 and took part in the Travancore State Congress agitation against Sir C.P. Ramaswamy Iyer's administration in Travancore.

In 1949 Padmanabhan became a member of the Travancore Legislative Assembly. In 1959 he led a united opposition against the State Communist Ministry. This struggle is called Vimochana Samaram which means liberation struggle he was travalled all over Kerala in chariot pulled by Bishops, priests of different Christian factions and other prominent members of different communities.

The immediate cause of the outbreak of the Vimochana Samaram was the introduction of an Education Bill by the Minister of Education Joseph Mundassery.

The immediate effect of the Vimochana Samaram was the dismissal of the Communist government under E.M.S. on July 31,

1959 and the beginning of President's rule in the state under Article 356 of the Indian Constitution. One notable feature of the movement was its massive student participation led by the student leaders like A.K. Antony, Oommen Chandy, etc.

Padmanabhan was involved with Nair Service Society as its Secretary for 31 years and as its President for 3 years. He was honoured with the title 'Bharata Kesari' from the President of India. He also received Padma Bhushan in 1966.

Guruvayur Satyagraha

The famous Guruvayur Satyagraha is a memorable episode in the history of the national movement. With the blessings of Mahatma Gandhi the Kerala Provincial Congress Committee decided to begin Satyagraha before the famous temple at Guruvayur with effect from 1st November, 1931. It was a movement for temple entry and abolition of untouchability.

The Satyagraha began accordingly under the leadership of Sri. K. Kelappan. Among the Kerala leaders other than Kelappan were Mannath Padmanabhan, A.K. Gopalan and N.P. Damodaran.

Guruvayur began to attract the attention of all India. There were certain untoward incidents during the early period of the Satyagraha. They served to heighten the tension in the minds of the people who were in sympathy with the movement. After the movement had run its course for about ten months, Kelappan entered on a fast before the temple on September, 21, 1932. The fast electrified the atmosphere. On October 2, 1932 Kelappan broke his fast in response to Gandhiji's wishes. There after a referendum was held among the Hindus to find out their views on the question of temple entry. More than 77 percent of the Hindus expressed themselves in favour of temple entry. The Guruvayur temple was thrown open to Harijans only in 1946. Though the Satyagraha did not immediately result in the opening of the Guruvayur temple to all Hindus, the movement helped to create a strong public opinion in the country in favour of temple entry and abolition of untouchablity.

Temple Entry Proclamation

In Travancore the movements for the mitigation of the severities of caste, if not its total abolition, have been popular. The teachings of Sree Narayana Guru gave a momentum to the forces which were generated by the extension of western education among the masses and the tolerant policy pursued by the state in recognising the legitimate claims of the backward communities. The promulgation of the Temple Entry Proclamation was a reform of far-reaching importance, not only to the teeming millions of Travancore but a momentous act of emancipation and hope to the whole of India.

The Proclamation runs as follows:-"Profoundly convinced of the truth and validity of our religion, believing that it is based on divine guidance and on all-comprehending toleration, knowing that in its practice it has through out the centuries, adapted itself to the needs of changing times, solicitous that none of our Hindu subjects should, by reason of birth or caste of community, be denied the consolations and the solace of the Hindu faith." 'Avarnas', to find out the extent of the demand for reforms, to ascertain the attitude of the Savarna castes, to examine the question in the light of the Hindu scriptures and formulate proposals as to the lines on which the reform might be effected.

The committee expressed their considered opinion that a Parishad of learned persons, well versed in the theory and practice of Hinduism, should be summoned, and that the reform might be effected by the ruler with their approval. They also suggested certain methods by which the rigour of the custom excluding the Avarnas from the temple might be softened. But the Maharaja did not believe in half measures. With an outlook which no Indian monarch had been able to entertain for a couple of thousands of conservative years, His Highness the Maharaja Sree Chitra Thirunal affixed the Sign Manual to the momentous Proclamation.

It was on the eve of the Maharaja's birth day in 1112(1936 AD) that the edict was promulgated. The Proclamation was received throughout India with delight and admiration. It was welcomed by the whole civilised world. To the Hindus it was matter of pride and fresh hope. The repercussions of the Proclamation were so great that the Christians and Muslims were so great that the Christians and Muslims were equally warm in giving it a hearty reception. Dr. C. P. Ramaswami Iyer referred to the day of the Proclamation as a unique occasion in the history of India and specially of Hinduism. Gandhiji expressed the hope that "all other Hindu Princes will follow the noble example set by this far-off ancient Hindu State." The Prime Minister of Madras described the

Proclamation as the "greatest religious reform in India after the time of Asoka". The Maharaja gave the biggest charity that any ruler could give to his subjects in opening the doors to every class and creed..

K. Kelappan

K. Kelappan (August 24, 1889-October 7, 1971) was born in a small village of in Muchukunnu Village in Calicut in Kerala. He studied in Calicut and Madras and graduated from the Madras University. He began his career as a teacher at in S.B High School Changanassery and was the founder President of Nair Service Society later he became the Principal of a school run by the society. He fought for social reforms on one hand and the British on the other. He was a great revolutionary, social reformer and crusader for justice to the backward classes. He was called Kerala Gandhi.

He joined studies in Law at Bombay which he gave up to join the Non-Cooperation Movement led by Mahatma Gandhi and joined the Freedom movement. During the Malabar rebellion he faced a group of rebels who came to loot the Ponnani Treasury and persuaded them to retreat by appealing to their good sense. He gave the lead to the Payyannur and Calicut salt Satyagraha and was chosen as the first Satyagrahi from Kerala in the individual satyagraha movement launched by Gandhiji. He played a dominant role in the famous Vaikom Satyagraha and was the leader of the Guruvayoor Satyagraha in 1932. It was at Gandhiji's request that he ended his fast at Guruvayoor.

He went to jail several times during the freedom struggle including the Quit India Movement. He worked hard for eradication of untouchability and worked for upliftment of Harijans and set up many Harijan hostels and schools in Kerala. He was in the forefront of Swadeshi Movement and did his best to build up a base of Khadi and Village industries.

After independence he left the Congress Party and joined the Kisan Masdoor Praja Party and was elected from the Ponnani Lok Sabha seat in 1952 later he quit politices and engaged only in social work and never aspired for position or power. He was the President of almost all major Gandhian organisations like Kerala Sarvodaya Sangh, Kerala Gandhi Samarak Nidhi, Kerala Sarvodaya Mandal and Gandhi Peace Foundation, Calicut. A part from above he was an educationist as well as an accomplished and forceful journalist.

He helped in starting 'Mathrubhoomi' and was its editor for a number of years. He worked for unification of Kerala into a new linguistic state..

B. R. Ambedkar

Bhimrao Ramji Ambedkar was an Indian jurist, political leader, Buddhist activist, philosopher, thinker, anthropologist, historian, orator, prolific writer, economist, scholar, editor, revolutionary and the revivalist of Buddhism in India. He was also the chief architect of the Indian Constitution. Born into a poor Mahar, then Untouchable, family, Ambedkar spent his whole life fighting against social discrimination, the system of *Chaturvarna* – the Hindu categorization of human society into four *varnas* – and the Hindu caste system. He is also credited with having sparked the bloodless revolution with his most remarkable and innovative Buddhist movement. Ambedkar has been honoured with the Bharat Ratna, India's highest civilian award.

Overcoming numerous social and financial obstacles, Ambedkar became one of the first "Dalit" to obtain a college education in India. Eventually earning law degrees and multiple doctorates for his study and research in law, economics and political science from Columbia University and the London School of Economics, Ambedkar returned home as a famous scholar and practised law for a few years before publishing journals advocating political rights and social freedom for India's untouchables. He is regarded as a Bodhisattva by Indian Buddhist Bhikkus and by millions of other Buddhists.

Early Life

Bhimrao Ramji Ambedkar was born in the British-founded town and military cantonment of Mhow in the Central Provinces (now in Madhya Pradesh). He was the 14th and last child of Ramji Maloji Sakpal and Bhimabai Murbadkar. His family was of Marathi background from the town of Ambavade in the Ratnagiri district of modern-day Maharashtra. They belonged to the Hindu, Mahar caste, who were treated as so called untouchables and subjected to intense socioeconomic discrimination. Ambedkar's ancestors had for long been in the employment of the army of the British East India Company, and his father Ramji Sakpal served in the Indian Army at the Mhow cantonment. He had received a degree of formal education in Marathi and English, and encouraged his children to learn and work hard at school.

Belonging to the Kabir Panth, Ramji Sakpal encouraged his children to read the Hindu classics. He used his position in the army to lobby for his children to study at the government school, as they faced resistance owing to their caste. Although able to attend school, Ambedkar and other untouchable children were segregated and given no attention or assistance by the teachers. They were not allowed to sit inside the class. Even if they needed to drink water somebody from a higher caste would have to pour that water from a height as they were not allowed to touch either the water or the vessel that contained it.

This task was usually performed for the young Ambedkar by the school peon, and if he could not be found Ambedkar went without water. Ramji Sakpal retired in 1894 and the family moved to Satara two years later. Shortly after their move, Ambedkar's mother died. The children were cared for by their paternal aunt, and lived in difficult circumstances. Only three sons – Balaram, Anandrao and Bhimrao – and two daughters – Manjula and Tulasa – of the Ambedkars would go on to survive them. Of his brothers and sisters, only Ambedkar succeeded in passing his examinations and graduating to a higher school. His native village name was "Ambavade" in Ratnagiri District so he changed his name from "Sakpal" to "Ambedkar" with the recommendation and faith of Mahadev Ambedkar, his teacher who believed in him.

Ramji Sakpal remarried in 1898, and the family moved to Mumbai (then Bombay), where Ambedkar became the first untouchable student at the Government High School near Elphinstone Road.

Although excelling in his studies, Ambedkar was increasingly disturbed by the segregation and discrimination that he faced. In 1907, he passed his matriculation examination and entered the University of Bombay, becoming one of the first persons of untouchable origin to enter a college in India.

This success provoked celebrations in his community, and after a public ceremony he was presented with a biography of the Buddha by his teacher Krishnaji Arjun Keluskar also known as Dada Keluskar, a Maratha caste scholar. Ambedkar's marriage had been arranged the previous year as per Hindu custom, to Ramabai, a nine-year old girl from Dapoli. In 1908, he entered Elphinstone College and obtained a scholarship of twenty five rupees a month from the Gayakwad ruler of Baroda, Sahyaji Rao III for higher studies in the USA. By 1912, he obtained his degree in economics and political science, and prepared to take up employment with the Baroda state government. His wife gave birth to his first son, Yashwant, in the same year. Ambedkar had just moved his young family and started work, when he dashed back to Mumbai to see his ailing father, who died on February 2, 1913.

Fight Against Untouchability

As a leading Indian scholar, Ambedkar had been invited to testify before the Southborough Committee, which was preparing the Government of India Act 1919. At this hearing, Ambedkar argued for creating separate electorates and reservations for Dalits and other religious communities. In 1920, he began the publication of the weekly *Mooknayak* (*Leader of the Silent*) in Mumbai. Attaining popularity, Ambedkar used this journal to criticize orthodox Hindu politicians and a perceived reluctance of the Indian political community to fight caste discrimination. His speech at a Depressed Classes Conference in Kolhapur impressed the local state ruler Shahu IV, who shocked orthodox society by dining with Ambekdar. Ambedkar established a successful legal practice, and also organised the Bahishkrit Hitakarini Sabha to promote education and socioeconomic uplifting of the depressed classes.

By 1927 Dr. Ambedkar decided to launch active movements against untouchability. He began with public movements and marches to open up and share public drinking water resources, also he began a struggle for the right to enter Hindu temples. He led a *satyagraha* in Mahad to fight for the right of the untouchable community to draw water from the main water tank of the town.

He was appointed to the Bombay Presidency Committee to work with the all-European Simon Commission in 1925. This commission had sparked great protests across India, and while its report was ignored by most Indians, Ambedkar himself wrote a separate set of recommendations for future constitutional reformers.

Poona Pact

By now Ambedkar had become one of the most prominent

untouchable political figures of the time. He had grown increasingly critical of mainstream Indian political parties for their perceived lack of emphasis for the elimination of the caste system. Ambedkar criticized the Indian National Congress and its leader Mohandas Gandhi, whom he accused of reducing the untouchable community to a figure of pathos. Ambedkar was also dissatisfied with the failures of British rule, and advocated a political identity for untouchables separate from both the Congress and the British. At a Depressed Classes Conference on August 8, 1930 Ambedkar outlined his political vision, insisting that the safety of the Depressed Classes hinged on their being independent of the Government and the Congress both:

We must shape our course ourselves and by ourselves... Political power cannot be a panacea for the ills of the Depressed Classes. Their salvation lies in their social elevation. They must cleanse their evil habits. They must improve their bad ways of living.... They must be educated.... There is a great necessity to disturb their pathetic contentment and to instill into them that divine discontent which is the spring of all elevation.

In this speech, Ambedkar criticized the Salt Satyagraha launched by Gandhi and the Congress. Ambedkar's criticisms and political work had made him very unpopular with orthodox Hindus, as well as with many Congress politicians who had earlier condemned untouchability and worked against discrimination across India. This was largely because these "liberal" politicians usually stopped short of advocating full equality for untouchables.

In 1932, M. C. Rajah concluded a pact with two right-wingers in the Indian National Congress, Dr. B. S. Moonje and Jadhav. According to this pact, Moonje offered reserved seats to scheduled castes in return for Rajah's support. This demand prompted Ambedkar to make an official demand for Separate Electorate System on an all-India basis. Ambedkar's prominence and popular support amongst the untouchable community had increased, and he was invited to attend the Second Round Table Conference in London in 1931. Here he sparred verbally with Gandhi on the question of awarding separate electorates to untouchables. Gandhi fiercely opposed separate electorate for untouchables but accepted separate electorate for all other minority groups like muslims,sikhs...etc. Gandhi feared that separate electorates for untouchables would divide Hindu society for future generations.

When the British agreed with Ambedkar and announced the awarding of separate electorates, Gandhi began a *fast-unto-death* while imprisoned in the Yerwada Central Jail of Pune in 1932 against the separate electorate for untouchables only; Gandhi is not against separate electorates for muslims, sikhs, and others. Exhorting orthodox Hindu society to eliminate discrimination and untouchability, Gandhi asked for the political and social unity of Hindus. Gandhi's fast provoked great public support across India, and orthodox Hindu leaders, Congress politicians and activists such as Madan Mohan Malaviya and Palwankar Baloo organized joint meetings with Ambedkar and his supporters at Yeravada. Fearing a communal reprisal and killings of untouchables in the event of Gandhi's death, Ambedkar agreed under massive coercion from the supporters of Gandhi to drop the demand for separate electorates, and settled for a reservation of seats. This agreement, which saw Gandhi end his fast, in the end achieved more representation for the untouchables, while dropping the demand for separate electorates that was promised through the British Communal Award prior to Ambedkar's meeting with Gandhi. Ambedkar was to later criticise this fast of Gandhi as a gimmick to deny political rights to the untouchables and increase the coercion he had faced to give up the demand for separate electorates.

Political Career

In 1935, Ambedkar was appointed principal of the Government Law College, a position he held for two years. Settling in Mumbai, Ambedkar oversaw the construction of a large house, and stocked his personal library with more than 50,000 books. His wife Ramabai died after a long illness in the same year. It had been her long-standing wish to go on a pilgrimage to Pandharpur, but Ambedkar had refused to let her go, telling her that he would create a new Pandharpur for her instead of Hinduism's Pandharpur which treated them as untouchables. His own views and attitudes had hardened against orthodox Hindus, despite a significant increase in momentum across India for the fight against untouchability and he began criticizing them even as he was criticized himself by large numbers of Hindu activists. Speaking at the Yeola Conversion Conference on October 13 near Nasik, Ambedkar announced his intention to convert to a different religion and exhorted his followers to leave Hinduism. He would repeat his message at numerous public meetings across India. In 1936, Ambedkar founded the Independent Labour Party, which won 15 seats in the 1937 elections to the Central Legislative Assembly. He published his book *The Annihilation of Caste* in the same year, based on the thesis he had written in New York. Attaining immense popular success, Ambedkar's work strongly criticized Hindu religious leaders and the caste system in general. He protested the Congress decision to call the untouchable community *Harijans* (*Children of God*), a name coined by Gandhi. Ambedkar served on the Defence Advisory Committee and the Viceroy's Executive Council as minister for labour. With *What Congress and Gandhi Have Done to the Untouchables*, Ambedkar intensified his attacks on Gandhi and the Congress, charging them with hypocrisy.

In his work *Who Were the Shudras?*, Ambedkar attempted to explain the formation of the Shudras i.e. the lowest caste in hierarchy of Hindu caste system. He also emphasised how Shudras are separate from Untouchables. Ambedkar oversaw the transformation of his political party into the All India Scheduled Castes Federation, although it performed poorly in the elections held in 1946 for the Constituent Assembly of India. In writing a sequel to *Who Were the Shudras?* in 1948, Ambedkar lambasted Hinduism in the *The Untouchables: A Thesis on the Origins of Untouchability*:

The Hindu Civilisation.... is a diabolical contrivance to suppress and enslave humanity. Its proper name would be infamy. What else can be said of a civilisation which has produced a mass of people... who are treated as an entity beyond human intercourse and whose mere touch is enough to cause pollution?

Pakistan or the Partition of India

Between 1941 and 1945, he published a number of books and pamphlets, including *Thoughts on Pakistan*, in which he criticized the Muslim League's demand for a separate Muslim state of Pakistan but considered its concession if Muslims demanded so as expedient.

In the above book Ambedkar wrote a sub-chapter titled *If Muslims truly and deeply desire Pakistan, their choice ought to be accepted*. He wrote that if the Muslims are bent on Pakistan, then it must be conceded to them. He asked whether Muslims in the army could be trusted to defend India. In the event of Muslims invading India or in the case of a Muslim rebellion, with whom would the Indian Muslims in the army side? He concluded that, in the interests of the safety of India, Pakistan should be acceded to, should the Muslims demand it. According to Ambedkar, the Hindu assumption that though Hindus and Muslims were two nations, they could live together under one state, was but a empty sermon, a mad project, to which no sane man would agree.

Architect of India's Constitution

Upon India's independence on August 15, 1947, the new Congress-led government invited Ambedkar to serve as the nation's first law minister, which he accepted. On August 29, Ambedkar was appointed Chairman of the Constitution Drafting Committee, charged by the Assembly to write free India's new Constitution. Ambedkar won great praise from his colleagues and contemporary observers for his drafting work. In this task Ambedkar's study of sangha practice among early Buddhists and his extensive reading in Buddhist scriptures were to come to his aid. Sangha practice incorporated voting by ballot, rules of debate and precedence and the use of agendas, committees and proposals to conduct business. Sangha practice itself was modelled on the oligarchic system of governance followed by tribal republics of ancient India such as the Shakyas and the Lichchavis. Thus, although Ambedkar used Western models to give his Constitution shape, its spirit was Indian and, indeed, tribal.

Granville Austin has described the Indian Constitution drafted by Dr. Ambedkar as 'first and foremost a social document.'... 'The majority of India's constitutional provisions are either directly arrived at furthering the aim of social revolution or attempt to foster this revolution by establishing conditions necessary for its achievement.'

The text prepared by Ambedkar provided constitutional guarantees and protections for a wide range of civil liberties for individual citizens, including freedom of religion, the abolition of untouchability and the outlawing of all forms of discrimination Ambedkar argued for extensive economic and social rights for women, and also won the Assembly's support for introducing a system of reservations of jobs in the civil services, schools and colleges for members of scheduled castes and scheduled tribes, a system akin to affirmative action. India's lawmakers hoped to eradicate the socioeconomic inequalities and lack of opportunities for India's depressed classes through this measure, which had been originally envisioned as temporary on a need basis. The Constitution was adopted on November 26, 1949 by the Constituent Assembly.

Ambedkar resigned from the cabinet in 1951 following the stalling in parliament of his draft of the Hindu Code Bill, which sought to expound gender equality in the laws of inheritance, marriage and the economy. Although supported by Prime Minister Nehru, the cabinet and many other Congress leaders, it received criticism from a large number of members of parliament. Ambedkar independently contested an election in 1952 to the lower house of parliament, the Lok Sabha, but was defeated. He was appointed to the upper house, of parliament, the Rajya Sabha in March 1952 and would remain a member until his death.

Conversion to Buddhism

In the 1950s, Ambedkar turned his attention to Buddhism and travelled to Sri Lanka (then Ceylon) to attend a convention of Buddhist scholars and monks. While dedicating a new Buddhist vihara near Pune, Ambedkar announced that he was writing a book on Buddhism, and that as soon as it was finished, he planned to make a formal conversion to Buddhism. Ambedkar twice visited Burma in 1954; the second time in order to attend the third conference of the World Fellowship of Buddhists in Rangoon. In 1955, he founded the Bharatiya Bauddha Mahasabha, or the Buddhist Society of India. He completed his final work, *The Buddha and His Dhamma,* in 1956. It was published posthumously.

After meetings with the Sri Lankan Buddhist monk Hammalawa Saddhatissa, Ambedkar organised a formal public ceremony for himself and his supporters in Nagpur on October 14, 1956. Accepting the Three Refuges and Five Precepts from a Buddhist monk in the traditional manner, Ambedkar completed his own conversion. He then proceeded to convert an estimated 500,000 of his supporters who were gathered around him. Taking the 22 Vows, Ambedkar and his supporters explicitly condemned and rejected Hinduism and Hindu philosophy. He then travelled to Kathmandu in Nepal to attend the Fourth World Buddhist Conference. He completed his final manuscript, *The Buddha or Karl Marx* on December 2, 1956.

Death

Since 1948, Ambedkar had been suffering from diabetes. He was bed-ridden from June to October in 1954 owing to clinical depression and failing eyesight. He had been increasingly embittered by political issues, which took a toll on his health. His health worsened as he furiously worked through 1955. Just three days after completing his final manuscript *The Buddha and His Dhamma*, it is said that Ambedkar died in his sleep on December 06, 1956 at his home in Delhi.

Since the Caste Hindus denied the cremation at Dadar crematorium, A Buddhist-style cremation was organised for him at Chowpatty beach on December 7, attended by hundreds of thousands of supporters, activists and admirers.

Ambedkar was survived by his second wife Savita Ambedkar and converted to Buddhism with him. His wife's name before marriage was Sharda Kabir. Savita Ambedkar died as a Buddhist in 2002. Ambedkar's grandson, Prakash Yaswant Ambedkar leads the Bharipa Bahujan Mahasangha and has served in both houses of the Indian Parliament.

A number of unfinished typescripts and handwritten drafts were found among Ambedkar's notes and papers and gradually made available. Among these were *Waiting for a Visa*, which probably dates from 1935-36 and is an autobiographical work, and the *Untouchables, or the Children of India's Ghetto*, which refers to the census of 1951.

A memorial for Ambedkar was established in his Delhi house at 26 Alipur Road. His birthdate is celebrated as a public holiday known as Ambedkar Jayanti or Bhim Jayanti. He was posthumously awarded India's highest civilian honour, the Bharat Ratna in 1990. Many public institutions are named in his honour, such as the Dr. Babasaheb Ambedkar Open University in Hyderabad, Andhra Pradesh, B. R. Ambedkar Bihar University, Muzaffarpur Dr.B.R.Ambedkar National Institute of Technology, Jalandhar the other being Dr. Babasaheb Ambedkar International Airport in Nagpur, which was otherwise known as Sonegaon Airport. A large official portrait of Ambedkar is on display in the Indian Parliament building. On the anniversary of his birth (14 April) and death (6 December) and on Dhamma Chakra Pravartan Din, 14th Oct at Nagpur, at least half a million people gather to pay homage to him at his memorial in Mumbai. Thousands of bookshops are set up, and books are sold. His message to his followers was " Educate!!!, Agitate!!!", Organize!!!.

Ambedkar v. Gandhi

Ambedkar was a fierce critic of Mahatma Gandhi (and the Indian National Congress). He was criticized by his contemporaries and modern scholars for this opposition to Gandhi, who had been one of the first Indian leaders to call for the abolition of untouchability and discrimination.

Gandhi had a more positive, arguably romanticised view of traditional village life in India and a sentimental approach to the untouchables, calling them Harijan (children of God) and saying he was "of" them. Ambedkar rejected the epithet "Harijan" as condescending. Ambedkar strongly opposed Gandhi's statement about dalit 'The harijan'. Ambedkar criticized Gandhi that calling dalit as children of Hindu God (Hari) indirectly implies as dalit must be under the circle of Hindu religion, not to go away from this. Then only the dalits said to be untouchables according to the Hindu varnasrama. He tended to encourage his followers to leave their home villages, move to the cities, and get an education.

Dr. Ambedkar and Gandhi had big differences and conflicts of thoughts. The details of some of those are written by Dr. Ambedkar in his book What Congress and Gandhi have Done to the Untouchables.

Criticism and Legacy

This section may contain original research. Please improve it by verifying the claims made and adding references. Statements consisting only of original research may be removed.

Ambedkar's legacy as a socio-political reformer, had a deep effect on modern India. In post-Independence India his socio-political thought has acquired respect across the political spectrum. His initiatives have influenced various spheres of life and transformed the way India today looks at socioeconomic policies, education and affirmative action through socioeconomic and legal incentives. His reputation as a scholar led to his appointment as free India's first law minister, and chairman of the committee responsible to draft a constitution. He passionately believed in the freedom of the individual and criticised equally both orthodox casteist Hindu society. His polemical condemnation of Hinduism and its foundation of caste system, made him controversial, although his conversion to Buddhism sparked a revival in interest in Buddhist philosophy in India and abroad.

Ambedkar condemned Gandhi's support for the caste system and perpetuating untouchability. Dr.Ambedkar warned people,"Don't call Gandhi a saint. He is a seasoned politician. When everything else fails, Gandhi will resort to intrigue." "Don't fall under Gandhi's spell, he's not God... Mahatmas have come and Mahatmas have gone but untouchables have remained untouchables."

Ambedkar's political philosophy has given rise to a large number of Dalit political parties, publications and workers' unions that remain active across India, especially in Maharashtra. His promotion of the Dalit Buddhist movement has rejuvenated interest in Buddhist philosophy in many parts of India. Mass conversion ceremonies have been organized by Dalit activists in modern times, emulating Ambedkar's Nagpur ceremony of 1956.

Some scholars, including some from the affected castes, took the view that the British were more even-handed between castes, and that continuance of British rule would have helped to eradicate many evil practices. This political opinion was shared by quite a number of social activists including Jyotirao Phule.

Some, in modern India, question the continued institution of reservations initiated by Ambedkar as outdated and anti-meritocratic.

Outside India, at the end of de 1990's, some Hungarian Romani people drew parallels between their own situation and the situation of the Dalits in India. Inspired by Ambedkar's approach, they started to convert to Buddhism.

Theorized Mahar Bias by 'Untouchable' Leaders

Narayan Rao Kajrolkar criticized Ambedkar, claiming that he was biased by utilising government funds to help the interests of his own caste, the Mahar, rather than dividing the funds equally among others such as the Chambars and the Mangs. Sitaram Narayan Shivtarkar criticized him on the same account at the Chambar conference held at Khond at the Ratnagiri District on 27 October, 1937. At the "First Chambar Conference" at Ratnagiri on

December 1937, chaired by S. G. Songaonkar, echoed this yet again.

Aftermath

The neutrality of this section is disputed. Please see the discussion on the talk page. Please do not remove this message until the dispute is resolved. *(August 2009)*

Frequent violent clashes between Buddhist groups and orthodox Hindus have occurred over the years. When in 1994 a garland of shoes was hung around a statue of Ambedkar in Mumbai, sectarian violence and strikes paralysed the city for over a week. When the following year similar disturbances occurred, a statue of Ambedkar was destroyed. In addition, some Dalits who had converted to Buddhism have rioted against Hindus (such as the 2006 Dalit protests in Maharashtra) and desecrated Hindu temples, often incited into doing so by anti-Hindu elements and replacing deities with pictures of Ambedkar. The radical Ambedkarite "Dalit Panthers Movement" has even gone so far as to attempt to assassinate academics who have been critical of Ambedkar's understanding of Buddhism.

Bibliography

Adikaram, E. W.: *Early History of Buddhism in Ceylon,* D. S. Puswella, Migoda, 1946.

Agrawala, V. S.: *Shiva Mahadeva: The Great God,* Veda Academy, Varanasi, 1966.

Ahmad, Imtiaz: *State and Foreign Policy: India's Role in South Asia,* Vikas, New Delhi, 1993.

Ahmad, Jamil-ud-din: *Some Recent Speeches and Writings of Mr. Jinnah,* Lahore, Ashraf, 1952.

Aiyar, R. Krishnaswami: *Outlines of Vedaanta,* Chetana, Bombay, 1978.

Archer, W. G.: *The Kama Sutra,* Unwin Hyman, London, 1990.

Ashton, S.R. : *British Policy Towards the Indian States, 1905-1939,* London, Curzon, 1982.

Aurobindo, Sri: *Vyasa and Valmiki,* Acharya Press, Pondicherry, 1956.

Avalon, Arthur and Ellen: *Hymns to the Goddess,* Ganesh and Co., Madras, 1964.

Aziz, Ashraf: *Light of the Universe: Essays on Hindustani Film Music,* Three Essays Collective, New Delhi, 2003.

Bagchi, P. C.: *Studies in Dharmashastra,* University of Calcutta Press, Calcutta, 1939.

Bahadur, K.P.: *The Wisdom of Vedaanta,* Sterling Publishers Private Limited, New Delhi, 1996.

Banerjea, J. N.: *Pauranic and Vedanta Religion,* University of Calcutta, Calcutta, 1996.

Bankimchandra, C.: *Essentials of Dharma,* Sanskrit Book Depot, Calcutta 1979.

Basu, Manoranjan: *Dharmashastra: A General Study,* Shrimati Mira Basu, Calcutta, 1976.

Beaumont, Roger : *Sword of the Raj: The British Army in India, 1747-1947*, Indianapolis, Bobbs-Merrill, 1977.

Benjamin, Joseph : *Scheduled Castes in Indian Politics and Society*, New Delhi, Ess Ess Publications, 1989.

Bhattacharyya, B.: *Nispannayogavali of Mahapandita Abhyakara Gupta*, Oriental Institute, Baroda, 1949.

Borchert, Bruno: *Mysticism: Its History and Challenge*, Samuel Wiser, York Beach, 1994.

Bose, D. N.: *Dharmashastra: Their Philosophy and Occult Secrets*, Kali Press, Calcutta, 1965.

Bowle, John: *The Imperial Achievement: The Rise and Transformation of the British Empire*, Little, Brown, 1974.

Brockington, J. L.: *Righteous Rama: The Evolution of an Epic*, Oxford, London, 1984.

Bromley, D.: *Krishna Consciousness in the West*, Bucknell University Press, Lewisburg, 1989.

Brooks, E.: *The Original Analects: Sayings of Confucius and His Successors*. Columbia University Press, New York, 1988.

Bruhn, Klaus: *The Jina-Images of Deogarh*, MacMillan, Leiden, 1969.

Burke, Mary Louise: *Swami Vivekananda in America: New Discoveries*, Advaita Ashrama, Calcutta, 1966.

Chaudhary, M.: *Partition and the Curse of Rehabilitation*, Calcutta, Bengal Rehabilitation Organization, 1964.

Chaudhuri, Nirad: *Thy Hand, Great Anarch! India: 1921-1952*, London, Chatto & Windus, 1987.

Coomeraswamy, Ananda K.: *Buddha and the Gospel of Buddhism*, MacMillan, London, 1928.

Crawford, Cromwell S.: *Ram Mohan Roy: His Era and Ethics*, Acharya Press, New Delhi, 1984.

Dalton, Dennis : *Gandhi's Power : Nonviolence in Action*, New Delhi, OUP, 2001.

Danielou, Alain: *The Complete Kama Sutra*, Park Street Press, Rochester, 2000.

Dasgupta, Shahana: *Rani Lakshmibai: The Indian Heroine*, Rupa & Company, Calcutta, 2002.

Datta, V.N.: *Sati: Widow Burning in India*, Manohar, New Delhi, 1990.

David, M. D.: *John Wilson and his Institutions*, Mumbai, 1957.

De Bary: *Self and Society in Ming Thought*, Columbia University Press, New York, 1970.

De, Sushil Kumar: *Ancient Indian Erotics and Erotic Literature*, Firma K. L. Mukhopadhyay, Calcutta, 1959.

Deak, Istvan: *The Lawful Revolution: Louis Kossuth and the Hungarians 1848-1849*, Columbia University Press, 1979.

Dhar, Niranjan: *Vedanta and Bengal Renaissance*, Minerva Associates, Calcutta, 1977.

Dikshit, D.P. *Political History of the Chalukyas of Badami*. New Delhi: Abhinav, 1980.

Donat, K.: *Meditate the Tantric Yoga Way*, George Allen and Unwin, London, 1973.

Doniger, W.: *The Rig Veda: An Anthology*, Penguin, New York, 1981.

Duboi, Abbe: *Hindu Manners, Customs and Ceremonies*, Fifth Indian Impression, CUP, 1985.

Dwivedi, M.: *The Principal Upanishads*, Adyar Library, Madras, 1931.

Eaton, Richard M.: *Sufis of Bijapur, 1300-1700: Social Roles of Sufis in Medieval India*, Princeton University Press, Princeton, 1978.

Edwardes, Michael: *Battles of the Indian Mutiny*, London; B. T. Batsford Ltd., 1963.

Erickson, Erik H.: *Gandhi's Truth: On the Origins of Militant Nonviolence*, Norton, New York, 1970.

Farquhar, J.N.: *Modern Religious Movements in India*, Munshiram, New Delhi, 1967.

Fay, Peter Ward: *The Opium War, 1840-42*, University of North Carolina Press, 1975.

Fisher, Michael H.: *The Politics of British Annexation of India - 1757-1857*, Oxford, 1996.

Frauwallner, E..: *History of Indian Philosophy*, Motilal, Delhi, 1973.

Gambhirananda, S.: *Brahma Sutra Shamkar Bhasya*, Adavita Ashrama, Calcutta, 1977.

Gambhirananda, Swami: *Brahma Sutra Shamkar Bhasya*, Adavita Ashrama, Calcutta, 1977.

Gandhi, M. K.: *The Story of My Experiment With Trust*, Washington, Public Affairs Press, 1948.

Garbe, R.: *The Philosophy of Ancient India*, Chicago University Press, Chicago, 1899.

Goradia, Nayana: *Lord Curzon: The Last of the British Moghuls*, New Delhi, Oxford University Press, 1993.

Goudriaan, T.: *Ritual and Speculation in Early Tantrism*, State University of New York Press, New York, 1992.

Gough, A.E.: *The Philosophy of the Upanisads and Ancient Indian Metaphysics*, MacMillan, London, 1882.

Grant, G. P.: *Philosophy in the Mass Age*, Copp Clark, Toronto, 1959.

Grisenold, H.D.: *Insights into Modern Hinduism*, Oxford, New York, 1934.

Growse, F. S.: *The Ramayana of Tulasidasa*, Motilal Banarsidass, Delhi, 1995.

Gurumurthy, S. : *Hindu Heritage, Assimilative, Not Divisive*, Vigil, Madras 1993.

Haich, E.: *Sexual Energy and Yoga*, Aurora Press, New York, 1982.

Hasan, Murhirul: *Legacy of a Divided Nation: India's Muslims Since Independence*, New Delhi, Oxford, 1997.

Hasan, Mushirul: *India's Partition: Process, Strategy and Mobilization*, New Delhi, Oxford UP, 1993.

Heifetz, Hank: *The Origin of the Young God: Kalidasa's Kumara-sambhava*, University of California Press, Berkeley, 1985.

Heimann, Betty: *Facets of Indian Thought*, Geroge Allen & Unwin, London, 1964.

Heinsath, Charles: *Indian Nationalism and Hindu Social Reform*, Princeton University Press, Princeton, 1964.

Heschel, J.: *God in Search of Man: A Philosophy of Judaism*, Noonday Press, New York, 1997.

Hirschman, Edwin: *White Mutiny: The Ilbert Bill Crisis in India and the Genesis of the Indian National Congress*, New Delhi, Heritage, 1980.

Hixon, L.: *Mother of the Universe: Visions of the Goddess, Tantric Hymns of Enlightenment*, Quest Books, Wheaton, 1994.

Hopkins, J.: *Kalachakra Tantra Rite of Initiation*, Wisdom Publications, Boston, 1982.

Hopkirk, Peter: *The Great Game: The Struggle for Empire in Central Asia*, Kodansha, 1992.

Hume, R.E.: *The Thirteen Principle Upanishads*, Oxford University Press, London, 1971.

Hutchins, Francis: *Spontaneous Revolution: The Quit India Movement*, New Delhi, Manohar, 1971.

Irene, S.: *Vedic Heritage Teaching Program*. Arsha Vidya Gurukulam, Coimbatore, 1994.

Iyar, K.: *Vedanta: The Science of Reality*, Ganesh and Co., Mardas, 1930.

Iyengar, B.K.S.: *Light on the Yoga Sutras of Patanjali*, Aquarian Press, London 1993.

Jacob, K.: *Religion and Ethics in Advaita*, C.M.S. Press, Kottayam, 1982.

Jafar, Malik Muhammad: *Jinnah as a Parliamentarian*, Lahore, Afzar Publications, 1977.

Jain, Kailash Chand, *Lord Mahavira and His Times*, Saraswati Press, Delhi, 1974.

James, Lawrence: *The Rise and Fall of the British Empire*, St. Martin's, 1997.

James, Robert Rhodes: *The British Revolution, 1880-1939*, New York, Knopf, 1976.

Jean, M.: *Tantrik Yoga*, The Aquarian Press, Wellingborough, 1970.

John, B.: *Mantras: Sacred Words of Power*, George Allen and Unwin, London, 1977.

John, Elsner: *Pilgrimage: Past and Present in the World Religions*, Harvard University Press, Cambridge, 1995.

John, K.: *The Origin and Development of the State Cult of Confucius*, Paragon Book, New York, 1966.

Karmarkar, D.: *Sankara's Advaita*, Karnatak University, Dharwar, 1976.

Kaushik, Asha : *Globalization, Democracy and Culture : Situating Gandhian Alternatives*, Jaipur, Pointer, 2002.

Kaviraj, G.: *Aspects of Indian Thought*, University of Burdwan, Calcutta, 1966.

Kavlekar, K.K. : *Non-Brahmin Movement in Southern India, 1873-1949*, Kolhapur, Shivaji University, 19790

Keith, A.B. : *Rigveda Brahmanas*, Harvard University Press, Cambridge, 1920.

Keith, Arthur Berriedale: *The Religion and Philosophy of the Veda and Upanishads*, MacMillan, Delhi, 1925.

Kishwar, Madhu : *Religion at the Service of Nationalism, and Other Essays*, OUP, Delhi, 1998.

Klaus, K.: *A Survey of Hinduism*, State University of New York Press, Albany, 1989.

Knipe, M.: *Hinduism: Experiments in the Sacred*, Harper, San Francisco, 1991.

Knott, K.: *Hinduism, A Very Short Introduction*, Oxford University Press, New York, 1998.

Kosambi, D. D. : *The Culture and Civilisation of Ancient India in Historical Outline*, London, Routledge and Kegan Paul, 1956.

Kottackal, Jacob: *Religion and Ethics in Advaita*, C.M.S. Press, Kottayam, 1982.

Kuiper, F.B.J. : *Aryans in the Rigveda*, Rodopi, Amsterdam, 1991.

Kuppuswamy, Sastri S.: *Compromises in the History of Advaitic Thought*, Kalyani Press, Madras, 1940.

Louis, Fischer: *Essential Gandhi: An Anthology of His Writings*, Vintage, New York, 1983.

Low, D. A. and Brasted, Howard: *Freedom, Trauma, Continuities: Northern India and Independence*, New Delhi, Sage Publications, 1998.

Maheshwari, Shriram: *Rural Development in India: A Public Policy Approach*, New Delhi, Sage, 1995.

Makhan, L.: *The Ramayana of Valmiki*, Munshiram Manoharlal, New Delhi, 1978.

Mathew, Arnold: *Culture and Anarchy*, The University Press, Cambridge, 1935.

Mayer, A. : *Caste in an Indian Village: Change and Continuity 1954-1992*, Delhi, OUP, 1996.

Mazumder, Sukhendu : *Politico-Economic Ideas of Mahatma Gandhi: Their Relevance in the Present Day*, New Delhi, Concept Pub., 2004.

Mearns, David J.: *Shiva's Other Children: Religion and Social Identity amongst Overseas Indians*, Sage, Walnut Creek, 1995.

Mearns, J.: *Shiva's Other Children: Religion and Social Identity amongst Overseas Indians*, Sage, Walnut Creek, 1995.

Mehra, Parshotam: *A Dictionary of Modern Indian History, 1707-1947*, New Delhi, Oxford University Press, 1985.

Metcalf, Thomas R.: *The Aftermath of the Revolt: India, 1857-1870*, Princeton, Princeton University, 1964.

Mohan, K.: *The Mahabharata*, Munshiram Manoharlal, Delhi 1997.

Mookerjee, Ajit: *Kali The Feminine Force*, Thames and Hudson, London, 1988.

Mookerji, Satkari: *Modern Polity and Vedanta*, Sanskrit College, Calcutta, 1972.

Moon, Penderel: *The British Conquest and Dominion of India*, London, Duckworth, 1989.

Morris-Jones, W.H.: *The Government and Politics of India*, London, Hutchinson, 1971.

Nanda, B. R. : *Gandhi and His Critics*, Oxford University Press, Delhi, 1993.

Neale, Walter C.: *Economic Change in Rural India: Land Tenure and Reform in the United Provinces, 1800-1955*, New Haven, 1962.

Nevile, P.: *Lahore: A Sentimental Journey*, New Delhi, Penguin, 1993.

Oddie, G.A. : *Hindu and Christian in South-East India*, London, Curzon Press, 1991.

Pathak, Dr S.P.: *Jhansi during the British Rule*, Ramanand Vidya Bhawan, Delhi, 1987.

Preston, Diana: *The Boxer Rebellion*, Berkley Books, 2000.

Raimundo Panikkar: *The Vedic Experience: Mantramanjari*, Longman Todd, London, 1977.

Raja, C. Kunhan : *The Taittiriya Sarvanukramani of Yaska*, Madras, 1931.

Ramamurti, A.: *Advaitic Mysticism of Sankara*, Visvabharati, Santiniketan, 1974.

Ranajit Guha: *A Construction of Humanism in Colonial India*, CASA, Amsterdam, 1993.

Renou, Louis: *The Nature of Dharmashastra*, Walker and Co., New York, 1997.

Robson, Brian: *Sir Hugh Rose and the Central India Campaign*, Sutton Publishing Ltd for the Army Records Society, UK, 2000.

Satyapal Verma: *Role of Reason in Sankara Vedanta*, Parimal Publication, Delhi, 1992.

Savarkar, Vinayak Damodar : *The Indian War of Independence* 1857 Rajdhani Granthagar, Delhi, 1988.

Scheftelowitz, Isidor : *Die Kasmirische Rezension von Katyayanas Sarvanukramani,* Zeitschrift fur Indologie und Iranistik, 1922.

Shukla, D. N.: *Vastu-Shastra,* Motilal Banarsidass, Delhi, 1966.

Singh, Birendra Kumar: *Early Chalukyas of Vatapi, circa A.D. 500 to 757,* Delhi, Eastern Book Linkers, 1991.

Smith, Col. J. T. : *Silver and the India Exchanges,* Effingham Wilson, London, 1876.

Strauss, L.: *Political Philosophy,* The Bobbs Merrill Co., New York, 1975.

Swami Vishnu Tirtha: *Devatma Shakti,* Swami Shivom Tirth, Rishikesh, 1962.

Talageri, Shrikant : *Aryan Invasion Theory and Indian Nationalism,* Voice of India, Delhi, 1993.

Tejomayananda, Swami: *Hindu Culture: An Introduction,* Chinmaya Publications, Piercy, 1993.

Thapar, Romila : *Ashoka and the Decline of the Mauryas,* London, Oxford University Press, 1961.

Thompson, Edward: *The Making of the Indian Princes,* Oxford University Press, London, 1943.

Trautmann, Thomas R.: *Kautilya and the Arthasastra: A Statistical Study,* Leiden, Brill, 1971.

Trimingham, J.: *Sufi Orders in Islam,* Oxford University Press, New York, 1998.

Utpat, V.N.: *Riddles of Buddha and Ambedkar,* Itihas Patrika Prakashan, Thane 1988.

Vable, D.: *The Arya Samaj. Hindu without Hinduism.* Vikas Publ., Delhi, 1983.

Vedalankar, Pandit Nardev : *Basic Teachings of Hinduism,* Veda Niketan, Durban, 1978.

Visvantha, K.: *Essentials of Hinduism,* Narosa Pub. House, New Delhi, 1989.

Wendy Doniger: *Siva: The Erotic Ascetic,* Oxford University Press, Delhi, 1998.

Zaidi, A. Moin: *Evolution of Muslim political Thought in India,* New Delhi: S. Chand, 1975.

Index

A

Acharya, 67, 68, 69, 70.
Achievements, 64, 90, 233.
Adi Brahmo Samaj, 7, 26, 73.
Adi Granth, 74.
Adi Shankara, 78, 254.
Administrative machinery, 187.
Administrator, 43, 187.
Advaita Vedanta, 4, 78, 254.
Ambedkar, 101, 162, 164, 171, 203, 273, 274, 275, 276, 277, 278, 279, 280, 281, 282, 283, 284.
Architecture, 155.
Armed Forces, 187.
Arya Samaj, 1, 3, 4, 6, 8, 10, 11, 12, 13, 14, 15, 16, 17, 19, 20, 21, 22, 23, 24, 44, 45, 58, 59, 73, 80, 135.
Arya Samaj Movement, 1, 15.
Assembly of Brahman, 49.
Atheism, 125, 134, 208.
Ayurveda, 248.

B

Battle of Plassey, 79.
Behramji Malabari, 135, 136, 147, 150, 151.
Bhagavad Gita, 79, 134.
Brahmanism, 163, 167, 218.
Brahmo Samaj, 7, 25, 26, 27, 28, 29, 32, 49, 50, 54, 56, 57, 73, 79, 80, 81, 84, 85, 86, 87, 88, 89, 90, 91, 95, 98, 100, 135, 147.
British India, 96, 132, 150.
British Policies, 217.
British Rule, 30, 42, 54, 62, 80, 87, 91, 102, 133, 164, 166, 219, 224, 276, 283.
Buddha, 20, 29, 53, 62, 115, 116, 117, 118, 120, 121, 211, 212, 253, 256, 274, 280, 281.
Buddhist Tradition, 120.

C

Civilization, 35, 44, 54, 57, 113, 138, 187, 200.
Constitution, 9, 23, 25, 28, 142, 148, 162, 206, 224, 226, 270, 273, 279, 280, 282.
Construction, 277.

D

Dalit Movement, 163.
Depressed Class Movement, 157.
Developments, 43, 55.
Dhondo Keshav Karve, 151.
Dravidar Kazhagam, 168, 175, 176, 199, 203, 204, 214, 215, 222.
Dravidian Movement, 174, 210.

E

East India Company, 16, 29, 30, 42, 64, 273.
Economy, 31, 35, 280.

F

Foundation, 25, 27, 43, 100, 110, 132, 165, 218, 250, 268, 272, 283.
Freedom Movement, 166, 272.

G

Ganesha, 214.
Gopal Hari Deshmukh, 146.
Government of India Act, 221, 275.
Governments, 64, 187.
Governor-general, 31.

H

Helena Blavatsky, 14, 103, 104, 106, 107, 114, 116, 123.
Hindu Philosophy, 51, 280.
Hindu Reformation, 54, 55, 56.
Hindu Reformers, 80, 83.
Hindu Scriptual Sources, 143.
Hindu Scriptures, 29, 79, 95, 131, 136, 144, 161, 245, 271.
Home Rule Movement, 132, 229.

I

Indian Culture, 18, 60, 94, 100, 112.
Indian Freedom Movement, 203.
Indian Independence Movement, 224.
Indian National Congress, 23, 81, 94, 98, 99, 100, 123, 132, 134, 146, 150, 164, 168, 170, 201, 216, 219, 220, 221, 224, 225, 229, 233, 234, 239, 246, 269, 276, 282.

J

Jinnah, 101, 203, 204, 217.
Judicial System, 98.
Justice Party, 168, 172, 173, 174, 175, 200, 201, 202, 203, 216, 217, 218, 219, 220, 221, 222, 223, 224, 225, 226, 227, 229.
Jyotirao Phule, 157, 160, 283.

K

Kabir, 71, 77, 274, 281.
Karma, 1, 6, 29, 34, 52, 84, 85, 113, 118, 154, 167, 208, 245.
Kesari, 270.
Koka Shastra, 142.

L

Laws, 35, 39, 63, 64, 93, 94, 104, 136, 171, 194, 199, 207, 238, 260, 268, 280.

M

Madras Presidency, 171, 172, 200, 201, 202, 203, 216, 218, 219, 220, 221, 225, 227, 238.
Mahabharata, 138, 144, 248.
Mahatma Hansraj, 15, 272.
Manav Dharma Sabha, 96.
Marathas, 79.
Mecca, 47.
Medicine, 90, 91, 228.
Member of Congress Party, 170.
Modern Hinduism, 79.
Moksha, 4, 11.
Moplah Rebellion, 230.
Muslim League, 133, 203.

N

National Movement, 229.
Newspaper, 17, 81, 112, 115, 124, 126, 132, 188, 214, 218, 220, 225, 226, 229, 236, 240, 257, 260, 262, 263, 266.

O

Organization, 7, 8, 13, 17, 23, 24, 55, 59, 60, 62, 80, 81, 92, 98, 99, 103, 104, 107, 110, 121, 122, 150, 176, 192, 215, 218, 219, 223, 224, 252, 258, 259, 260, 261, 262, 264, 268.
Ownership, 173, 194.

P

Paramahansa Mandali, 96.
Partition of India, 278.
Peace on Earth, 47.
Permanent Settlement, 42, 94.
Pilgrimages, 4.
Policy, 22, 43, 46, 57, 127, 131, 174, 188, 196, 207, 218, 221, 231, 236, 271.
Political and Economic, 47.
Politics, 33, 47, 93, 98, 99, 100, 123, 124, 126, 128, 161, 173, 174, 175, 199, 202, 210, 216, 218, 222, 225, 230, 265.
Powers, 87, 104.
Prarthana Samaj, 9, 10, 95, 96, 98, 99, 100, 147, 163, 164.
Princely State, 6, 170.
Projects, 96, 197.
Promotion, 57, 131, 155, 253, 283.
Public Welfare, 193.
Puranas, 40, 78, 181, 184, 210.

R

Raja Ram Mohan Roy, 3, 26, 29, 30, 31, 32, 33, 43, 47, 73, 80, 83, 84, 85, 87, 90, 91, 92, 93, 164.
Rajputs, 21, 22, 83.
Ram Mohan Roy, 3, 25, 26, 29, 30, 31, 32, 33, 43, 47, 49, 50, 52, 54, 56, 58, 62, 65, 73, 74, 75, 79, 80, 83, 84, 85, 87, 88, 90, 91, 92, 93, 164, 213.
Rama, 68, 69, 70, 76, 77, 176, 214.
Ramakrishna Gopal Bhandarkar, 96, 97, 98.
Ratirimanjeri of Jayadeva, 142.
Reform Movement, 1, 3, 6, 16, 17, 29, 33, 41, 43, 44, 45, 46, 50, 54, 84, 85, 95, 96, 145, 169.
Relationship, 12, 19, 87, 116, 126, 150, 211, 265.
Research, 40, 97, 98, 112, 119, 215, 273, 282.
Revolt of 1857, 44, 46.
Rigveda, 33, 34, 35, 36, 39, 138, 139.

S

Salient Features, 39.
Sati, 28, 32, 33, 79, 81, 82, 83, 84, 93.
Satyarth Prakash, 1, 5, 8, 19.
Satyashodhak Samaj, 157, 158, 163.
Scholarly Career, 97.
Shaivism, 66.
Shaktism, 66.
Shiv Narayan Agnihotri, 147.
Shivaji, 95, 102, 162.
Shuddhi Movement, 17, 21.
Sikh Community, 14, 237.
Sikhism, 14, 54, 74.
Smartism, 78.
Social Oppression, 162.
South Indian Liberal Federation, 202, 216, 218, 219, 223, 224, 225, 226, 229.
Split with Annadurai, 175.
Sri Aurobindo, 1, 4, 34.
Statesmen, 151.
Sufism, 75.

Swami Dayananda Saraswati, 1, 18, 20, 73.
Swami Shraddhanand, 1, 15, 16, 17, 18, 20, 21, 237.

T

Technology, 199, 281.
The pioneer, 75, 152, 157.
The Saktas, 72.
The Shaivas, 71.
Theagaroya Chetty, 216, 218, 222, 224, 225, 226, 227, 229.
Theosophical Society, 1, 12, 13, 14, 60, 103, 104, 106, 107, 108, 110, 111, 112, 114, 115, 116, 117, 119, 121, 122, 123, 130, 131, 132.
Traditions, 59, 71, 81, 84, 95, 102, 120, 166, 191, 201.

U

Untouchability, 4, 12, 20, 33, 59, 96, 155, 158, 161, 164, 165, 170, 171, 172, 175, 194, 207, 208, 209, 230, 234, 237, 240, 259, 267, 269, 270, 272, 275, 276, 277, 278, 279, 282, 283.
Upanishads, 26, 49, 51, 52, 57, 58, 61, 66, 79, 84, 88, 210, 248, 254.

V

Vaikom Satyagraha, 171, 207, 220, 230, 238, 239, 241, 247, 272.
Vaishnavism, 66, 97.
Valmiki, 48.
Varnas, 273.
Vedanta, 4, 49, 53, 54, 57, 58, 60, 61, 62, 66, 75, 78, 80, 161, 254.
Vedas, 1, 2, 3, 4, 5, 6, 7, 8, 11, 13, 14, 19, 26, 30, 33, 34, 35, 36, 37, 38, 40, 50, 51, 52, 53, 58, 59, 67, 73, 74, 78, 80, 85, 95, 100, 106, 113, 149, 159, 160, 181, 195, 209, 210, 248.
Vedic Culture, 6, 7.
Vedic Literature, 35, 51, 138.
Vedic People, 48.
Vitthal Ramji Shinde, 163.

W

Welfare, 32, 88, 90, 152, 160, 193, 216.
William Quan Judge, 103, 110, 111, 116, 121, 130.
Wisdom, 11, 13, 74, 75, 80, 85, 106, 134, 139, 162, 178, 211, 241, 254.
World War, 90, 202, 221, 228.
Worship, 1, 2, 4, 6, 9, 12, 19, 25, 26, 29, 32, 49, 52, 53, 59, 61, 66, 67, 68, 69, 70, 71, 73, 76, 77, 78, 85, 87, 92, 113, 164, 170, 196, 231, 246, 248, 251, 257.

Y

Yajurveda, 5, 34.

Z

Zamindars, 42, 47, 220.